TABLE OF CONTENTS

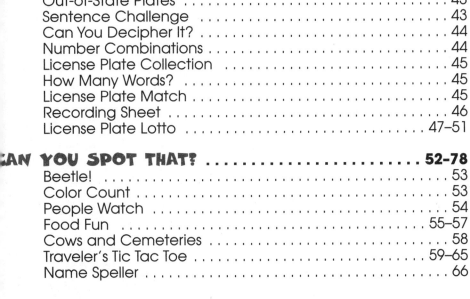

TABLE OF CONTENTS

TABLE OF CONTENTS

TABLE OF CONTENTS

TRAVEL GAMES TIPS

Going on a trip? Don't forget to include some fun activities for the time you'll be spending on the road, water or in the air. Here are some tips for getting the most out of your vacation travels.

PORTABLE FUN PAK

Before your trip, gather together a "fun pak"—a set of things that will help you occupy your time while traveling. Choose items that are small and portable. Place them in a knapsack or a tote bag.

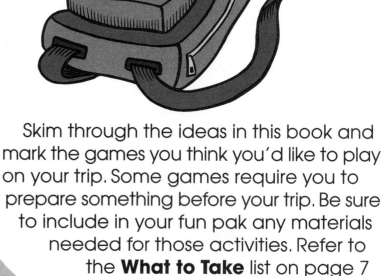

Skim through the ideas in this book and mark the games you think you'd like to play on your trip. Some games require you to prepare something before your trip. Be sure to include in your fun pak any materials needed for those activities. Refer to the **What to Take** list on page 7 for some suggestions.

What and how much you take will depend on how long you plan to travel. Also, some things that are appropriate for one form of travel may not be for another. For example, you can listen to a cassette or CD of your favorite music if you're traveling in your family car, but you won't be able to do that on a plane unless you have a portable cassette or CD player with headphones.

WHAT TO TAKE

Make a checklist of the items you are taking in your fun pak. Check off these items to make sure you have everything you need for your trip. Keep your checklist in your knapsack or tote bag for the rest of the trip. Later, when you are ready to move to the next place or return home from your trip, you can use your checklist to make sure you don't leave anything behind.

Here are some suggestions for your fun pak. Remember not to take too much. You don't want your fun pak to be more burden than fun.

Items needed to use with this book:

✔ calculator
✔ crayons
✔ a deck of playing cards
✔ drinking straws

✔ a large pad of paper (200+ sheets)
✔ paper lunch bags
✔ pencils/pens/ markers

✔ safety scissors
✔ steno pad or lined journal
✔ watch with a second hand

OTHER SUGGESTED ITEMS

✔ small clipboard
✔ crossword puzzles
✔ magnetic games (such as checkers)
✔ your favorite paperback book

✔ portable cassette or CD player (with headphones) and your favorite music
✔ word search puzzles
✔ hand-held video game player and your favorite games

ALPHABET GAMES

Awesome! Brilliant!
Challenging!
These alphabet games
let you have loads
of fun from A to Z!

ALPHABET SCAVENGER HUNT

Find each letter of the alphabet on signs you see as you travel. Begin with A, then go on to B, and so on. Just call out the letter and the word it's in as you spot it. See how long it takes to find all 26 letters.

Variation: Write the letters of the alphabet vertically on a sheet of paper. As you find the letters in order, write the corresponding words.

ALPHABET COLLECTION

Collect your own alphabet by looking for objects that start with the various letters, beginning with the letter A. Call out the items as you spot them.

This game can be played by everyone working together to finish the alphabet, or it can be done with each player collecting his or her own alphabet. If you decide to play individually, then the first person to spot the object gets to "collect" it. For a letter that may be hard to collect, such as x, players can agree to allow objects whose names contain the letter, such as box.

ANIMAL ALPHABET

One player calls out a letter. Then, everyone has to name animals beginning with that letter. When no one can think of any more animals, another player calls out a different letter.

CANARY	CAT
CENTIPEDE	CHEETAH
CHIMPANZEE	
COUGAR	CRAB

GOING ON A TRIP

This fun game tests your memory and your alphabet skills.

The first player starts off by saying, "I'm going on a trip and I'm taking along. . . ." That player then has to state an object beginning with the letter A. The next player repeats the first player's statement but adds an object beginning with B. The game continues with each player in turn adding an object that begins with the next letter in the alphabet. If a player can't think of an appropriate object, or forgets any of the items, he or she is out. The last player left is the winner.

THE NAME GAME

The first player begins by saying, "My name is _____, I live in _____, and I like _____." That player completes the sentence with a name, a place and an item beginning with A. (Example: "My name is Ann, I live in Alaska and I like apples.")

The second player repeats the statement but changes the name, place and item to ones beginning with the letter B. The game continues until the alphabet is completed.

ALPHABET SOUP

In this game, players try to be the first to "drink" their alphabet soup.

Each player needs a pencil and a sheet of paper. Each player draws a large circle on his or her paper to represent a soup bowl. Inside the bowl, each player writes 12 letters. Now, everyone's ready to begin the game!

As you travel, look for signs that contain the letters in your soup bowl. If you spot a letter, call it out and cross it off your sheet of paper. Each sign is good for only one player and one letter. The first player to cross off all the letters has finished "drinking" the alphabet soup and is the winner.

ALPHABET VEHICLES

This spotting game will help you become familiar with the various makes and models of cars and trucks.

First, write the letters of the alphabet vertically on a sheet of paper. Then, for each letter, try to spot a car or truck with a name that begins with that letter. Write the name on your paper beside the corresponding letter. For example, with the letter "S," you could use the name sports car. Set a time limit on the game. The person with the most names listed wins.

SAY IT BACKWARDS

Can you say the alphabet backwards without making a mistake? That's the challenge in this game. Each person can try individually or one player can say Z, the next Y, the following person X, and so on.

For an extra challenge, try singing the alphabet backwards to the tune of the alphabet song.

WOW!

MAKE AN ALPHABET SPINNER

Before your trip, make this alphabet spinner to add the element of chance to your games.

Materials: tagboard or file folder, paper clip, scissors, pen, ruler, brad fastener

Directions: Cut out a 6" tagboard circle and divide it into 26 sections. Label each section with a letter. Punch a hole in the center of the circle with a pen. Put the brad fastener through the paper clip and the hole. Secure it in place.

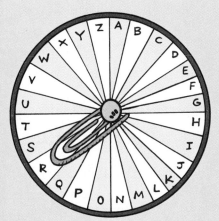

Use the spinner to select a letter.

TRICKY TONGUE TWISTERS

Give your tongue a workout with this game!

Make up a sentence in which every word begins with A, such as "Alan asked Adam about ants." Then say the sentence three times fast and challenge others to do the same. Everyone who successfully says the sentence gets a point.

The game continues with another player making up a sentence for B. The winner is the person with the most points.

I SELL SEASHELLS BY THE SEASHORE!

SUSIE'S SHELLS

DING! DONG!

This counting game is harder than it sounds.

Start counting aloud with the first player saying 1, the second player 2, and so on. When a number ending in 7 is reached, the person has to say "Ding!" instead of the number. When a number that is a multiple of 7 is reached, such as 14 or 21, the person has to say "Dong!" If a player makes a mistake, the counting starts all over again.

See how fast and how high everyone can count.

ONE HUNDRED CHALLENGE

This game is great entertainment if you're traveling on the road. Just look out the window and try to spot the numbers from 1 to 100 in order. Look at road signs, addresses, license plates and other sources for the numbers. If you reach 100 and you still have some distance to travel, you can keep playing the game to see how much higher you can go.

Variation: Begin by spotting 100, then 99, and so on until you reach 1.

IMPORTANT NUMBERS

Make a list of numbers that are important to you in some way. Then, as you travel, look for those numbers on road signs, license plates, billboards and buildings. Check off the numbers on your list as you see them.

MY IMPORTANT NUMBERS

_____   _____
_____   _____
_____   _____
_____   _____
_____   _____
_____   _____
_____   _____

WHAT'S MY NUMBER?

In this version of "Twenty Questions," one player thinks of a number and the others guess what it is by asking questions that are answered yes or no. For example, a player can ask, "Is your number greater than 10?" or "Does your number end in a 5?" You can vary the game by choosing one or more of the following options:

- Limit the number of questions to 10.

- Allow only questions that involve addition, subtraction, multiplication or division. (Example: Is your number greater than 4 + 5? Is your number divisible by 2?)

- Begin the game by having one player write a number on a piece of paper and place it inside a lunch bag. Any player who makes a guess can peek at the paper without showing the others. If the guess is correct, that player wins. If the guess is wrong, the player is out and the remaining players can continue guessing.

PICK A NUMBER

You'll need a deck of cards for this game. First, take out the joker, ace, king, queen and jack. Then, place the remaining cards in a lunch bag.

Each player takes a turn picking a card from the bag. The one who selects the highest card keeps the cards of the other players. If more than one card shows the same number, those players draw another card. The player with the highest card keeps all the cards.

Continue until all the cards from the bag have been selected or there are not enough cards for another round. The players count their cards. The winner is the one with the greatest number of cards.

NUMBER LOTTO

Use the lotto game board below and on pages 19–21. Have each player write a number from 0 to 20 in the 16 sections. Next, have everyone try to spot the numbers that are on his or her gameboard. The first person to spot a particular number calls it out and crosses it off his or her lotto gameboard. Players who have that same number do not cross it off their gameboards; only the first person to spot the number gets to cross it off. The player who crosses off the most numbers on his or her lotto gameboard is the winner.

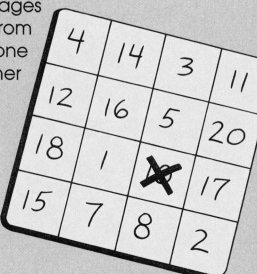

4	14	3	11
12	16	5	20
18	1	✗	17
15	7	8	2

NUMBER LOTTO GAMEBOARDS

(Directions are found on page 18.)

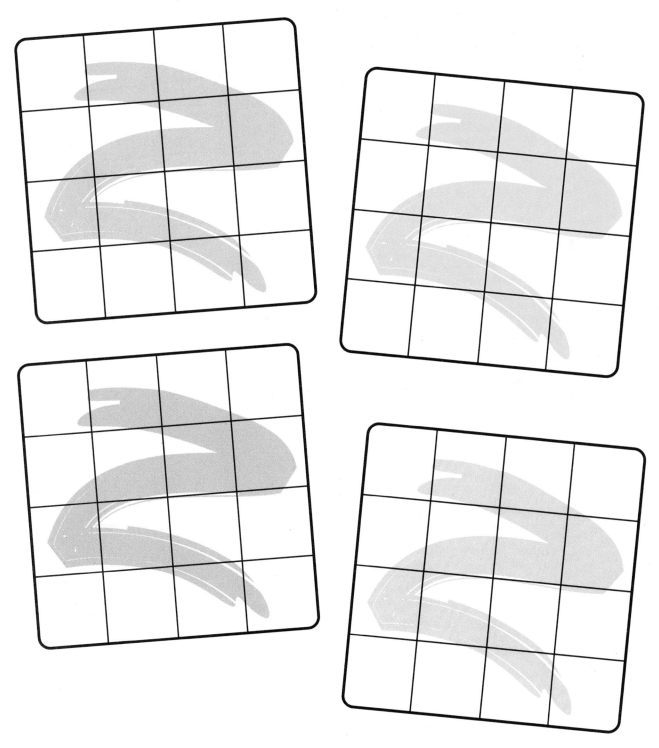

NUMBER LOTTO GAMEBOARDS

(Directions are found on page 18.)

NUMBER LOTTO GAMEBOARDS

(Directions are found on page 18.)

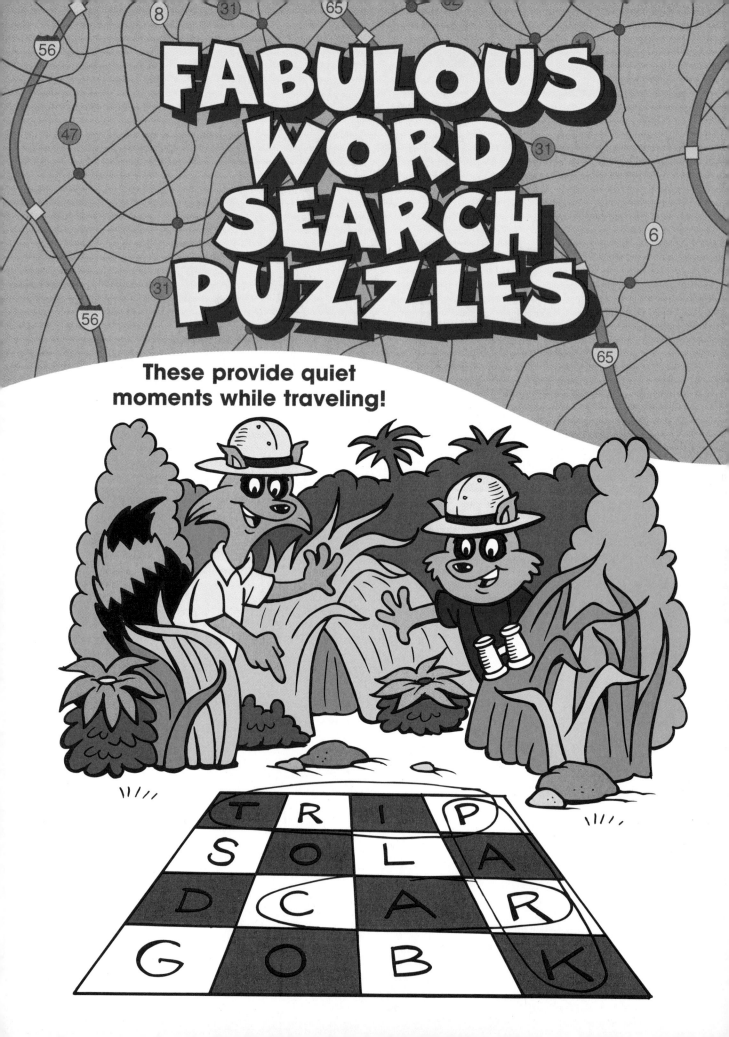

HOW HIGH CAN WE GO?

Look across and down to find the words from the Word Bank in the puzzle. Circle them.

f	i	n	d	l	d	
h	t	r	e	y	p	u	f
e	w	u	z	o	l	f	o
r	o	n	d	u	a	u	r
e	c	o	m	e	y	n	w
s	k	m	a	k	e	n	e
o	j	u	m	p	p	y	o
e	h	e	l	p	a	

WORD BANK

here	come		
find	funny	for	jump
two	you	so	help
we	make	play	run

I CAN READ IT!

Look across to find the words from the Word Bank in the puzzle. Circle them.

I CAN!

a	n	d	b	u	p
s	e	e	k	a	t
c	i	s	p	w	r
t	o	d	n	o	t
e	r	u	n	h	f
j	i	n	t	h	e
i	t	m	v	g	o

WORD BANK

and	to	at	go
in	is	it	not
run	see	the	up

LOOK WHAT I SEE!

Look down to find the words from the Word Bank in the puzzle. Circle them.

d	b	u	m	w	i	a	y
o	d	l	u	e	m	w	o
w	a	i	s	n	l	a	u
n	f	t	a	t	o	y	b
a	t	t	i	e	o	c	i
m	e	l	d	m	k	a	g
y	r	e	o	e	s	n	r

25

CAREFUL!

Circle the words from the Word Bank in the puzzle.
Color the spaces you circled blue. What did you find? _____

d	i	o	e	c	r	b	z	w	c	n	p	q	t	e	a
b	h	j	e	c	a	r	r	o	t	c	o	r	f	g	i
m	r	m	c	c	l	o	c	k	c	o	f	d	u	w	j
s	i	n	x	c	h	a	i	r	o	b	c	s	c	r	h
a	c	c	c	c	a	k	e	c	t	c	c	o	l	o	r
v	o	a	l	c	h	o	p	u	t	i	c	l	e	a	n
p	o	s	a	c	o	s	t	p	o	t	c	h	e	s	t
t	k	t	m	c	r	a	s	h	n	y	c	l	o	u	d
m	n	b	c	o	t	f	h	g	o	t	c	a	t	m	s
c	b	r	c	a	n	j	i	e	c	t	c	u	t	o	e

WORD BANK

cot	clam	cast
cat	color	chest
carrot	cook	cob
chair	can	cup
clean	cloud	chop
city	cost	crash
cake	clock	cut
	cotton	

26

TRUCKIN' ALONG

Circle the words from the Word Bank in the puzzle.
Color the spaces that you circled green. What did you find? _____

p	t	n	d	f	h	j	u	i	v	j	d	o	l	e
x	r	e	j	k	e	i	s	t	y	a	o	u	z	a
e	o	o	j	a	d	e	p	t	u	b	c	d	j	j
w	a	j	u	n	g	l	e	j	u	m	p	j	j	k
i	c	j	o	l	l	y	j	e	e	p	s	a	o	t
e	d	f	j	e	l	l	y	j	o	k	e	m	g	s
j	f	s	g	j	e	t	j	o	k	j	a	r	r	v
k	g	t	h	j	o	b	k	j	l	j	u	g	t	u
b	a	s	d	f	j	g	h	i	l	o	p	s	y	z

WORD BANK

jump	jug	jolly
jade	jet	jog
joke	jungle	job
jelly	jar	jeeps
jab	jam	

WHAT'S THE WORD?

Circle the words from the Word Bank in the puzzle.
Color the squares you circled red. What did you find? _____

y	g	h	u	p	y	t	i	d	r	e	o	n	m	t	c
d	y	c	y	i	b	y	e	l	l	w	g	y	u	l	e
b	o	t	a	s	r	e	y	e	t	n	m	a	o	m	f
c	w	s	r	j	f	l	a	d	g	h	o	w	s	e	o
x	l	y	n	l	k	l	y	e	s	t	y	n	y	a	k
d	y	e	h	u	p	o	y	o	u	i	m	t	a	y	y
v	p	a	g	e	o	w	u	n	m	j	l	u	b	i	a
h	k	s	o	m	p	y	o	k	e	k	m	v	c	p	m
g	m	t	t	c	s	y	a	r	d	c	z	y	a	p	s
i	l	u	r	f	k	g	u	l	f	d	u	x	o	r	e

WORD BANK

yak	yawn	yes
yams	yeast	yet
yap	yell	yip
yard	yellow	yoke
yarn	yowl	yule
you		

28

CREATIVE COLORS

Find and circle the color words from the Word Bank in the puzzle.
Look across and down. Color the squares you circled blue.
What did you find? _____

o	r	a	n	g	e	b	d	c	a	e	g	i	k	r	z	t
p	x	h	o	e	b	u	n	w	n	f	a	d	f	e	q	x
i	l	m	n	b	l	v	c	x	z	a	s	f	g	d	h	a
n	y	u	i	o	u	r	e	w	q	t	p	w	h	i	t	e
k	g	r	a	y	e	x	p	b	n	v	m	x	k	y	u	p
b	u	d	r	u	g	t	u	b	r	o	w	n	m	e	n	o
l	a	s	d	m	r	r	r	v	n	e	t	y	w	l	l	h
a	b	d	f	g	e	h	p	j	k	m	u	z	m	l	n	e
c	g	h	k	o	e	i	l	e	w	n	l	v	f	o	g	n
k	s	d	u	e	n	l	e	j	o	m	c	s	x	w	y	w

WORD BANK

blue   black
brown   yellow
red   pink
orange   gray
green   purple
white

TICKET, PLEASE!

Find and circle the number words from the Word Bank in the puzzle. Look across and down. Color the squares you circled black. What did you find? _____

a	l	m	j	e	f	o	p	q	d	g	u	i
c	f	h	i	k	f	f	c	e	b	m	n	p
b	e	r	t	y	s	e	v	e	n	z	c	b
h	o	e	r	s	j	t	e	n	l	h	n	g
u	x	e	t	c	d	o	n	e	t	h	i	k
w	f	l	n	y	x	f	e	z	h	d	i	o
p	i	e	i	s	t	o	i	e	r	a	u	p
d	v	v	n	i	w	u	g	r	e	n	k	l
a	e	e	e	x	o	r	h	o	e	d	f	h
b	c	n	d	f	g	i	t	j	l	m	n	o

WORD BANK

zero
one
two
three

four
five
six
seven

eight
nine
ten
eleven

TICKET

30

A GENTLE BREEZE

Find the words from the Word Bank in the puzzle.
Color the squares you circled red. What did you find? _____

WORD BANK

grin	yell
shut	street
fast	unhappy
steps	beautiful
starts	go
cap	talk
same	small

t	w	p	x	m	a	u	o	s	g	r	a	t	a	k	g	a
n	s	r	e	p	g	h	b	a	a	r	v	r	h	i	o	l
v	w	b	n	s	f	p	r	m	d	u	i	d	t	e	f	m
b	o	t	m	f	d	g	i	e	n	h	r	n	p	o	q	c
a	b	z	p	c	i	e	s	s	k	c	f	h	c	t	m	e
j	l	t	e	a	y	m	i	m	u	q	w	b	o	a	l	t
e	g	f	d	r	t	u	s	a	s	t	a	r	t	s	p	l
h	r	y	c	f	m	o	t	l	w	f	y	e	b	h	j	e
k	j	p	g	i	e	q	a	l	s	o	f	m	l	p	n	i
s	h	u	t	b	e	a	u	t	i	f	u	l	y	e	l	l
f	a	s	t	s	t	r	e	e	t	u	n	h	a	p	p	y
c	m	a	s	t	e	p	s	t	a	l	k	g	o	g	a	t

WHAT WILL I BE?

Find and circle the words Word Bank in the puzzle. Look across and down.
Color the squares you circled black. What did you find? _____

c	o	m	p	u	t	e	r	o	p	e	r	a	t	o	r	e
p	o	l	i	c	e	o	f	f	i	c	e	r	m	c	h	l
m	e	c	h	a	n	i	c	p	i	l	o	t	u	a	o	e
f	i	r	e	f	i	g	h	t	e	r	d	l	s	r	m	c
g	k	j	r	i	u	p	l	m	r	e	a	o	i	p	e	t
a	s	d	f	g	h	j	k	l	u	r	n	g	c	e	m	r
g	w	e	r	t	y	u	l	m	o	p	c	g	i	n	a	i
a	d	g	j	i	o	t	e	r	w	m	e	e	a	t	k	c
l	o	l	j	u	r	x	b	f	g	h	r	r	n	e	e	i
f	a	r	m	e	r	m	e	r	c	h	a	n	t	r	r	a
a	s	t	r	o	n	a	u	t	t	e	a	c	h	e	r	n
p	o	s	t	a	l	w	o	r	k	e	r	c	l	e	r	k
d	o	c	t	o	r	t	r	e	w	u	i	o	p	m	n	e
a	r	t	i	s	t	m	n	e	r	y	p	h	g	l	o	r
m	e	n	t	i	o	n	s	i	y	r	e	m	n	j	k	l
a	b	a	k	e	r	c	t	j	u	s	f	o	u	k	r	e
c	n	u	r	s	e	d	f	h	g	r	i	y	b	e	w	k

WORD BANK

computer operator	artist	astronaut	nurse	electrician
postal worker	farmer	carpenter	logger	mechanic
police officer	clerk	teacher	baker	merchant
musician	dancer	fire fighter	doctor	homemaker
pilot				

WAY TO GO!

Find and circle the words from the Word Bank in the puzzle.
Look across and down. Color the squares you circled yellow.
What did you find? _____

s	g	a	b	g	t	h	o	v	i	w	a	k	l	o	h
f	t	r	u	c	k	e	l	e	v	a	t	o	r	n	e
s	s	h	i	p	e	s	c	a	l	a	t	o	r	b	c
u	b	o	a	t	c	a	b	l	e	c	a	r	s	h	w
p	t	a	x	i	s	c	h	o	o	l	b	u	s	e	g
x	t	r	a	i	n	s	a	i	r	p	l	a	n	e	v
o	t	r	a	m	h	e	l	i	c	o	p	t	e	r	a
f	s	u	b	w	a	y	m	o	n	o	r	a	i	l	n
n	o	s	b	u	s	o	e	f	a	c	a	b	t	p	s
y	n	e	c	a	r	u	n	f	t	j	e	t	o	i	e

WORD BANK

monorail	trains	cable cars	schoolbus	tram
airplane	bus	elevator	ship	truck
boat	cab	escalator	subway	van
car		helicopter	taxi	jet

A MAJESTIC VIEW

Find and circle the words from the Word Bank in the puzzle.
Look across and down. Color the squares you circled green.
What did you find? _____

s	r	t	u	i	r	x	l	m	p	i	e	k	n	b
t	g	h	n	l	y	s	e	t	m	n	r	e	w	a
n	y	u	o	p	r	u	a	r	s	e	t	f	x	t
a	z	h	s	m	i	n	v	u	e	p	b	g	h	v
b	e	a	o	o	n	s	e	n	e	i	a	f	y	t
c	f	g	i	s	g	e	s	k	d	n	r	i	g	u
e	d	e	l	s	s	e	n	f	s	e	k	r	g	h
h	r	o	o	t	s	d	e	o	p	l	a	n	t	s
s	t	r	e	e	s	l	e	r	w	a	t	e	r	u
x	c	o	n	e	s	i	d	e	w	o	o	d	s	g
t	f	u	m	a	b	n	l	s	u	p	r	n	f	r
x	d	y	u	i	e	g	e	t	a	e	t	r	i	o
r	e	f	t	u	e	s	s	s	b	j	h	g	t	y

WORD BANK

age	fir	moss	plant	seedlings	sun	water
bark	forests	needles	rings	seeds	trees	woods
cones	leaves	pine	roots	soil	trunk	

A REFRESHING DIP

Find and circle the words from the Word Bank in the puzzle.
Look across and diagonally. Color the squares you circled orange.
What did you find? _____

e	m	w	a	t	e	r	s	i	q	t	a	s	t
t	s	c	l	e	a	r	w	e	a	q	c	j	a
a	b	u	b	b	l	e	s	i	u	a	y	x	c
b	r	e	a	t	h	e	l	a	l	o	p	d	h
r	o	c	k	s	c	a	r	e	f	n	o	e	u
p	l	a	n	t	s	i	s	e	e	i	p	n	m
x	a	i	r	f	u	n	i	l	y	a	n	t	o
b	c	p	u	m	p	s	e	r	w	e	t	s	j
y	i	d	s	w	i	m	u	i	o	g	h	r	k
t	e	f	t	g	i	l	l	j	m	h	i	o	x

WORD BANK

eat	fins
clear	breathe
pumps	scales
eye	aquariums
fun	plants
bubbles	water
gill	air
swim	tail
care	rocks

HEADING FOR THE SLOPES

Find and circle the words from the Word Bank in the puzzle. Color the squares you circled one color. What did you find? _____

g	i	o	w	t	r	z	u	y	
s	s	s	s	s	s	s	t	o	p	r	t
a	h	h	h	h	h	t	r	o	e	c	s	v	p
c	o	i	o	a	a	b	e	p	r	w	n	m	x
y	u	r	u	r	l	l	t	z	e	m	a	n	d
g	l	l	t	t	e	l	s	h	e	l	l	o	s	h
r	o	d	s	s	s	o	s	h	a	r	p	h	h	s
s	h	s	h	o	w	w	s	h	e	e	p	s	o	h
s	h	o	r	t	s	h	a	p	e	s	h	i	n	e

WORD BANK

shell	should	shallow	sharp
shouts	sheep	shares	shirts
she	short	shape	show
shine			

WHAT A RECIPE

Read the clues. Write the words that mean the same. Find and circle your answers in the puzzle.

Hint: All words start with the prefixes "un," "dis" or "re."

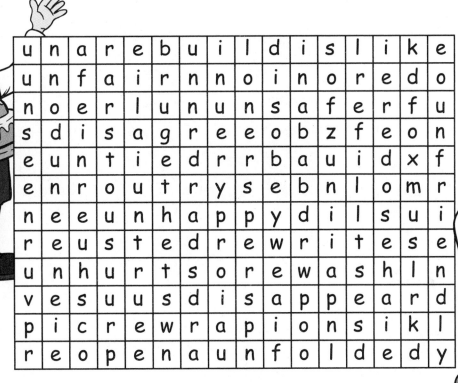

u	n	a	r	e	b	u	i	l	d	i	s	l	i	k	e
u	n	f	a	i	r	n	n	o	i	n	o	r	e	d	o
n	o	e	r	l	u	n	u	n	s	a	f	e	r	f	u
s	d	i	s	a	g	r	e	e	o	b	z	f	e	o	n
e	u	n	t	i	e	d	r	r	b	a	u	i	d	x	f
e	n	r	o	u	t	r	y	s	e	b	n	l	o	m	r
n	e	e	u	n	h	a	p	p	y	d	i	l	s	u	i
r	e	u	s	t	e	d	r	e	w	r	i	t	e	s	e
u	n	h	u	r	t	s	o	r	e	w	a	s	h	l	n
v	e	s	u	u	s	d	i	s	a	p	p	e	a	r	d
p	i	c	r	e	w	r	a	p	i	o	n	s	i	k	l
r	e	o	p	e	n	a	u	n	f	o	l	d	e	d	y

CLUES

1. Not happy _____
2. Not true _____
3. To not obey _____
4. Not hurt _____
5. To not like _____
6. Not safe _____
7. To fill again _____
8. Not fair _____
9. To wrap again _____
10. Not seen _____
11. To stop appearing _____
12. To write again _____
13. Wash again _____
14. Not tied _____
15. Not folded _____
16. To not agree _____
17. To do again _____
18. To open again _____
19. Not friendly _____
20. To build again _____

TAGALONG WORD SEARCH

Antonyms are words that have opposite meanings.

Draw a line through the words in the word search that are antonyms of the words in the Word Bank. In tagalong, use the words in the order they are listed. The last letter of the word just found will be the first letter of the next word to be found.

Attract/repel has been done for you.

WORD BANK

attract	niece
lad	best
awakes	listen
opens	donate
hears	richer
madam	work
ewe	head
women	first
old	fat
kindness	day
rooster	short
later	more
divorce	north
sharp	she
dark	beginning
relaxed	shrunk
difficult	dry
brave	from
foolish	in
west	push
tender	ill
soften	borrow

R	R	H	A	R	D	E	N	O	W	E	D	E
E	E	C	G	S	L	E	E	P	S	U	N	H
R	P	S	S	U	P	I	H	H	L	D	J	T
O	E	A	T	H	O	T	U	L	I	E	O	U
O	L	A	E	D	A	T	A	N	I	T	S	O
P	I	W	O	R	S	T	G	G	U	G	O	S
L	E	B	W	A	A	H	R	O	T	L	H	W
E	A	E	E	L	Y	G	E	E	S	N	E	T
M	N	S	K	S	S	I	W	F	A	L	P	K
S	A	E	T	H	I	N	A	O	L	S	N	T
Q	U	H	M	A	R	W	O	L	L	E	Y	R

TAGALONG WORD SEARCH

Draw a line through the words in the word search that are antonyms of the words in the Word Bank. In tagalong, use the words in the order they are listed. The last letter of the word just found will be the first letter of the next word to be found.

Shy/bold has been done for you.

WORD BANK

shy	dull
alike	meaner
head	wrong
die	bottom
late	whole
no	overweight
different	woman
beginning	all
bad	difficult
up	adult
old	cold
east	rested
mend	dine
poor	gives
share	go
washed	future
mom	heel
dash	giant
from	last
even	loose
smart	short
front	truth

A	Y	L	R	A	E	T	I	G	H	T	T
U	R	E	A	S	T	V	S	E	E	A	N
E	M	A	S	R	N	R	I	R	I	L	E
N	D	R	I	E	D	Y	A	L	I	L	R
D	R	M	B	A	S	O	P	P	M	F	E
I	A	K	D	A	D	U	O	B	D	L	F
N	O	N	E	O	U	T	I	T	Q	E	F
G	H	R	K	J	T	H	H	C	S	L	I
C	O	C	H	E	O	A	G	O	A	D	
O	A	O	I	D	E	R	I	T	I	R	P
B	M	U	D	R	I	N	I	C	E	R	O
A	G	R	A	O	T	E	Y	F	L	K	T
I	R	E	W	G	W	C	T	A	K	E	S
E	T	S	E	W	E	N	B	E	A	L	M

TAGALONG WORD SEARCH

Homophones are words that sound alike but are spelled differently and have different meanings.

Draw a line through the word in the word search that is a homophone of the word in the Word Bank. In tagalong, use the words in the order they are listed. The last letter of the word just found will be the first letter of the next word to be found.

Fur/fir has been done for you.

H	O	E	S	X	O	H	B	K	S	T	E	A	K	N	U	N
G	C	O	N	R	A	E	G	T	R	E	I	G	N	O	A	A
U	N	E	M	W	W	E	E	U	Z	I	S	E	I	T	D	O
O	W	H	R	O	L	L	I	Y	O	L	E	J	G	U	E	L
R	A	R	R	I	J	S	P	E	E	D	O	H	H	C	W	E
G	E	R	I	A	F	A	T	I	W	A	T	I	T	K	O	E
N	F	E	S	N	E	A	G	A	D	E	H	D	P	S	W	T
A	E	O	D	H	G	H	H	E	I	R	G	A	A	E	H	S
E	U	I	V	E	G	G	L	G	A	R	I	S	R	D	I	K
L	K	S	G	L	I	M	H	Y	R	L	S	H	E	O	C	C
U	E	N	C	H	B	T	S	H	O	O	T	R	I	A	H	A
F	N	V	E	Q	U	I	T	W	E	I	G	H	S	A	I	L

WORD BANK

fur	knead	here	you	know	raise	oar	steal
role	doe	roe	ate	ores	chute	wrap	lone
let's	heals	wee	tide	sole	through	pale	none
stake	stares	urn	dear	lien	witch	lo	knot
night	site	knew	ruff	nay	hare	ways	tux
there	tows	ring	hose	hi	read	sale	sew
rain	slay	gait	sun	air	due	lax	ode

TAGALONG WORD SEARCH

A **synonym** is a word that means about the same as another word.

Draw a line through the word in the word search that is a synonym of the word in the Word Bank. In tagalong, use the words in the order they are listed. The last letter of the word just found will be the first letter of the next word to be found.

Rank/rate has been done for you.

R	A	I	S	E	S	R	E	T	S	E	P	P	E	E	W
G	A	S	D	N	E	O	H	B	K	G	A	A	Q	U	O
A	F	E	T	N	T	R	A	P	A	R	D	O	N	U	N
M	P	Z	T	I	A	I	I	R	T	A	P	K	I	C	K
J	I	E	I	V	R	C	X	R	O	T	C	C	W	A	G
E	D	M	E	L	K	E	Y	E	S	O	L	I	O	R	R
J	D	A	E	L	Y	E	S	O	S	L	S	R	R	S	O
A	A	N	O	B	L	C	E	T	U	P	D	T	H	D	W
W	R	E	X	L	U	T	A	P	S	H	O	U	T	O	I
F	E	L	E	C	T	R	A	S	H	U	R	T	H	H	S
K	N	L	S	I	T	E	A	C	H	I	T	S	S	A	H

WORD BANK

rank	want	haul	rip	separate	choose
finishes	possesses	misplace	lifts	attempt	destroy
mix	halt	leave	fly	scream	harm
relaxes	plan	snare	perch	pack	surpasses
holler	pave	forgive	fool	plunge	begin
toss	knock	doze	punt	pare	instruct
wave	select	bother	recognize	guide	smacks
mature	save	lease	cry	challenge	exhibit

FUN WITH LICENSE PLATES

Check out some license plates as you play these super games!

OUT-OF-STATE PLATES

Be on the lookout for out-of-state license plates. When you find one, call out the state where the license plate was issued. Score 1 point for every out-of-state plate you spot first. The first person who scores 20 points wins.

SENTENCE CHALLENGE

In this game, players use the letters from a license plate to make up interesting sentences. For example, if the license plate reads 2ABC345, each player must come up with a sentence made up of words that start with the letters A, B and C. The letters can be in any order. One player might say, "Adorable babies coo," while another might call out, "Can alligators bite?"

Variation: Instead of sentences, players can create phrases or come up with individual words for the letters. (Examples: awkward brown cats or apple, banana, cherry.)

CAN YOU DECIPHER IT?

In this game, the first person to decipher a personalized license plate scores a point. For example, the license plate ILVMYCR can be deciphered as "I love my car." If you can create another phrase or sentence from the letters on the plates, such as "Ian loves very mild, yellow, crunchy rice," you earn an extra point. The letters should be kept in the order they appear on the plate.

NUMBER COMBINATIONS

In this game, only the numbers on license plates count. The first player writes the license plate number of the first car, the second player writes the number of the second car, and so on. When everyone has had a turn, each player tallies his or her combinations.

One Pair
(two numbers that are the same)
— **1 point**

Two Pairs
(two sets of like numbers)
— **2 points**

Three of a Kind
(three numbers that are the same)
— **3 points**

Four of a Kind
(four numbers that are the same)
— **4 points**

Three or More in a Row (three or more numbers in sequence, such as 4, 5, 6)
— **5 points**

Play the game several times. The person with the highest score wins.

LICENSE PLATE COLLECTION

Try to spot as many different kinds of license plates as you can. Here are some things you can look for: place name, color, slogan, picture or symbol. List the kinds of license plates you see. Use the recording sheet on page 46.

Variation: Collect license plates by state or province. List the ones you see. At the end of your trip, tally how many you've collected.

HOW MANY WORDS?

One person calls out three or four license plates while another person writes them down. (If no vowels are present, continue writing down the license plates until one or more are found.) Then, using only the letters on the plates, everyone works together to make as many words as possible. Use the recording sheet on page 46.

LICENSE PLATE MATCH

Make up a license plate number and write it down. Then, write the license plate number of the first vehicle you see. How close were you at matching the plate? Score 1 point for each number and letter you were able to match. Score 2 points for each number and letter that is also in the correct position. Use the recording sheet on page 46.

RECORDING SHEET

(Directions are found on page 45.)

LICENSE PLATE COLLECTION

_____
_____
_____
_____
_____
_____
_____
_____
_____
_____
_____
_____
_____
_____
_____
_____

HOW MANY WORDS?

_____
_____
_____
_____
_____
_____
_____
_____
_____
_____
_____
_____
_____
_____
_____
_____

LICENSE PLATE MATCH

_____
_____
_____
_____
_____
_____
_____
_____
_____
_____
_____
_____
_____
_____
_____
_____

LICENSE PLATE LOTTO

Use the lotto gameboard below and on pages 48–51. Each player fills in the 25 sections with numbers from 1 to 9 and letters of the alphabet. The numbers and letters may be used more than once.

Next, one player calls out a number or a letter from the license plate of a passing vehicle. Players with the corresponding number or letter cross it off their gameboard. The game continues with different players calling out numbers or letters. The first player to cross off all the letters or numbers on his or her lotto gameboard wins.

P	S	9	Z	C
M	3	H	T	E
8	L	R	Z	U
G	A	F	J	V
I	R	B	N	4

LICENSE PLATE LOTTO GAMEBOARDS

(Directions are found on page 47.)

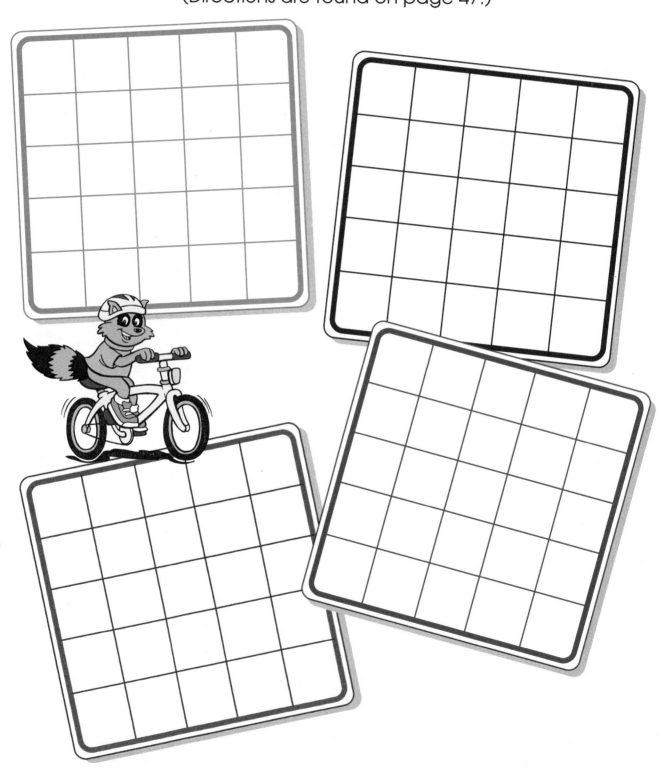

LICENSE PLATE LOTTO GAMEBOARDS

(Directions are found on page 47.)

LICENSE PLATE LOTTO GAMEBOARDS

(Directions are found on page 47.)

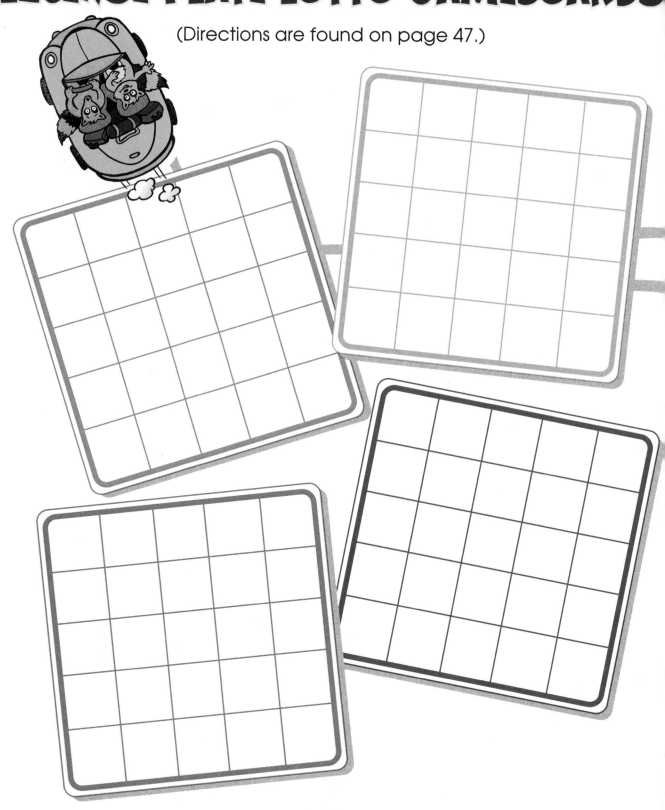

LICENSE PLATE LOTTO GAMEBOARDS

(Directions are found on page 47.)

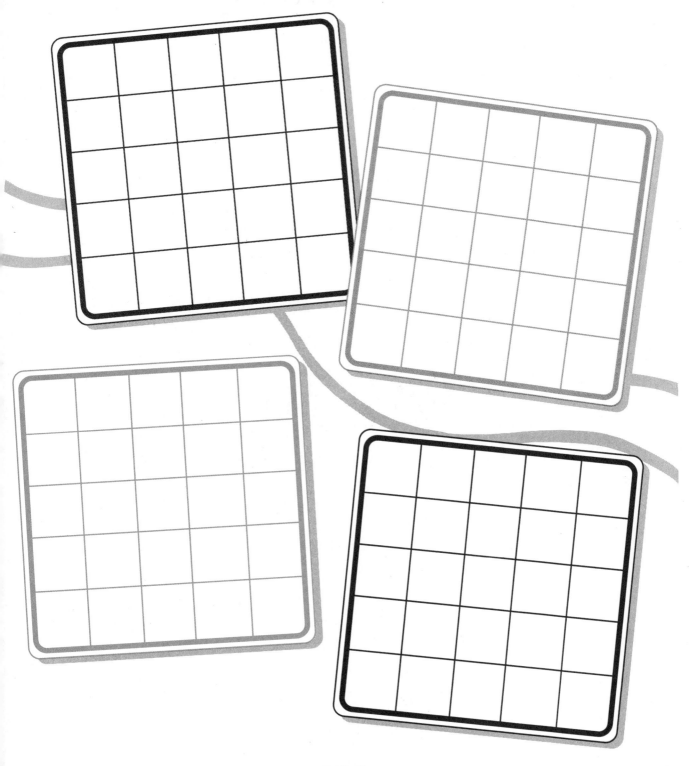

BEETLE!

In this traditional car-spotting game, the goal is to find a Volkswagen "beetle!" and call out "beetle!" Players score 1 point for each Volkswagen® spotted. The person who scores the most points in a given time period wins.

Volkswagen is a registered trademark of Volkswagenwerk Aktiengesellschaft.

Variation: Choose a different type of car or a specific color. For example, you can decide to look for vans or for red cars.

COLOR COUNT

Each player chooses a color. (To make the game even more challenging, have the players choose a specific shade of color, such as dark green or light blue.) Then, players score 1 point for each car they spot that is their color. The first person to score 100 points wins.

Variation: Each player chooses a color and a side of the road. Players can only count the cars they see on their side of the road. For example, a player can choose to look for cars of a certain color that are on the side of oncoming traffic.

PEOPLE WATCH

List at least 15 different kinds of people you might see while traveling. Then, when you spot them, check them off your list. Here are some suggestions: police officer, taxi driver, truck driver, jogger, person with sunglasses, baby.

MY PEOPLE WATCH LIST

FOOD FUN

Use the Food Fun lists below and on pages 56 and 57. See how many food words or pictures of food you can find while traveling. Look for them on billboards, restaurant signs and other sources. See how many items you can spot in 30 minutes.

BURGERS

TACOS

PIZZA

SANDWICHES

ICE CREAM

HOT DOGS

FOOD FUN LIST

FOOD FUN LIST

FOOD FUN LISTS

(Directions are found on page 55.)

FOOD FUN LIST	FOOD FUN LIST	FOOD FUN LIST
_____	_____	_____
_____	_____	_____
_____	_____	_____
_____	_____	_____
_____	_____	_____
_____	_____	_____
_____	_____	_____
_____	_____	_____
_____	_____	_____
_____	_____	_____
_____	_____	_____
_____	_____	_____
_____	_____	_____
_____	_____	_____
_____	_____	_____

FOOD FUN LISTS

(Directions are found on page 55.)

FOOD FUN LIST	FOOD FUN LIST	FOOD FUN LIST

COWS AND CEMETERIES

This game is ideal for a car trip through the countryside. The game can be played by two players or two teams.

Each person or team picks one side of the car. Players look out their side of the car and keep track of the number of cows they find. If a cemetery is passed, the players on that side lose all their cows and have to start counting from the beginning. The team with the greatest number of cows wins.

Variation: If you're traveling in the city or in an area where cows are not usually found, choose other items to count. For example, you could score points for gas stations and lose points for police cars.

TEAM 1

TEAM 2

TRAVELER'S TIC TAC TOE

This game requires two players sitting next to each other. One person is **X** and the other is **O**.

Use the grids below and on pages 60–65. Write in each section the name of something you might see during your travels, such as a stop sign or a fire hydrant. The first player to see one of the items calls it out and writes his or her designated letter in the corresponding place on the grid. The first person to get three in a row wins.

TRAVELER'S TIC TAC TOE GRIDS

(Directions are found on page 59.)

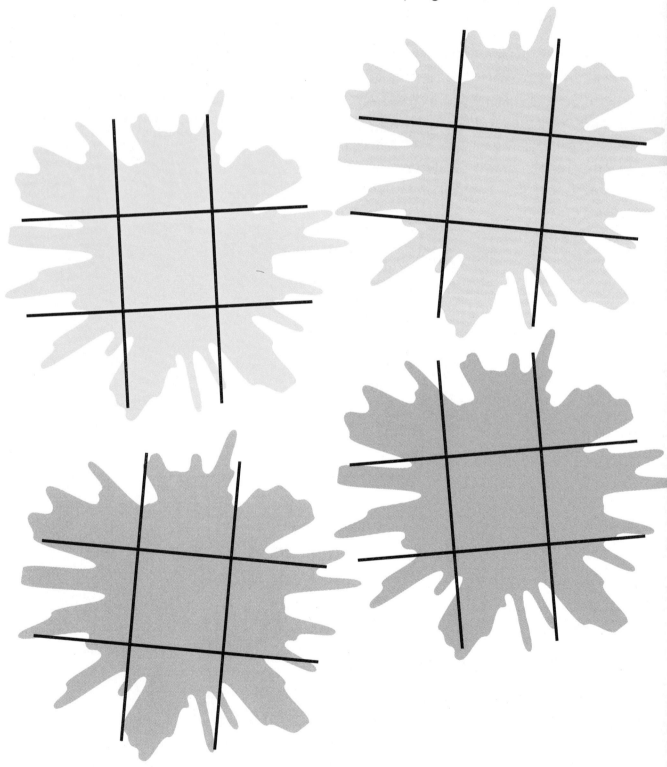

TRAVELER'S TIC TAC TOE GRIDS

(Directions are found on page 59.)

TRAVELER'S TIC TAC TOE GRIDS

(Directions are found on page 59.)

TRAVELER'S TIC TAC TOE GRIDS

(Directions are found on page 59.)

TRAVELER'S TIC TAC TOE GRIDS

(Directions are found on page 59.)

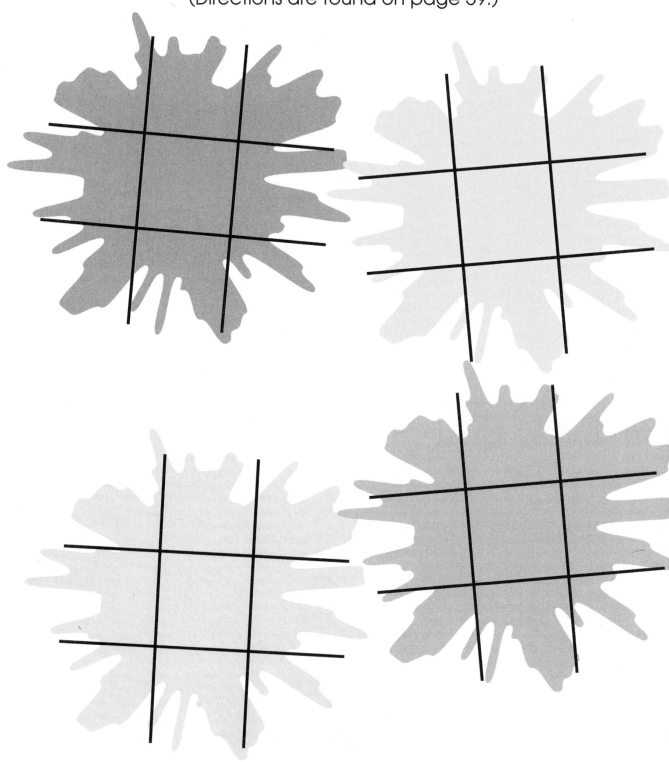

TRAVELER'S TIC TAC TOE GRIDS

(Directions are found on page 59.)

NAME SPELLER

Use the space below or another sheet of paper. Start this game by writing a name vertically on a sheet of paper. Then, spot things beginning with the letters in that name. When an item is spotted, a person calls it out and records it. If the name has more than one of the same letter, different items have to be found for each of them. Everyone helps to complete the name.

Write your name in this space.

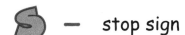
S — stop sign

C — cream-colored car

O — office building

T — telephone pole

T — tree

TRAVELER'S SCAVENGER HUNT

Here's a fun scavenger hunt that everyone in the car will enjoy playing. Together, make a list of 15 or more things you will most likely see on your trip. The list can include general things, such as a billboard or a farm, and very specific items, such as a black-and-white cow or a sign that displays the letter "Z."

While traveling, everyone helps look for the things on the list. The first person to spot an item calls it out, then writes his or her initial beside that item on the list. If two people call out an item at the same time, both their initials are written down. The goal is to find as many things on the list as possible within a given amount of time or before the trip is over. (Lists are found on page 68.)

WHAT'S THE TALLY?

Before you go on a car trip, make a list of 10–15 things you think you might see while traveling. Then when you're on the road, look for the items on your list. When you spot one, put a tally mark beside the word. Keep track of how many of each item you see. At the end of the trip, total the tally marks.

Here are some things you can include on your list:

✔	barn	✔	bike
✔	bird	✔	boat
✔	bus	✔	cow
✔	dog	✔	gas station
✔	golf course	✔	helicopter
✔	hotel	✔	motorcycle
✔	plane	✔	police car
✔	train	✔	truck

MAKING LISTS

(Directions are found on page 67.)

MY LIST

1. _____
2. _____
3. _____
4. _____
5. _____
6. _____
7. _____
8. _____
9. _____
10. _____
11. _____
12. _____
13. _____
14. _____
15. _____

MY LIST

1. _____
2. _____
3. _____
4. _____
5. _____
6. _____
7. _____
8. _____
9. _____
10. _____
11. _____
12. _____
13. _____
14. _____
15. _____

MY LIST

1. _____
2. _____
3. _____
4. _____
5. _____
6. _____
7. _____
8. _____
9. _____
10. _____
11. _____
12. _____
13. _____
14. _____
15. _____

ROADSIDE BINGO

Use the bingo card below and on pages 70–75. Players fill in the sections with various things they might see on their trip, such as a black cat, a flagpole, a white van and a fire hydrant. When players see one of the items on their bingo card, they cross it off. The first person to make a straight line vertically, horizontally or diagonally calls out "Bingo!" and wins.

ROADSIDE BINGO CARDS

(Directions are found on page 69.)

ROADSIDE BINGO CARDS

(Directions are found on page 69.)

B	I	N	G	O

ROADSIDE BINGO CARDS

(Directions are found on page 69.)

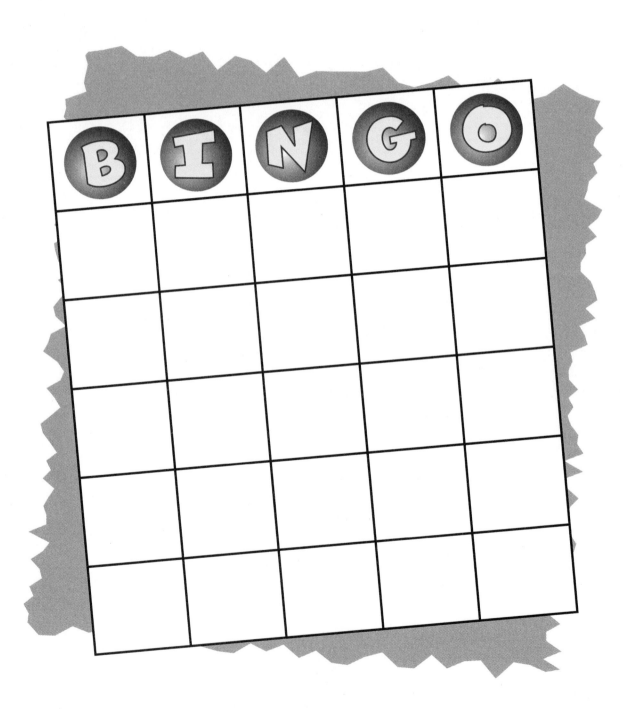

ROADSIDE BINGO CARDS

(Directions are found on page 69.)

ROADSIDE BINGO CARDS

(Directions are found on page 69.)

ROADSIDE BINGO CARDS

(Directions are found on page 69.)

SPOT THE SIGNS

Take a copy of this page with you when you're traveling. Then see how many of the following signs you can spot. (The meaning of each sign is shown by its picture.) Check off each sign that you find.

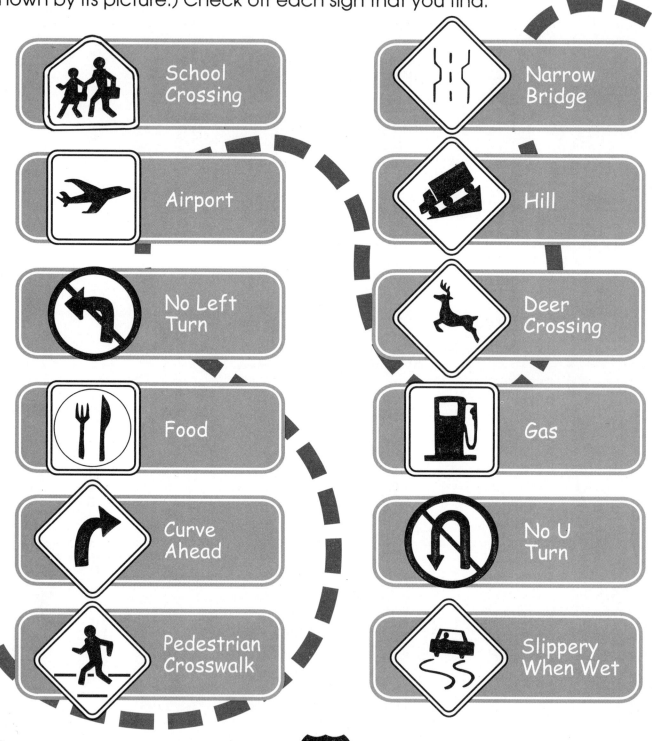

School Crossing

Airport

No Left Turn

Food

Curve Ahead

Pedestrian Crosswalk

Narrow Bridge

Hill

Deer Crossing

Gas

No U Turn

Slippery When Wet

MY FAVORITE COLOR

Each player writes the name of his or her favorite color on a sheet of paper. Then, players see how many things of their color they can find. When an appropriate object is spotted, the player calls it out and writes it on his or her list.

One type of object counts for 1 point. For example, if a player's color is red and three red cars are spotted, only 1 point is scored. If two players have the same color, the player who spots the object first and calls it out earns the point. Set a time limit, and see who can find the greatest number of objects for his or her color.

RED	GREEN
fire truck	grass
apples	house
stop sign	corn field
	beans

CITY, STATE AND COUNTRY

Be the first to spot the name of a city, state or country and call it out. When you do, you score one point. Sources for the names include road signs, bumper stickers, license plates and buildings. The person who finds the most place names wins.

WELCOME TO
COLUMBUS
OHIO

525·AFP
IOWA

NATURE SEARCH

Go on a nature search when you're traveling. Make a list of the items you find. Can you spot 20 different things before your trip is over?

Here are some things you might see:

- birds
- broadleaf trees
- evergreen trees
- cactuses
- cliffs
- clouds
- dandelions
- fields
- flowers
- fruit trees
- grass
- hills
- islands
- lakes
- mountains
- rivers
- oceans
- rainbows
- rocks
- sand
- waterfalls

NATURE SEARCH

_____
_____
_____
_____
_____
_____
_____
_____
_____
_____
_____
_____
_____
_____
_____
_____

NATURE SEARCH

_____
_____
_____
_____
_____
_____
_____
_____
_____
_____
_____
_____
_____
_____
_____
_____

WHAT A PACE!

Number the pictures 1, 2, 3, 4 to show the order from fastest to slowest.

_____ _____ _____ _____

_____ _____ _____ _____

 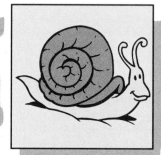  

_____ _____ _____ _____

_____ _____ _____ _____

PLEASE HELP ME FIND MY OWNER

Help each pet find its owner. Start at the picture of each animal. Follow the directions at the bottom to find each pet's owner.

Example: S 4 means to go south 4 spaces.

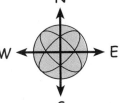

Cat E 4 → S 3 → W 3 → S 3 → E 6 → S 4 → W 4 → S 1 → E 8 → N 7 → W 2

Dog S 6 → W 3 → N 5 → W 3 → S 6 → E 6 → S 2 → W 5

The cat's owner is _____ . The dog's owner is _____ .

ON THE WAY TO THE BIG GAME

Jan and Jeff are meeting at the baseball field. Start at the picture of each child. Follow the directions at the bottom to find out how each one entered the field.

Example: (S 4) means to go south 4 spaces.

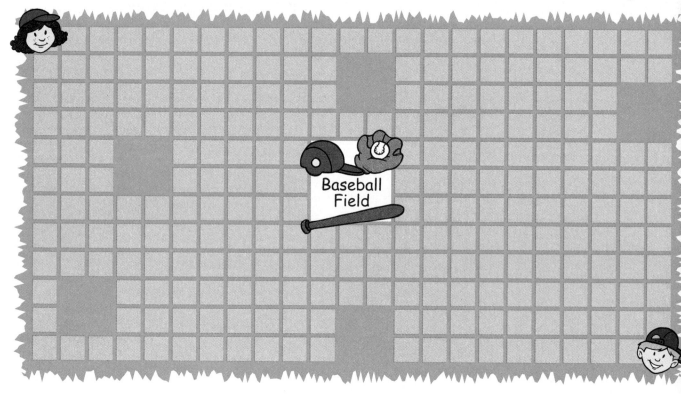

Baseball Field

Jan (E 2) (S 1) (E 6) (S 1) (W 7) (S 4) (E 6) (S 3) (E 3) (N 2)

Jeff (W 8) (N 3) (E 6) (N 7) (W 2) (S 6) (W 2) (N 2) (W 3)

Who entered the field from the south? _____

GOING FOR REPAIRS

Your bike needs to go to the repair shop. Your parents' car needs to go to a garage for new tires. Follow the lines to see how the bike and the car reached the correct repair shops.

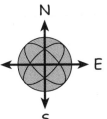

Write the directions in the ⭕'s to show how they reached the repair shops. The first ones have been done for you.

Example: 4 spaces to the west is written (W 4).

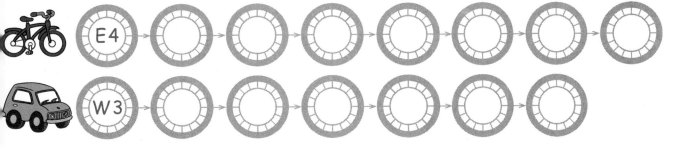

E 4 → ⭕ → ⭕ → ⭕ → ⭕ → ⭕ → ⭕ → ⭕

W 3 → ⭕ → ⭕ → ⭕ → ⭕ → ⭕ → ⭕

How many spaces was the bike from the repair shop? _____

How many spaces was the car from the garage? _____

Which repair shop was farthest away? _____

ISLAND-HOPPING HELICOPTER RIDE

Hawaii, our 50th state, is really a group of islands in the Pacific Ocean. Many people like to island-hop, which means traveling from one island to another. One way to island-hop is to fly in a helicopter.

Look at the map. Starting at Hilo, follow the route shown by the dashed line. Write the names of the islands in the order of the route.

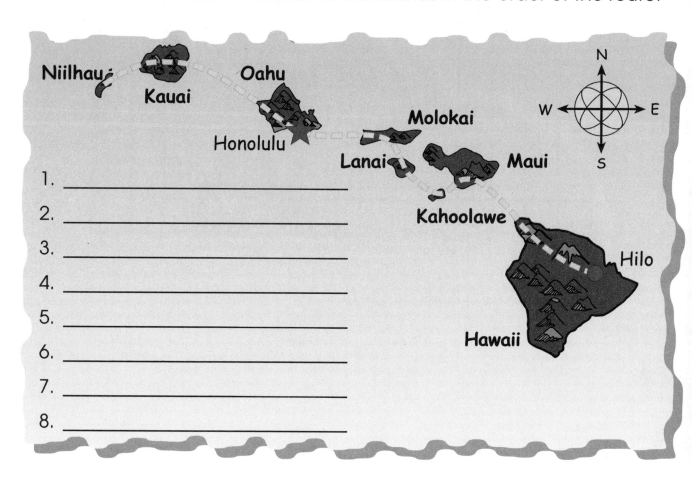

1. _____
2. _____
3. _____
4. _____
5. _____
6. _____
7. _____
8. _____

Honolulu is the capital of Hawaii. On what island will we find Honolulu?

_____

On which side of the island is Honolulu located? _____

PONY EXPRESS

The "pony express" carried the mail across our country between April 3, 1860 and October 28, 1861. A young man would ride a horse from one station to the next, changing horses at each station. It was a very dangerous ride. The trip went from Sacramento, California to St. Joseph, Missouri.

Look at the map. Write the names of the states in the order the pony express rider traveled through them while carrying the mail from California to Missouri.

1. _____   4. _____   7. _____

2. _____   5. _____   8. _____

3. _____   6. _____   9. _____

Which state did you write two times? _____

How long did the pony express deliver mail? _____

_____

OLD-TIME STAGECOACH RIDE

Follow the horseshoe trail to tour the old western town. Write the names of the places in the order they are passed along the trail. Remember the ride starts and ends at the same place.

1. _____
2. _____
3. _____
4. _____
5. _____
6. _____
7. _____
8. _____
9. _____
10. _____

HELPING A LOST STUDENT

Recess is over. A first grade student cannot find her way to Room 1. Can you help her? Look at the map. The dotted line shows the way from the playground to Room 1.

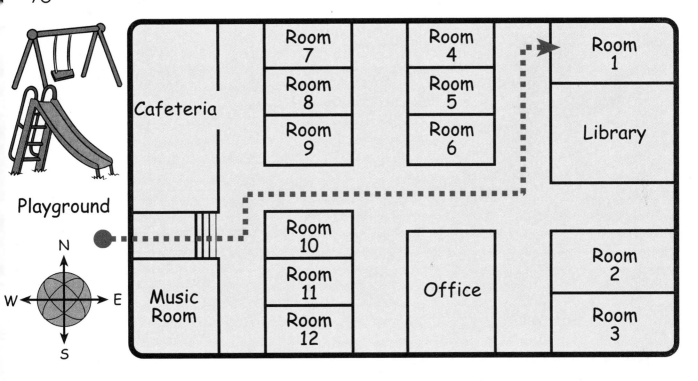

Number the directions by following the path of the dotted line.

_____ Turn north at the bottom of the steps.

_____ First, you open the door and come into the school.

_____ Continue walking down the long hall past the office.

_____ Turn north when you reach the library.

_____ Walk by the music room.

_____ Keep walking until you come to Room 1.

_____ Go down three steps.

_____ Turn east and walk down the hall between Rooms 9 and 10.

How does it feel to be lost? _____

_____

PLAN A ROUTE

A truck driver has to decide which roads he will use to deliver his cargo to the depot. He has to be sure his truck will go under the bridges and through the tunnels. His truck is 12 feet high. The heights of the bridges and tunnels are marked on the map.

14 feet — Redding

Brownsville

11 feet

10 feet

Fair City

Comstock

16 feet

Carson

Peaks

10 feet

15 feet

Silver City

Dayton

DEPOT

Trace the route the truck driver will need to take to reach the depot. Write the names of the towns the truck will pass through in order.

1. _____

2. _____

3. _____

4. _____

5. _____

Why can't the truck driver take any other route? _____

_____

_____

_____

What kind of cargo do you think the truck driver might be carrying?

_____

_____

_____

88

ARRIVING ON TIME

There are TV monitors at the airport that show when planes are arriving and departing. Here is one showing arrivals.

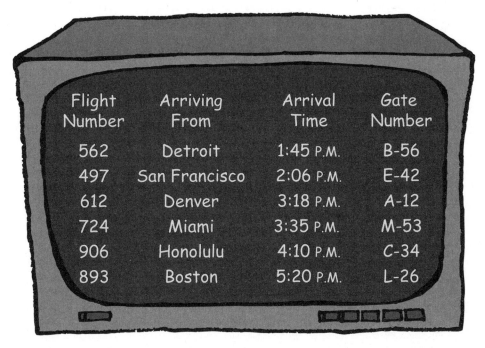

Flight Number	Arriving From	Arrival Time	Gate Number
562	Detroit	1:45 P.M.	B-56
497	San Francisco	2:06 P.M.	E-42
612	Denver	3:18 P.M.	A-12
724	Miami	3:35 P.M.	M-53
906	Honolulu	4:10 P.M.	C-34
893	Boston	5:20 P.M.	L-26

Use the information on the monitor to answer the questions.

What is the . . .

1. city listed before Denver? _____

2. flight number listed before 906. _____

3. gate number listed before M-53? _____

4. arrival time listed before 4:10 P.M.? _____

5. flight number listed after 562? _____

6. gate number listed after C-34. _____

7. city listed after Miami? _____

8. arrival time listed after 2:06 P.M.? _____

9. city listed before San Francisco? _____

10. arrival time listed after 4:10 P.M.? _____

FINDING THE GOLD

Can you find the gold?

Mine Entrance

Follow the directions to draw a line to the gold.

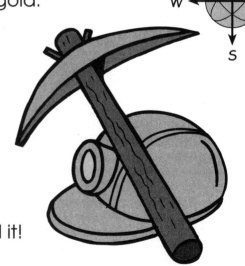

1. Start at the mine entrance.
2. Follow the dashed line east 7 spaces.
3. Next, go north 5 spaces.
4. Then, go east 3 spaces.
5. Now, go north 3 spaces.
6. Turn and go east 3 spaces.
7. Turn again and go south 6 spaces.
8. Now, go west 2 spaces. You have found it!
9. Color that space yellow.

THE BUS ROUTE

This map shows all the stops this bus makes on its route to South Station.

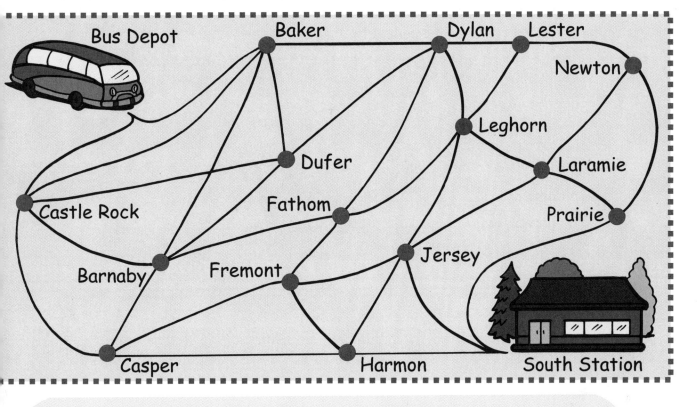

Write the names of the stops in alphabetical order to show the bus route.

1. _____   9. _____

2. _____   10. _____

3. _____   11. _____

4. _____   12. _____

5. _____   13. _____

6. _____   14. _____

7. _____   15. _____

8. _____

Use a crayon to connect the stops in the order of the bus route.

CRUISING

There are many islands in the Caribbean Sea. These islands are favorite vacation spots for many people. Cruise ships take several different routes to the different islands.

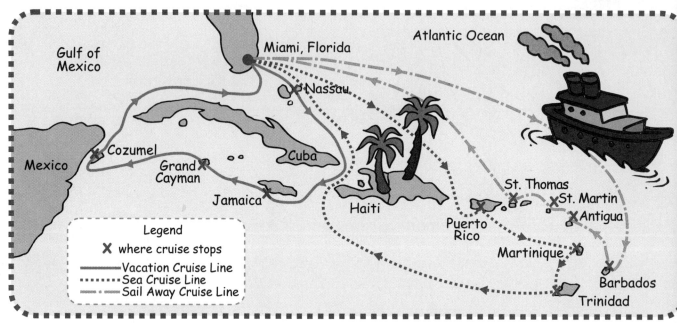

Write in order the names of the islands where each cruise ship stops. Be sure to include where each cruise line begins and ends.

Vacation Cruise Line	Sea Cruise Line	Sail Away Cruise Line
1. _____	1. _____	1. _____
2. _____	2. _____	2. _____
3. _____	3. _____	3. _____
4. _____	4. _____	4. _____
5. _____	5. _____	5. _____
6. _____	6. _____	6. _____

If your ship left port without you, what would you do? _____

_____

THEY SHOWED THE WAY

Meriwether Lewis and William Clark were chosen by President Jefferson to find a route to the Pacific Ocean. They had to draw maps of the land, record weather conditions and write about the plants and animals they found along the way. People wanted to know what it was like west of the Mississippi River. On May 14, 1804, they started their expedition. They arrived at the Pacific Ocean in the winter of 1805. They set up a camp which they named Fort Clatsop.

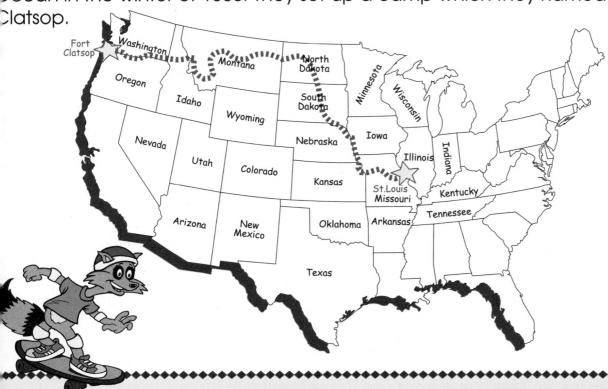

Write the names of the states in the order Lewis and Clark traveled through them on their expedition from St. Louis, Missouri to Fort Clatsop, Oregon.

1. _____
2. _____
3. _____
4. _____
5. _____

6. _____
7. _____
8. _____
9. _____
10. _____

PACKING A SUITCASE

In this traditional game, a player starts off by saying, "I'm packing a suitcase and I'm putting in a. . . ." The player then completes the sentence with an object. The second player repeats the sentence plus adds another item. The game continues with a new item being added each time. A player who forgets an item or says it out of order is out of the game. The winner is the last person left who can state all the items that are in the suitcase.

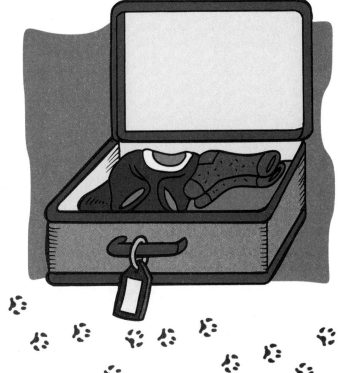

GUESS WHO I SAW?

This game is similar to "Packing a Suitcase" except that you have to remember people's names. The first player begins by saying, "I went to the store and guess who I saw! My friend _____!" The player completes the sentence with a person's name. The second player then repeats what the first player said but adds another person's name: "I went to the store and guess who I saw! My friends _____ and _____!" The game continues with a different person's name being added each time. The winner is the person who can say all the names.

MY AMAZING PET

Think of how many ways you can describe a pet.

The first player chooses a descriptive word that begins with "A," such as amazing, and uses it in a sentence: "My pet is an amazing pet." The second player repeats the sentence but also adds a descriptive word that begins with "B." For example, "My pet is an amazing, brilliant pet." The game continues with a "C" word, and so on. If a player forgets a word, gets the words out of order or can't think of a new word, he or she is out of the game. The last player left in the game is the winner.

carrots	macaroni
milk	frozen peas
ice cream	salad dressing
chicken	sesame
paper towels	crackers
hamburger	two dozen eggs
apple juice	rye bread
apples	vegetable soup
cheese	bag of sugar
pickles	lettuce

GROCERY LISTS

Use the lists on page 97 or another sheet of paper to prepare a grocery list that contains 20 items. The first player reads his or her list aloud. The other players have 5 minutes to write as many of the items from memory as they can. The person who gets the greatest number of correct items wins. The game continues with another player reading his or her list to the others.

Variation: Use a grocery list with 26 items. The first item begins with "A," the second with "B," and so on. (For "X," an item containing the letter can be used, such as wax paper.)

GROCERY LISTS

(Directions are found on page 96.)

CAR-TUNES

See how quickly you can recognize tunes with this musical challenge. Turn on your radio until a song comes on. Listen for a few seconds and turn off the radio. Can you name that tune? If not, turn on the radio and listen again. The first person to identify the song scores 1 point. Keep playing until someone scores 10 points.

Variation: Instead of naming the title of the song, players have to identify the recording artist.

MYSTERY TAPE

This game requires some preparation, but the effort will be worth it for music lovers.

Before you leave on your trip, tape-record short bursts of songs from cassettes, compact discs, videos or the radio. Write the song titles on a sheet of paper in the order the songs appear.

When you're traveling, play the tape for your family. Pause the tape after each song to allow everyone to think about the song. Keep track of how many songs each person can name. The person who identifies the most songs first is the winner.

HUM A MELODY

One player begins by humming a tune. The tune may be from a popular song or from a melody used in a commercial, TV show or movie. The player who identifies the tune gets to hum the next one.

SONGS ON THE GO

Does your family enjoy singing in the car? If so choose from a great selection of songs that describe people on the go. If your family is shy about singing, that's okay. Instead of singing the songs, just write them down and see how long your list grows. Here are some suggestions:

- "Row, Row, Row Your Boat"
- "She'll Be Comin' Round the Mountain"
- "The Wheels on the Bus"
- "Michael, Row Your Boat Ashore"
- "A Bicycle Built for Two"

SILLY VERSES

Everyone decides on a favorite tune and makes up new verses for the song. Each person can contribute a line or everyone can add lines as he or she thinks of them. You can include the names of family members or add lines that describe the trip you're taking. For example, here's a verse that's sung to the tune of "Jingle Bells":

Mom and Dad, Jed and I
Ride for miles and miles,
It's so fun for everyone,
We're always full of smiles!

ANSWER:

ANSWER:

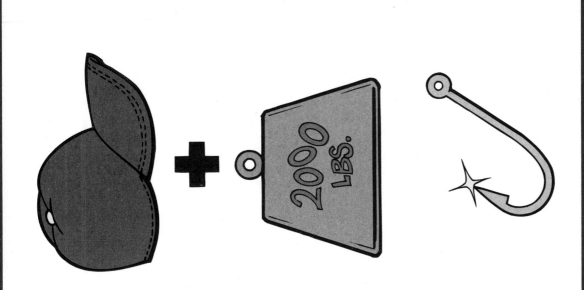

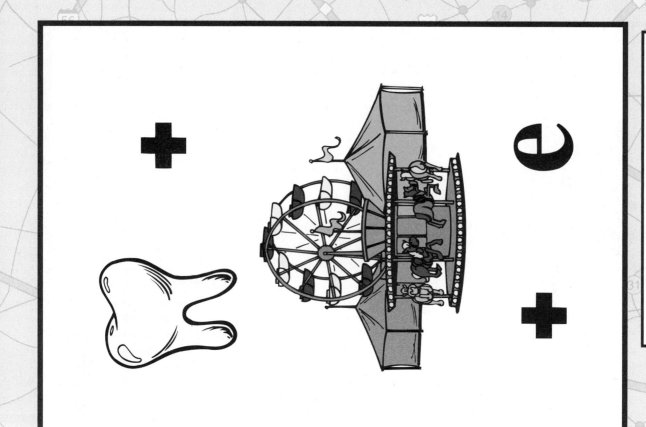

ANSWER:

ANSWER:

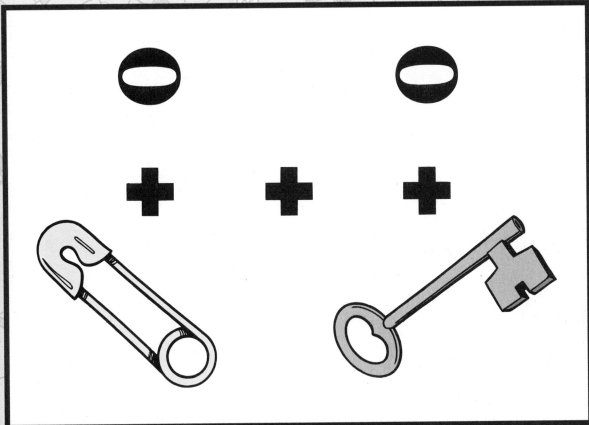

ANSWER:

ANSWER:

Top puzzle

a + − + n

ANSWER:

Bottom puzzle

+ us

ANSWER:

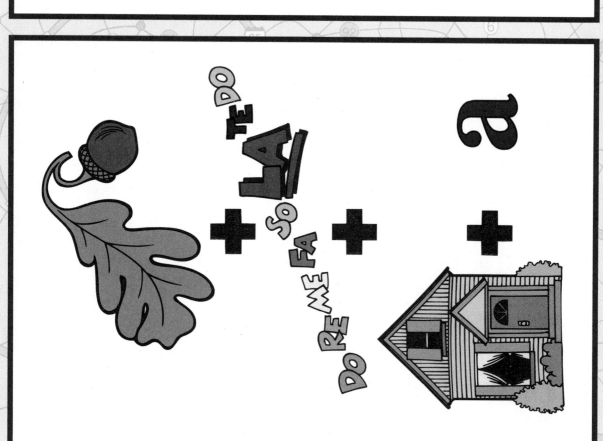

ANSWER:

ANSWER:

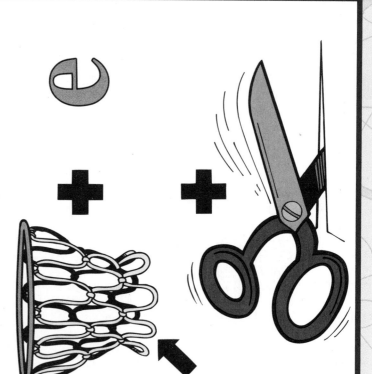

ANSWER:

ANSWER:

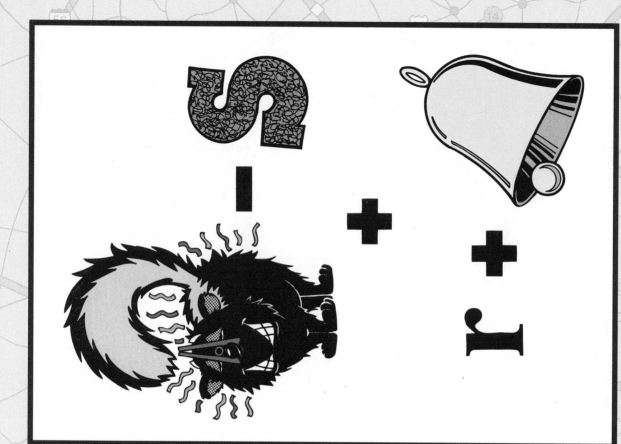

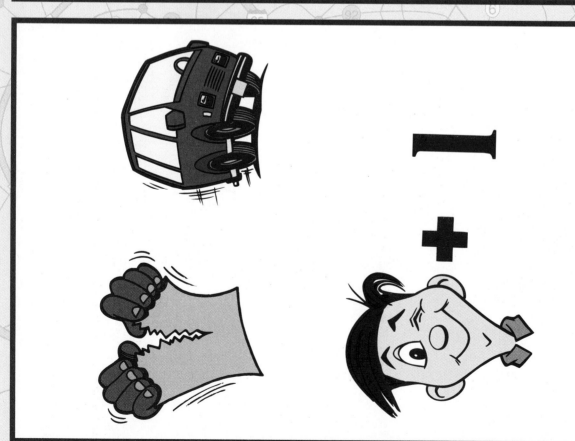

ANSWER:

ANSWER:

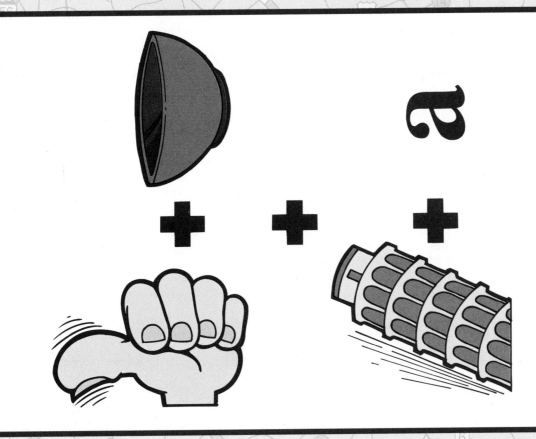

113

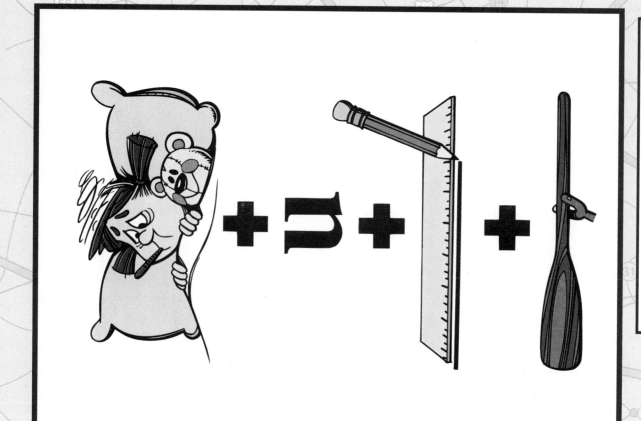

ANSWER:

ANSWER:

ANSWER:

ANSWER:

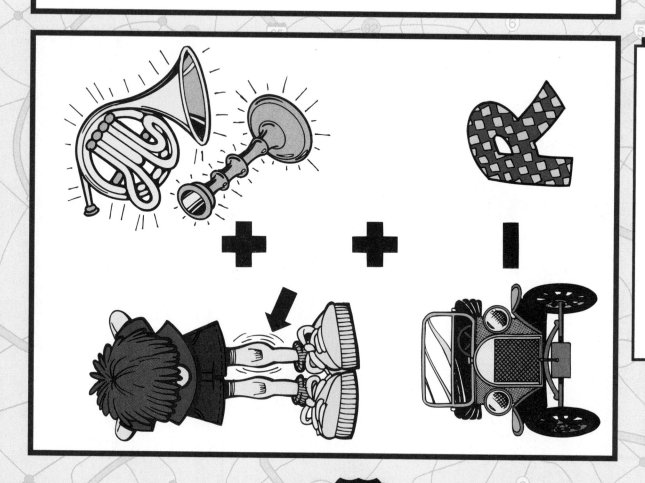

ANSWER:

ANSWER:

R -

C - + j +

j + I +

ANSWER:

ANSWER:

ANSWER:

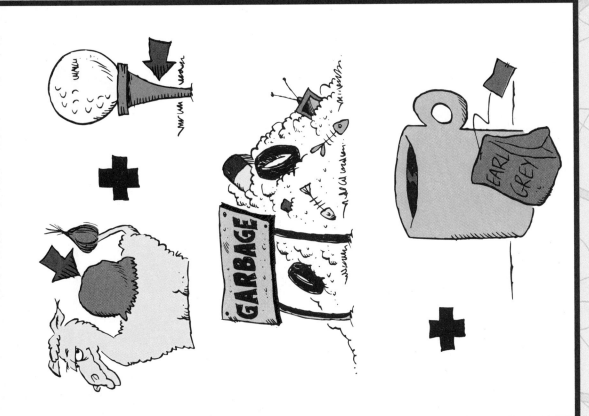

119

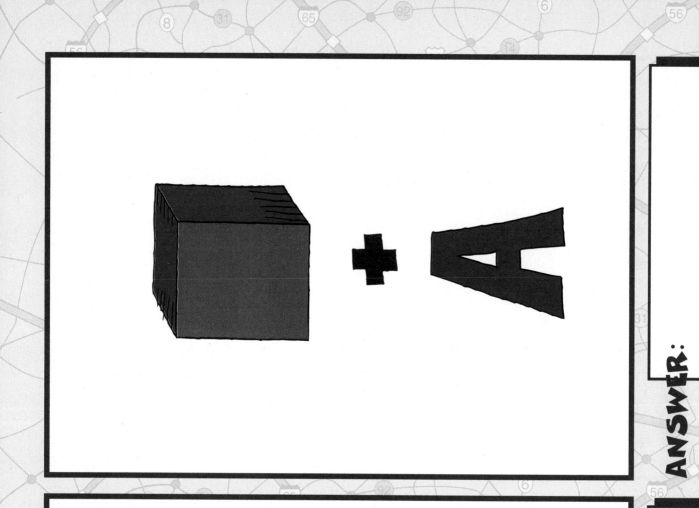

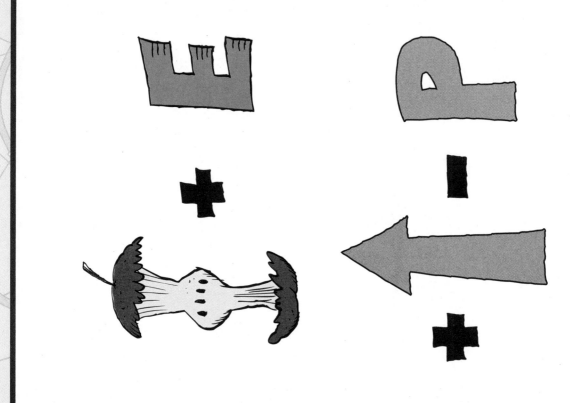

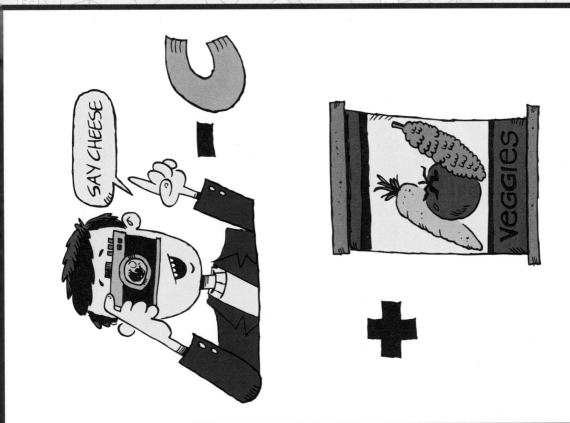

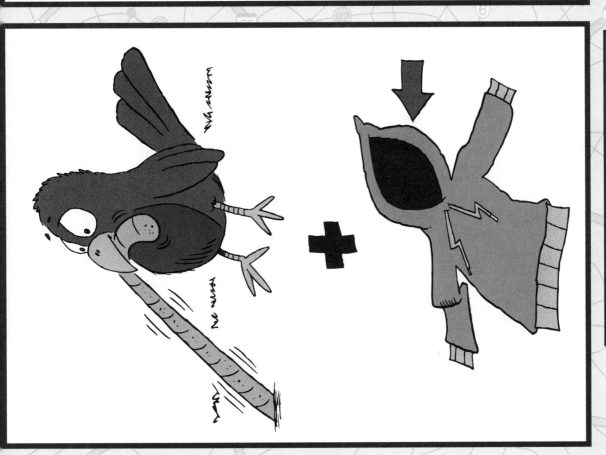

ANSWER:

ANSWER:

ANSWER:

ANSWER:

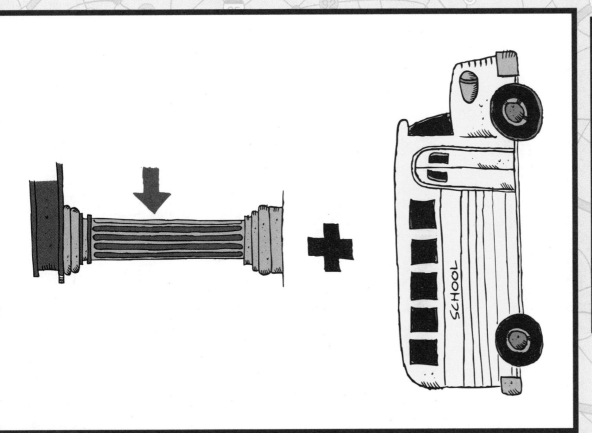

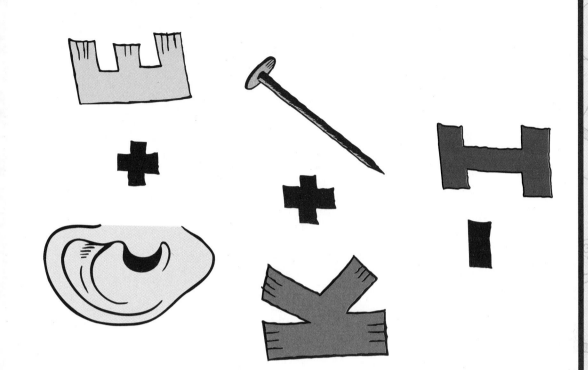

ANSWER:

ANSWER:

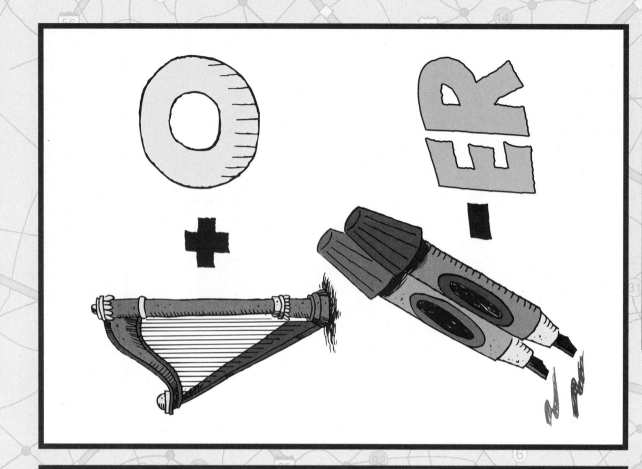

ANSWER:

ANSWER:

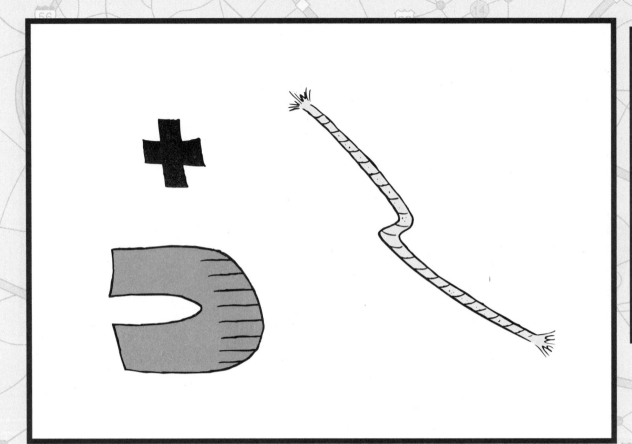

ANSWER:

ANSWER:

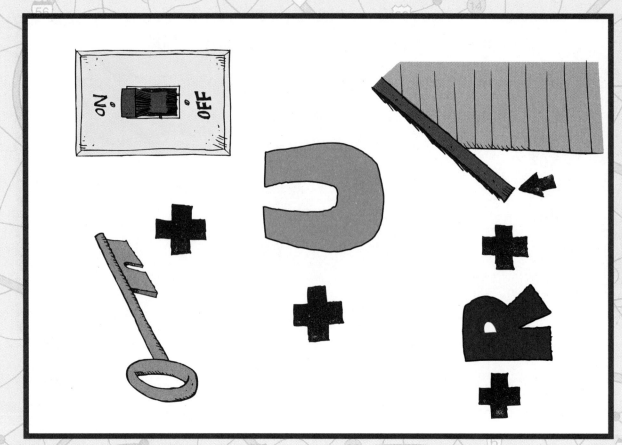

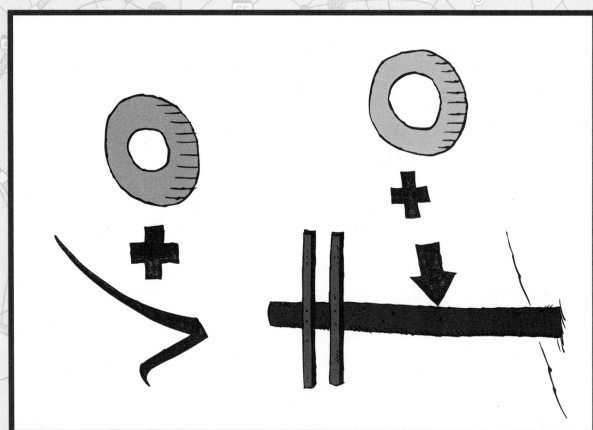

ANSWER:

ANSWER:

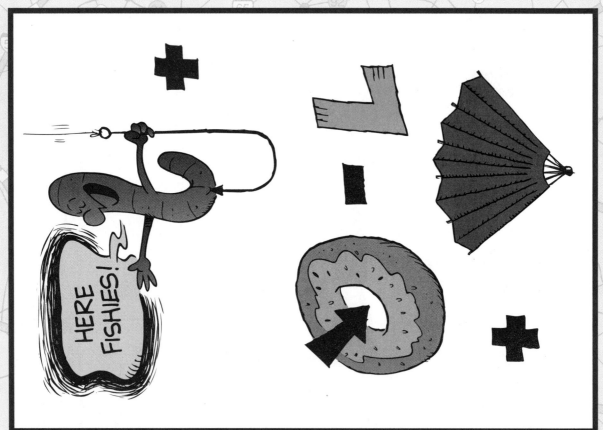

ANSWER:

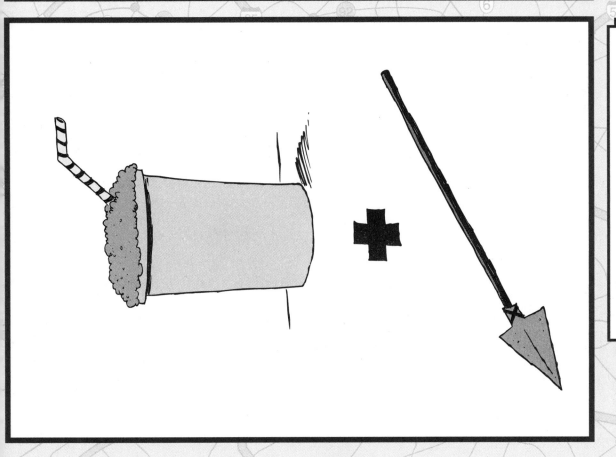

ANSWER:

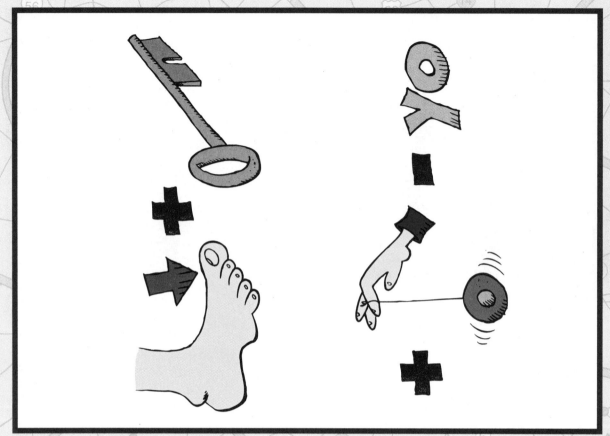

ANSWER:

ANSWER:

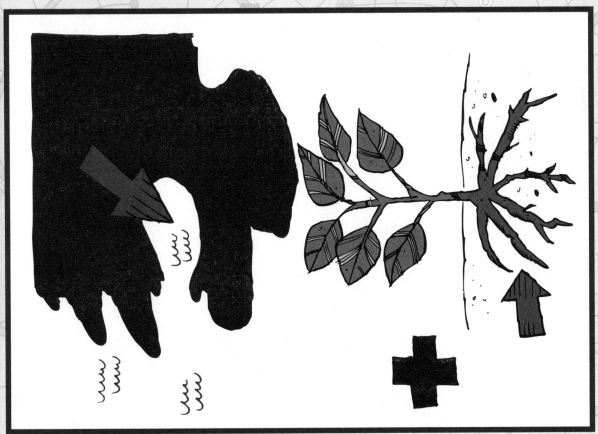

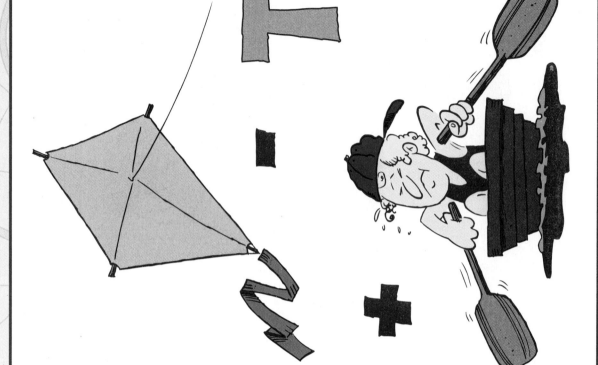

A WORD PYRAMID

Use the pyramid below and on pages 142–145.

To begin this game one player names a general category, such as animals or action words. The players then have to fill in their pyramids with names of animals or action words. The top row will have a two-letter word, the second row will have a three-letter word, and so on. The first person to finish the pyramid wins the game.

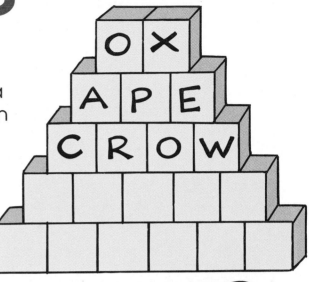

WORD PYRAMIDS

(Directions are found on page 141.)

WORD PYRAMIDS

(Directions are found on page 141.)

WORD PYRAMIDS

(Directions are found on page 141.)

WORD PYRAMIDS

(Directions are found on page 141.)

COLOR MY WORLD

One person states a color and everyone takes turns naming one thing that is that color. Keep playing until you can't think of anything else to name. Then, another person chooses a different color.

Variation: Make the game more challenging by allowing only things that naturally come in a particular color. For example, if the color were yellow, you could say "banana" or "daffodil" but not "car."

CATEGORIES CHALLENGE

One person chooses a category, such as ocean animals, cartoon characters or countries. Then, everyone takes turns naming something in that category. A player who can't name an item in 15 seconds is out. The game keeps going until only one player is left. That person is the winner and gets to name the category for the next game.

Here are some variations you can try for an extra challenge:

Name items according to the order of the alphabet.
The first player names an item that starts with A, the next player with B, and so on.

Choose a category and a letter.

All the items have to start with the letter.

Write down the items.
Set a time limit and let everyone write as many answers as they can. The player with the most items wins.

WORD DIAMONDS

Use the diamond below and on pages 148 and 149. This game is similar to the word pyramid (see page 141), but the blocks form a diamond instead. The top and bottom rows are made up of two blocks, the next rows have three blocks, and so on. The middle row is the longest and has seven blocks.

As before, a category is named and the number of letters in each word must fit the number of blocks provided. The first person to complete the word diamond wins.

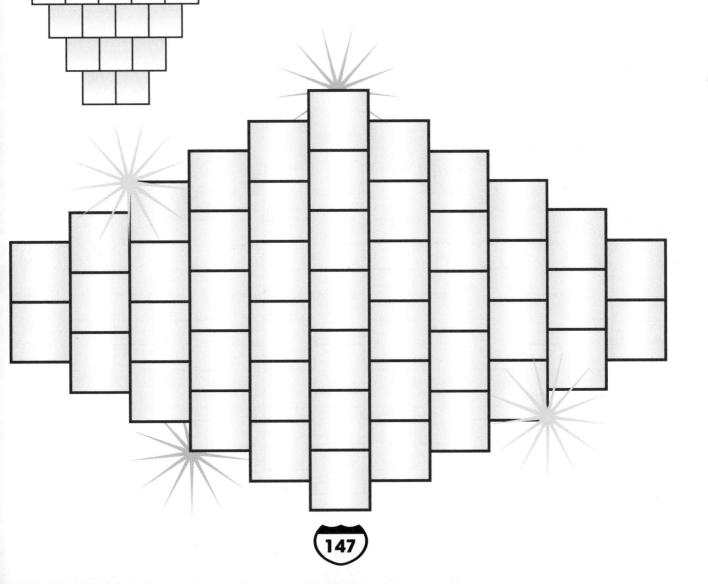

WORD DIAMONDS

(Directions are found on page 147.)

WORD DIAMONDS

(Directions are found on page 147.)

WHAT'S IN A NAME?

Use the grids below and on page 151. Write the name of a family member vertically on the grid. Then, write three categories at the top. (Examples: city, food, animal.) Next, write down items that fit the three categories and begin with the letters of the person's name. See how long it takes you to complete the sheet.

This game can be played with people working together or individually.

	CITY	FOOD	ANIMAL
L	Lakeville	Lima Beans	Lion
I			
N			
D			
A			

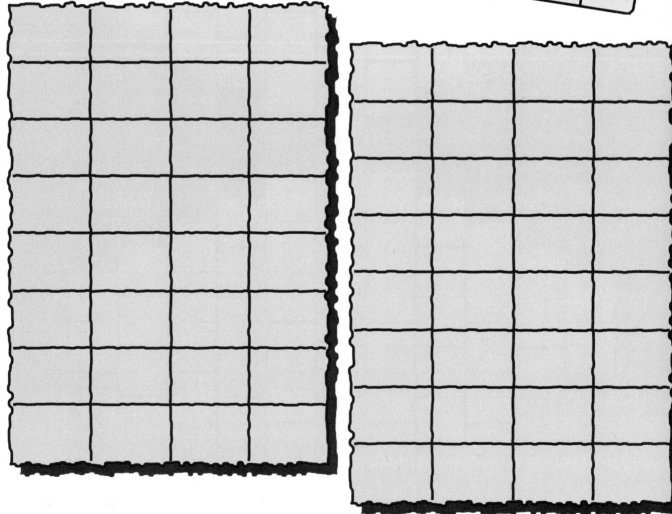

WHAT'S IN A NAME?

Directions are found on page 150.)

MOVIE TRIVIA

Do you like movies? Then, this category game is just for you!

One person begins by naming a movie. Then, each player takes a turn naming a character or an actor from the movie. Everyone helps to collect as many names as possible.

Variation: Play this game with two teams, and have each team write down the names on a sheet of paper. The team with the longest list wins.

CAPITAL CITIES

Challenge your knowledge of the states and their capital cities with this activity.

Each player must name a state and its capital. Write the capitals on a sheet of paper. Afterward, tally your answers. For an extra challenge, try countries and their capitals.

(Answer key for the states and their capitals is found on page 338.)

GOT IT!

Try to beat the time limit in this category game.

Use the lists on pages 154–159. Each player begins by writing six categories—one under the other—on a sheet of paper. Next, a person chosen to be the Caller calls out a letter. The players then have 1 minute to write down one item for each category that begins with the letter that was called out. If one player gets all six items before the minute is up, he or she yells, "Got it!" Then, everyone stops writing and the score is tallied. A player scores 1 point for every item listed; if a player writes an item that no one else has, he or she scores 2 points.

The game continues with the same categories but a different letter. Later, after several games have been played, the person with the most points wins.

beverages – tea
birds – toucan
countries – Thailand
people's names – Tim

Categorically Speaking

Stuck on what category to choose for a game? These suggestions may help you!

- adjectives (describing words)
- animals
- beverages
- birds
- book titles
- capital cities
- cars
- cartoon characters
- cities
- clothing
- colors
- comic book heroes
- countries
- famous people
- food
- lakes
- landmarks
- money
- movie stars
- movie titles
- people's names
- presidents
- sports
- sports figures
- recording stars
- rivers
- song titles
- states
- TV shows
- verbs (action words)

GOT IT! PAPER

(Directions are found on page 153.)

GOT IT! PAPER

(Directions are found on page 153.)

GOT IT! PAPER

(Directions are found on page 153.)

GOT IT! PAPER

(Directions are found on page 153.)

GOT IT! PAPER

(Directions are found on page 153.)

GOT IT! PAPER

(Directions are found on page 153.)

SCHOOL SPIRIT

Count the items. Use the Word Bank to help you write the number words in the puzzles.

Across

2.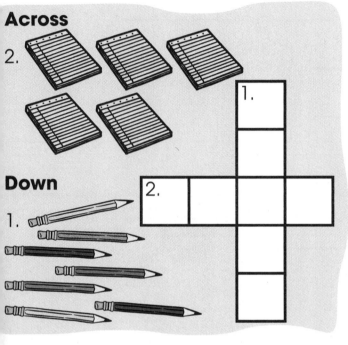

Down

1.

Word Bank
seven   eight   one
two   four   five

Across

2.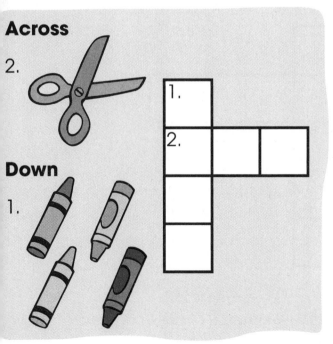

Down

1.

Across

1.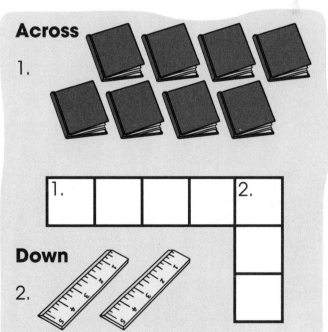

Down

2.

161

OOPS!

Use the Word Bank to help you find answers to the clues. Write them in the puzzles.

Across

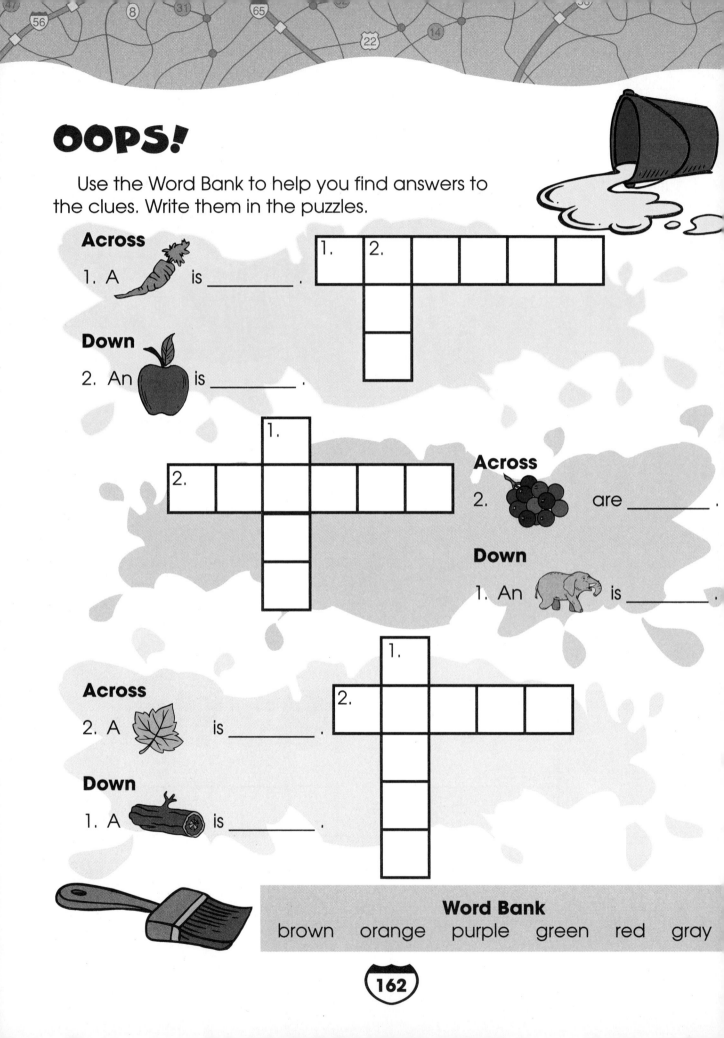

1. A ![carrot] is _____ .

Down

2. An ![apple] is _____ .

Across

2. ![grapes] are _____ .

Down

1. An ![elephant] is _____ .

Across

2. A ![leaf] is _____ .

Down

1. A ![log] is _____ .

Word Bank

brown   orange   purple   green   red   gray

ASTRO ADVENTURE

Use the Word Bank to help you find words that match the pictures. Write them in the puzzle.

Across

1.
3.
5.
7.
9.

Down

2.
4.
6.
8.
0.

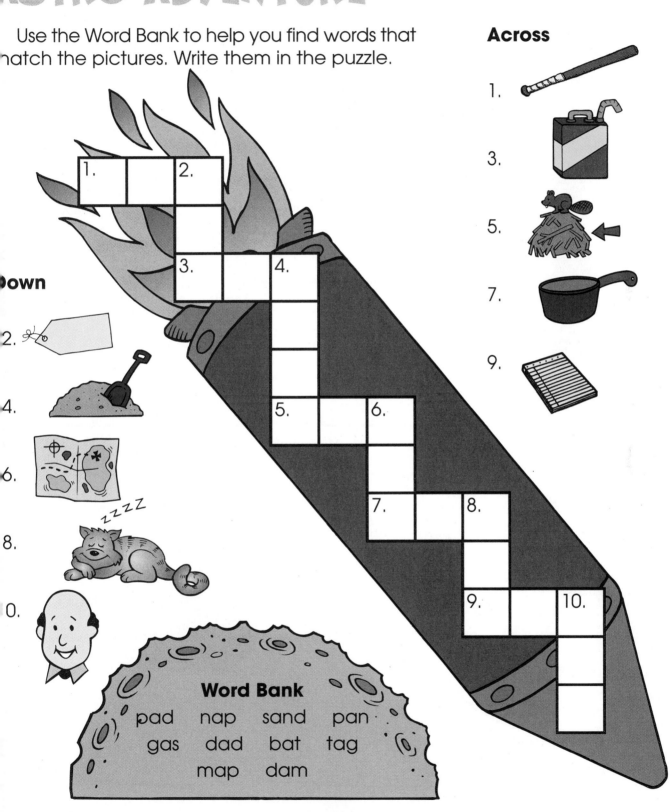

Word Bank

pad   nap   sand   pan
gas   dad   bat   tag
map   dam

UMBRELLAS UP!

Use the Word Bank to help you find words that match the pictures. Write them in the puzzle.

Across

1.

3.

5.

7.

9.

Down

2.

4.

5.

6.

8.

10.

Word Bank

mug   bus   sun   pup   hut

gum   hump   bug   sub   plum

nuts

DON'T JUST SIT THERE!

Use the Word Bank to help you find words that match the pictures. Write them in the puzzle.

Across

Word Bank

dinner   dime   desk
dock   dust   donkey
deer   dent   down
drum   dress

Down

HIT THE HAY!

Use the Word Bank to help you find words that match the pictures. Write them in the puzzle.

Across

1. 
6. 
3. 
7. 
4. 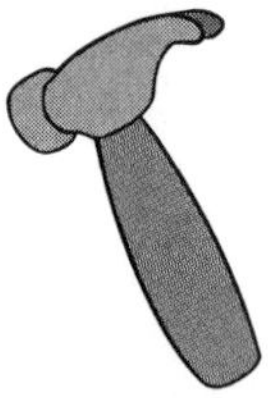
5. 
5.
6.
7.

Word Bank

hop   hole   hill
happy   helmet
hen   hose
hut   hay   hand
hammer   hat

Down

1. 
2. 
3. 
4. 
6. 
7.

CLIMBING KOALA

Use the Word Bank to help you find words that match the pictures. Write them in the puzzle.

Across

Down

Word Bank

king   keys   kite   kettle
kangaroo   kits   koala bear
kick   kitten   kind

IS IT REALLY MAGIC?

Use the Word Bank to help you find words that match the pictures. Write them in the puzzle.

Across

1.

2.

3.

5.

7.   8.

Down

1.   4.

2.   6.

3.   7.

Word Bank

mittens melt
map   mitt
mug   mop
mail   moon
mask   match
monster mouse

NAP TIME IN THE NEST

Use the Word Bank to help you find words that match the pictures. Write them in the puzzle.

Across

2.

4.

5.

6.

Down

1.

5.

2. 1, 2, 3, 4, …

6.

3.

Word Bank
note   nose   numbers   needle
net   nail   nine   nurse   nest

READY YOUR ROBOT

Use the Word Bank to help you find words that match the pictures. Write them in the puzzle.

Across

2.

4.

5.

6.

7.

Down

1.

2.

3.

4.

5.

Word Bank

rope
road
robe
race
rake
raft
raindrop
ribbon
rabbit
read

VEGGIE DELIGHT

Use the Word Bank to help you find words that match the pictures. Write them in the puzzle.

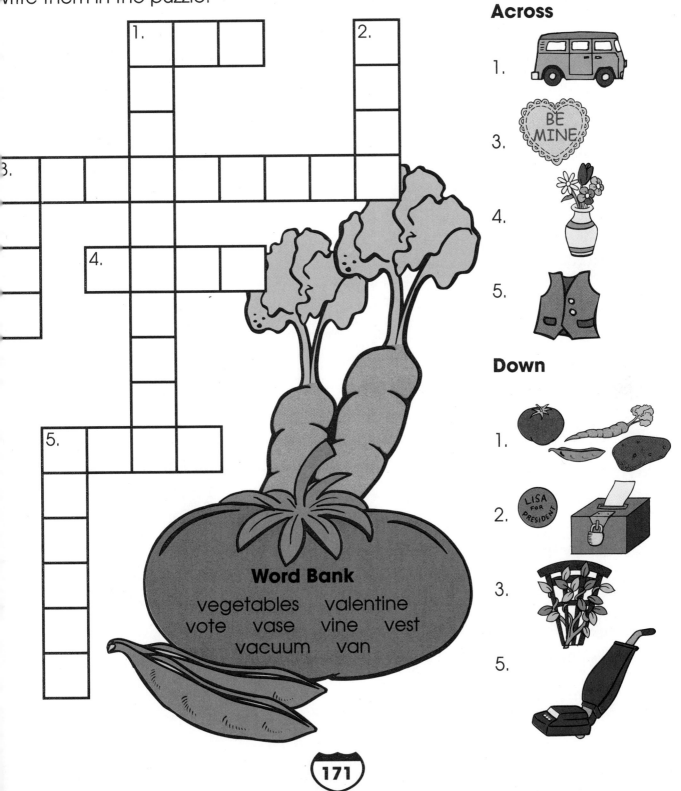

Across

1.

3.

4.

5.

Down

1.

2.

3.

5.

Word Bank

vegetables   valentine
vote   vase   vine   vest
vacuum   van

JUST CLOWNING AROUND

Count the 's. Write the number words in the puzzle. Use the Word Bank to help you.

Word Bank

three   eight
one   six   zero   ten
five   nine   four
seven   two

Across

2.

3.

5.

6.

8.

Down

1.

2.

3.

4.

7.

8.

FACING THE SUN

Use the Word Bank to help you find words that match the clues. Write them in the puzzle.

Across

1. A farm animal
2. A buzzing bug
4. A fruit
6. A very tall plant
7. The color of grass
8. A big bird

Down

1. At night you . . .
3. A mouse eats . . .
5. You _____ food.
6. 2 + 1 = _____ .
9. A part of a plant

Word Bank

bee   cheese   eat
sheep   green   peach   tree
sleep   eagle   leaf   three

SOOOO . . . COZY

Use the Word Bank to help you find words that match the clues. Write them in the puzzle.

Word Bank

stone	open	home
bones	toes	road
doe	hole	notes
rope	soap	boat
pole	globe	stove
toad		

Across

3. Not shut
5. Dogs like these
7. A street
10. These are on your feet
12. A rock
13. A mother deer
14. A long, rounded piece of wood

Down

1. Your house
2. A mole digs this
4. Musical
5. A ship
6. You cook on this
7. You can jump with this
8. A round map
9. Like a frog
11. You wash with this

PLACES, EVERYONE!

Use the Word Bank and the pictures below to help you fill in the puzzle.

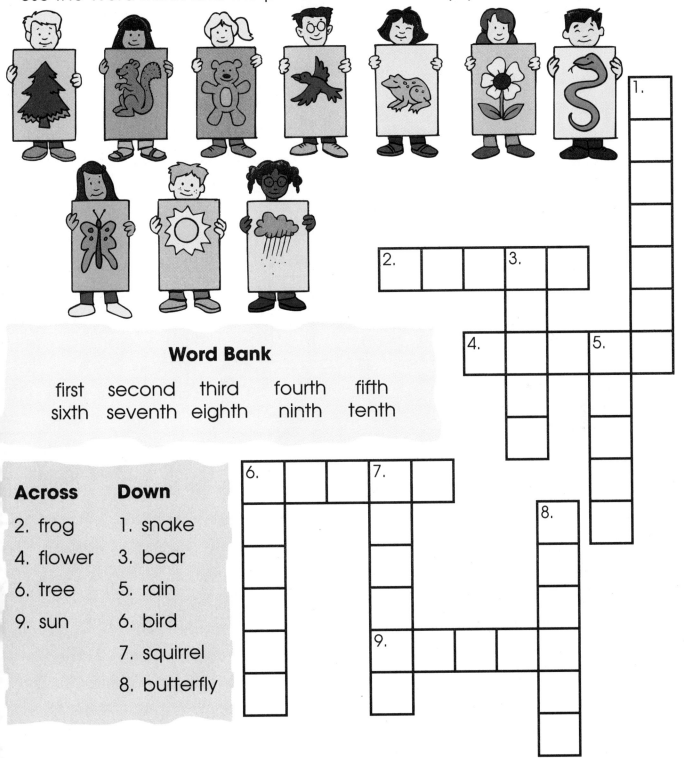

Word Bank

first   second   third   fourth   fifth
sixth   seventh   eighth   ninth   tenth

Across

2. frog
4. flower
6. tree
9. sun

Down

1. snake
3. bear
5. rain
6. bird
7. squirrel
8. butterfly

NICE HAT!

Use the Word Bank to help you fill in the puzzle.

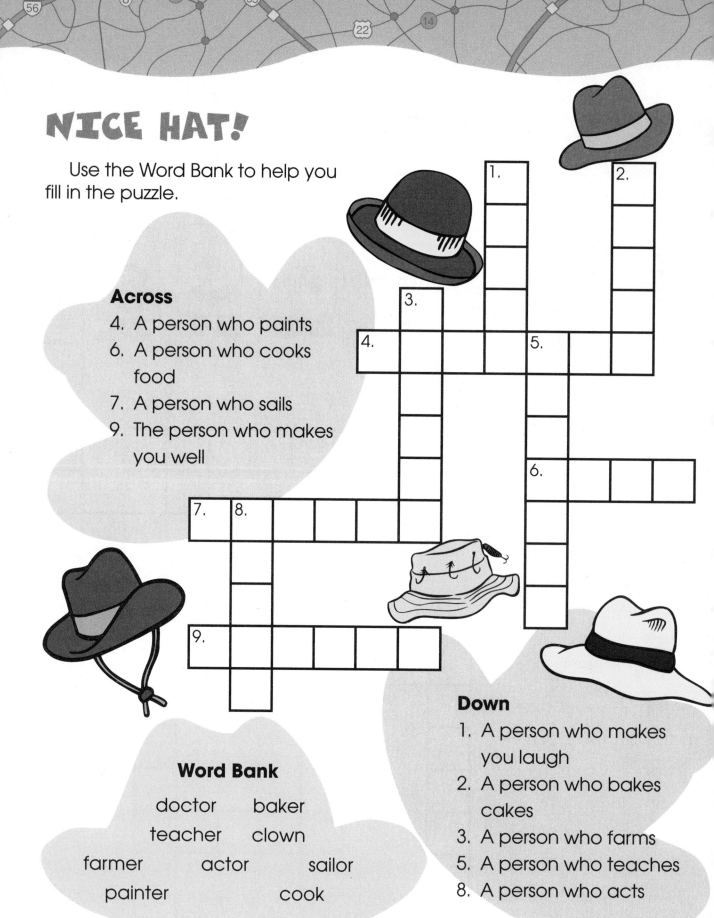

Across

4. A person who paints
6. A person who cooks food
7. A person who sails
9. The person who makes you well

Down

1. A person who makes you laugh
2. A person who bakes cakes
3. A person who farms
5. A person who teaches
8. A person who acts

Word Bank

doctor   baker

teacher   clown

farmer   actor   sailor

painter   cook

HELPFUL FRIENDS

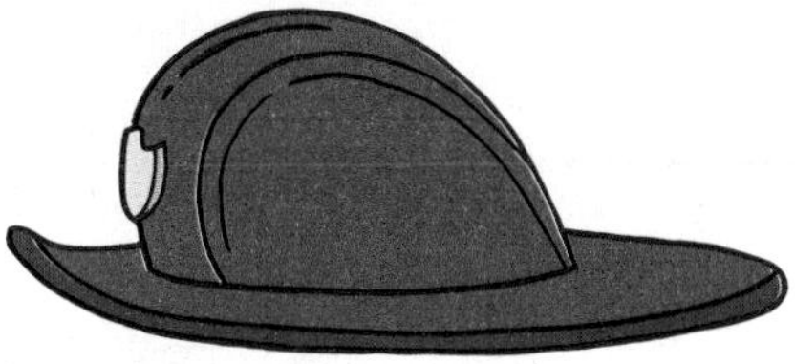

Use the Word Bank to help you fill in the puzzle.

Across

. A person who works for the police

. A person who puts out fires

. Always be _____ with fire.

Down

. Makes a police car's sound

. Policemen and firemen _____ everyone.

. People need to _____ _____ the rules.

. Police help when there is an _____ .

. Never play with _____ .

. An _____ goes off when there is a fire.

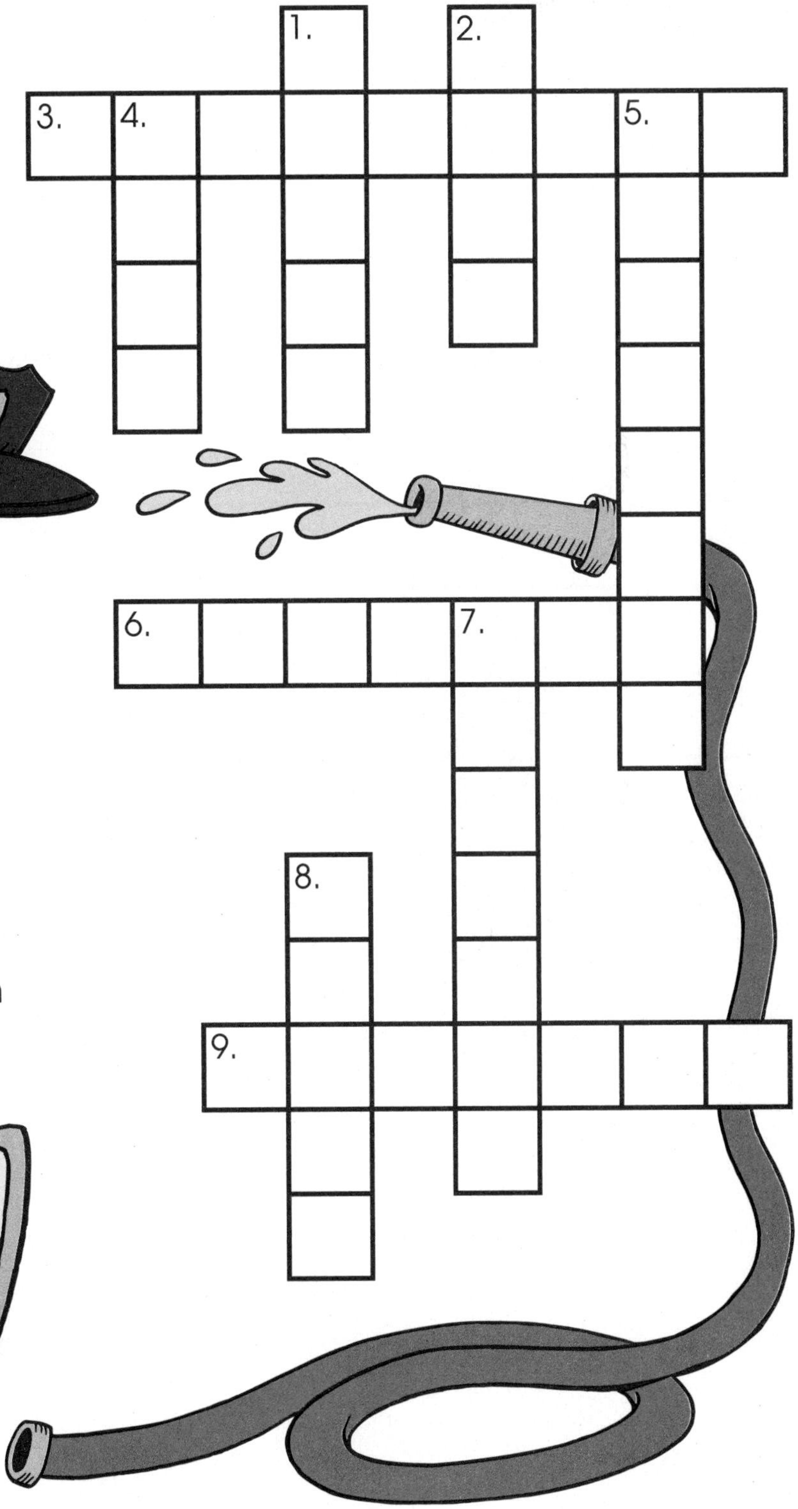

Word Bank

fireman   alarm
help   careful
accident   obey
matches   siren
policeman

AN ATTACK OF THE MUNCHIES

Use the Word Bank to help you fill in the puzzle.

Across

3. It comes from cows.
5. It can go in a pie.
7. It is good with jelly.

Down

1. It is brown and sweet.
2. Rabbits like them.
4. It is made from milk.
6. It can be red, yellow or green.
8. It is yellow and grows in a bunch.

Word Bank

apple	peanut butter	cheese	carrots
cherry	raisin	milk	banana

A GOOD SCOUT

Use the Word Bank to help you fill in the puzzle.

Across

1. A word you say when you get hurt
3. The shape of a circle
5. The opposite of quiet
7. To find out how many, you must . . .
9. The opposite of north
11. The opposite of in
12. Animal like a rat
14. A very high land form

Down

2. Fluffy white object in the sky
4. Ground wheat that is used in making bread
6. Not having something
7. A sofa
8. A fish
10. A home
12. A part of your face
13. To make a ball go down and up

Word Bank

cloud   without
out   loud   south   trout
flour   couch   ouch
bounce   round
mouse   count   house
mouth   mountain

SLUMBERING SLIPPERS

Use the Word Bank to help you fill in the puzzle.

Across

4. Opposite of frown
5. A small, slow-moving creature
6. Opposite of rough
9. Resting
10. To slant or lean
11. What your nose does
13. Intelligent
14. Ah . . . choo!

Down

1. To shut with a bang
2. A smooth, layered rock
3. A cracking sound
4. Very clever, like a fox
6. To trip
7. A kind of shoe
8. Reptiles
11. Frozen white flakes
12. Something burning gives off

Word Bank

smooth	snail	sly
slam	smart	slip
slipper	snow	smile
slope	slate	smoke
snakes	smells	sneeze
snap	sleeping	

STRETCH!

Use the Word Bank to help you fill in the puzzle.

Across
2. A shape that has equal sides
4. A road
5. To scatter little pieces
7. Light-weight rope
10. A bushy-tailed animal
11. A stalk of grain

Down
1. Opposite of weak
2. The sound a mouse makes
3. A small river
4. Yell
5. Opposite of crooked
6. A season of the year
7. To throw water
8. Very odd
9. To separate
10. A homeless cat or dog

Word Bank

splash	spring
squeak	square
strong	sprinkle
straight	straw
split	string
scream	squirrel
strange	stream
street	stray

READ ALL ABOUT IT

Use the Word Bank to help you fill in the puzzle.

Across

2. To send a letter
5. Not messy
6. What you are called
7. A polite word
8. Pretty
9. Related to a donkey
10. A kind of coat you wear around the house
12. To sparkle
13. Not shallow
15. To steer a car
16. Opposite of dirty

Down

1. Used to catch a fish
3. Jump
4. To rob
5. Friendly and kind
6. Opposite of far
9. Opposite of kind
11. A dog's treat
12. To slip
13. Ten-cent coin
14. More than one mouse

COOL CIDER

Use the Word Bank to help you fill in the puzzle.

Across
3. A baby's bed
5. The cost of something
6. A castle
8. A yellow vegetable
9. You can mold things with this
10. A very small house

Down
1. Something to drink
2. Frozen water
4. A cold dessert that comes in a cone
7. A very large town
8. A desert animal with a humped back
9. A line that goes around

Word Bank

city   ice   ice cream
corn   circle   palace
cabin   clay   camel
price   crib   juice

IT'S A SNAP FOR A GIRAFFE!

Use the Word Bank to help you fill in the puzzle.

Across

1. A valuable jewel
4. A leader in the army
6. A long-necked bird
10. A store where you buy food
11. A round map

Down

1. A silly laugh
2. A huge, tall person
3. A long-necked animal
4. A chewy treat
5. Glasses to wear underwater
6. A spice or kind of cookie
7. A visitor
8. A place to exercise
9. Having a bright yellow color

Word Bank

general	ginger
gum	guest
goggles	golden
giant	gem
goose	giraffe
gym	grocery
giggle	globe

LAUGHABLE FELLOW

Use the Word Bank to help you fill in the puzzle.

Across
2. Opposite of darken
4. To make wider
5. Can be sunk
7. To make hard
8. Can be read
11. Can be broken

Down
1. Put in writing
3. To make something not crooked
4. Can be washed
6. A lot of fun
9. To make darker
10. Opposite of harden

Word Bank

breakable
widen
readable
sinkable
harden
lighten
soften
washable
darken
enjoyable
written
straighten

LIGHTHOUSE

Use the Word Bank to help you fill in the puzzle.

Across

1. Opposite of downstairs
4. An orange-yellow fish
5. A room in a school
6. What a spider weaves
9. Place to store a boat
11. A bird that lives near the sea
12. Lands that are low
13. A book in which you write notes
14. To walk very quietly

Down

2. Coastline
3. Work to be done at home
5. Someone who works on a ranch
7. A place to bathe
8. Forest
10. The covering of an egg
11. A boat moved by the wind

Word Bank

cobweb
boathouse
tiptoe
seashore
goldfish
eggshell
homework
lowlands
upstairs
woodland
bathtub
cowboy
sailboat
notebook
seagull
classroom

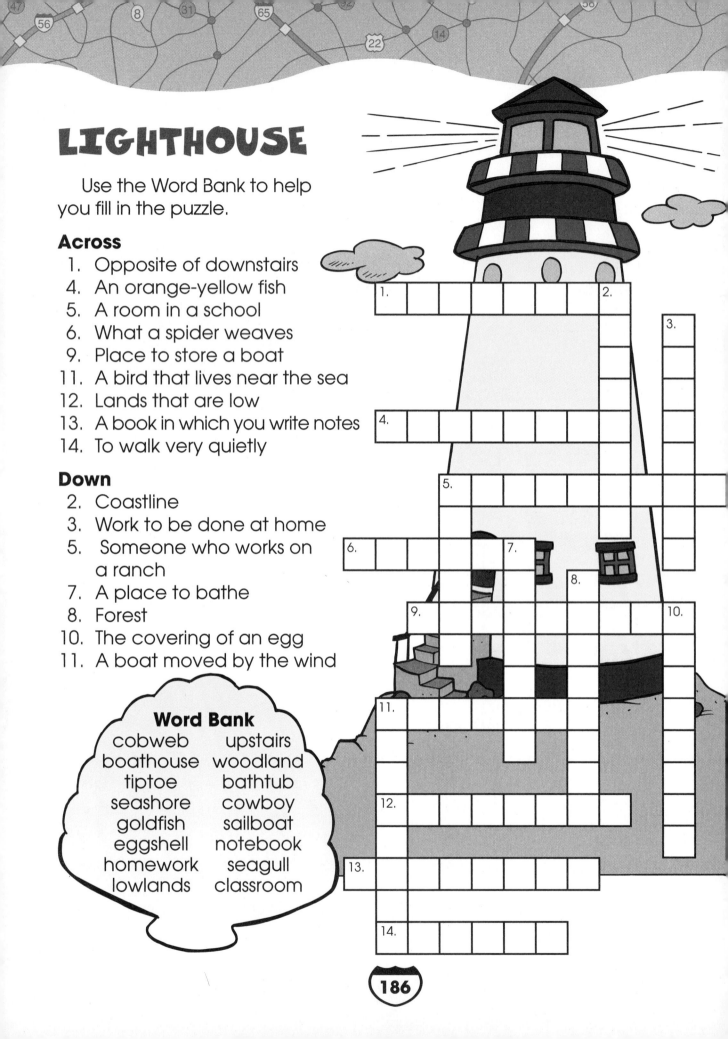

HOMOPHONE CROSSWORD

Homophones are words that sound alike but are spelled differently and have different meanings. Fill in the blanks to form homophones for the words listed below. To help, some of the letters have been given.

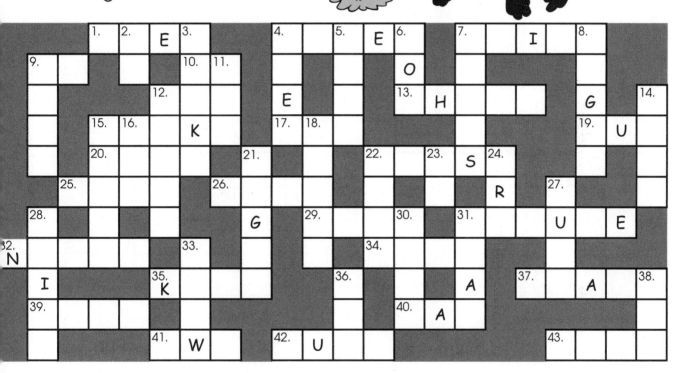

Across

1. tows	19. hew	35. not
4. hairs	20. rows	37. peeks
7. fryer	22. cents	39. gait
9. bee	25. feat	40. lei
10. too	26. wring	41. oh
12. wore	29. here	42. serf
13. wear	31. troop	43. seem
15. break	32. kneads	
17. lead	34. you're	

Down

2. oar	12. waist	27. loot
3. steak	14. peal	28. nay
4. heal	15. bred	30. role
5. rode	16. row	31. trey
6. sew	18. ate	33. new
7. fleas	21. mite	36. four
8. write	22. sleigh	38. some
9. bear	23. know	
11. or	24. air	

SYNONYM CROSSWORD

Synonyms are words that mean about the same as another word. Fill in the blanks to form synonyms for the words listed below. To help, some of the letters have been given.

Across

2. easy
7. drenched
9. damp
11. beautiful
13. quiet
14. hurried
15. blaring
16. strange
17. enjoyable
18. annual
21. unusual
22. mad
24. final
25. alike
26. ruddy
28. mended
32. uncovered
33. independent
34. extreme
37. sick
39. arid
40. naughty
41. feminine
42. mild
43. happy
44. ordinary
45. curved

Down

1. dull
2. sturdy
3. untidy
4. older
5. all
6. entire
7. broad
8. secure
9. insane
10. aged
12. youthful
13. rough
17. less
19. simpler
20. misplaced
22. plentiful
23. tidy
24. high
26. lifted
27. lifeless
29. reliable
30. peaceful
31. proper
35. speechless
36. just
38. tardy
41. plump

PALINDROME CROSSWORD

Palindromes are words that are spelled the same both forward and backward. Examples: tat, Bob.

Use the clues below to help you fill in the crossword. Hint: Two words you may have trouble finding are ABBA and CIVIC.

Across

1. More red
4. Short for statistics
6. Paper showing land ownership
8. Sound a chick makes
0. Aramaic name for father
1. Flies alone
2. Day before a holiday
4. A prank
7. Even
8. Midday
0. Past tense of do
22. Short for chrysanthemum
23. Sound of a horn
26. Title of respect for a lady
27. A napkin tied under the chin
28. A little dog

Down

1. It detects airplanes
2. Common name for father
3. A blade on a helicopter
4. Watches
5. An Eskimo's canoe
7. A female sheep
8. A soda
9. Energy
13. A seeing organ
15. Short for mother
16. Describes a citizen's duties
19. A religious sister
21. Expression of surprise
24. A small child
25. A failure

189

TWENTY QUESTIONS

One player starts the game by thinking of a person, place or thing. Then, the other players take turns asking questions that can be answered by "yes" or "no." (Examples: Are you thinking of a person? Is the person a movie star?) You can keep asking questions until someone makes a correct guess or until you've reached 20 questions.

Players who think they have the answer can make a guess when it's their turn. A player who makes an incorrect guess is out. The player who guesses correctly gets to think of the next person, place or thing.

FAMOUS INITIALS

This game is a variation of "Twenty Questions." Player A gives the initials of a famous person such as a historical figure, a movie star or an author. The other players then have to guess who that person is by asking questions that can be answered by "yes" or "no." If a person guesses the correct answer, he or she gets to think of a new set of initials. If no correct guesses are made before 20 questions are asked, Player A gets to think of another celebrity.

ESP

You'll need a deck of cards to play "ESP" (Extra-Sensory Perception). Hold the cards facedown. Then, sort the cards into two piles. Place the ones you think are black in one pile and the ones you think are red in the other. Turn over the piles and count how many cards you sorted correctly. What was your ESP score?

Try this game with one or more other players. See who can get the highest ESP score.

SIT-DOWN CHARADES

Play charades while sitting down. Use only your hands and face to give clues. Here are some ideas you might try.

What Am I Doing?

Players have to guess what you are doing. Choose simple actions such as washing the dishes, painting or climbing a ladder.

Who Am I?

Players have to guess who you are. Use hand gestures to show what the person looks like or does. For example, you can touch the lower part of your face to indicate a beard or act out playing a guitar to indicate a rock musician.

What Is It?

Players have to guess what item you're thinking about. For example, for banana, you can pretend to peel the fruit and eat it. Fo hair dryer, you can pretend to blow-dry your hair.

IN THE DOGHOUSE

Stay out of the doghouse!

Use the space below and those on pages 194–199. Or use another sheet of paper.

Player A begins by thinking of a word or name (at least 7 letters long). Here are some examples: an action word or famous person.

Player A draws the number of blanks needed for the answer.

The other players take turns guessing the letters. Player A writes the correct letter guesses in the correct blanks. An incorrect guess means a part (wall, wall, floor, ceiling, side of roof, side of roof and door) of the doghouse will be drawn. The last person to guess incorrectly and not guess the answer will have his or her name written on the doghouse sign.

The person who guesses the word or name correctly is the next person to think of a word or name.

IN THE DOGHOUSE

(Directions are found on page 193.)

IN THE DOGHOUSE

(Directions are found on page 193.)

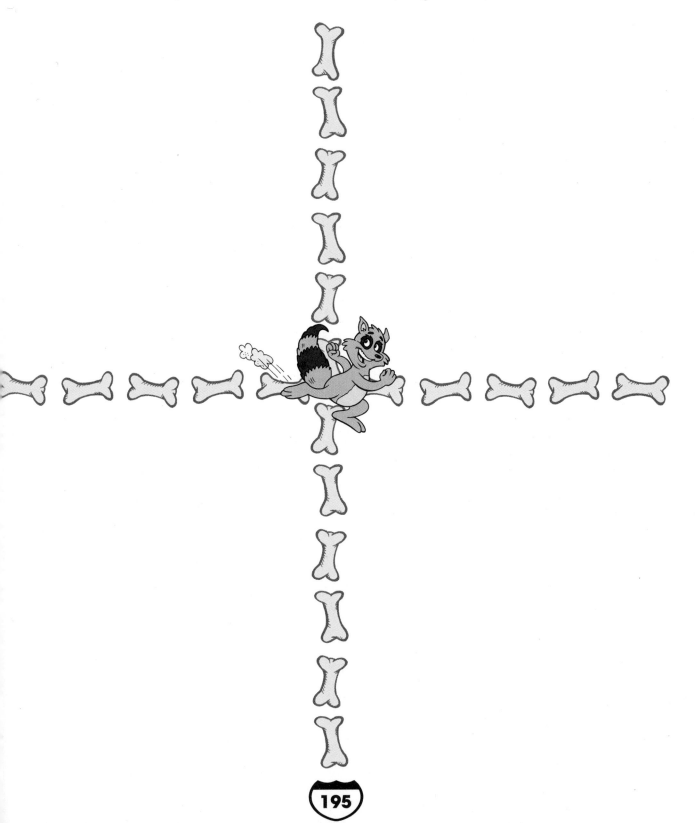

IN THE DOGHOUSE

(Directions are found on page 193.)

IN THE DOGHOUSE

(Directions are found on page 193.)

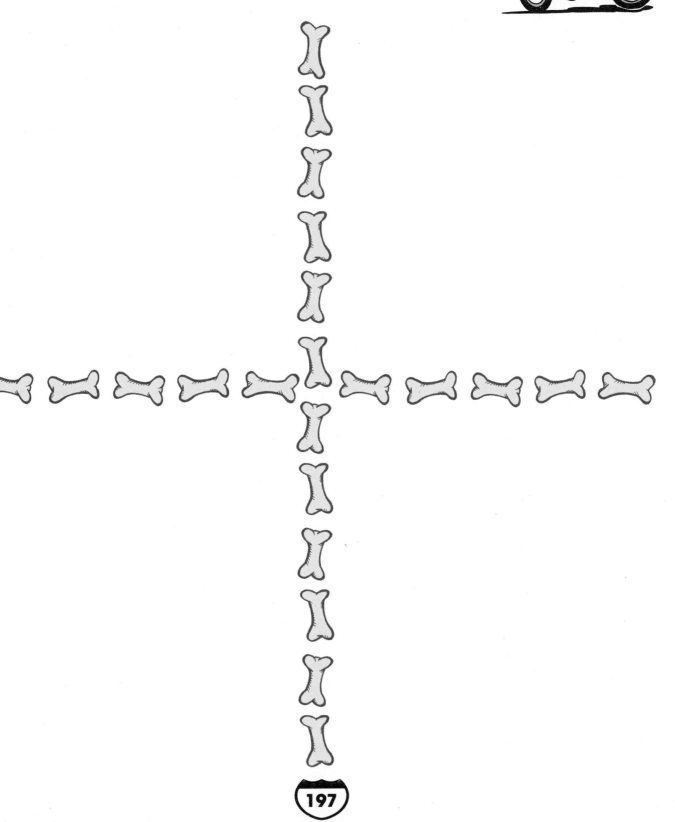

IN THE DOGHOUSE

(Directions are found on page 193.)

IN THE DOGHOUSE

(Directions are found on page 193.)

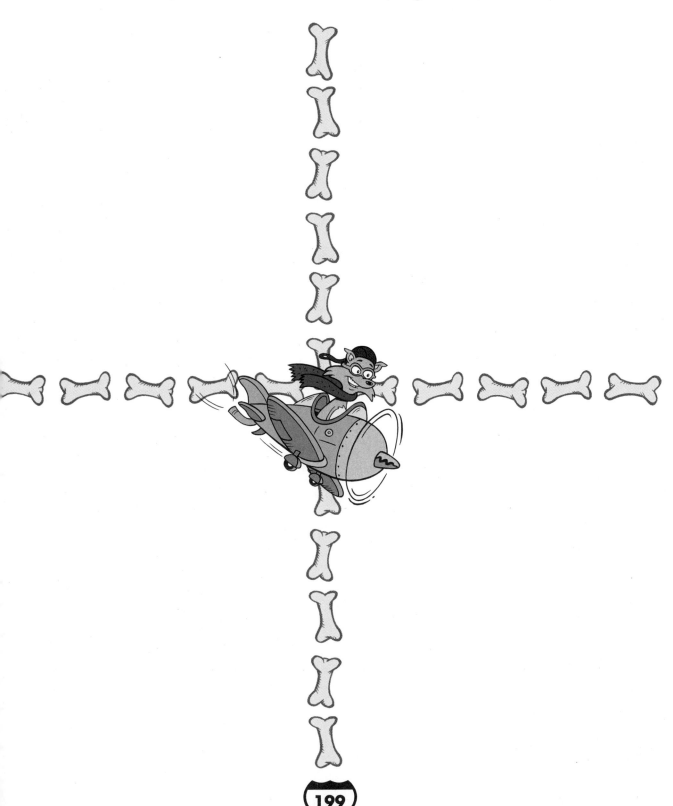

TRAVELER'S PASSWORD

Teamwork and sharp thinking are needed for this vocabulary game.

Players are divided into two teams. Team A writes a word on a slip of paper and gives it to a player on Team B. That player gives a one-word clue to his or her teammates. Team B must then guess the word; if the guess is correct, Team B gets 5 points. If the guess is wrong, the player gives another one-word clue and Team B has a chance to score 4 points, and so on. A maximum of five clues is allowed, and a guess must be made for every clue. If five clues are given and no correct guess is made, Team B scores 0 points for that round. Then, Team B writes a new word for Team A, and the game continues as before.

After each team has played five rounds, the points are totaled and the team with the most points wins.

NOW, PICTURE THIS

This game is similar to "Traveler's Password" except that picture clues are given instead of word clues.

Team A writes a noun, a verb or an adjective on a slip of paper and gives the paper to a player on Team B. Then, that player draws a picture on a sheet of paper for his or her teammates to try to guess. There is a 1-minute time limit for guesses. If a correct guess is made, Team B scores 1 point. If the team cannot come up with the correct answer in 1 minute, it is Team A's turn. Team B then gives a player on Team A a word to draw.

NOT JUST ANY STAR

Color the space **blue** if the word means only one.
Color the space **red** if the word means more than one.

What kind of star is this? _____

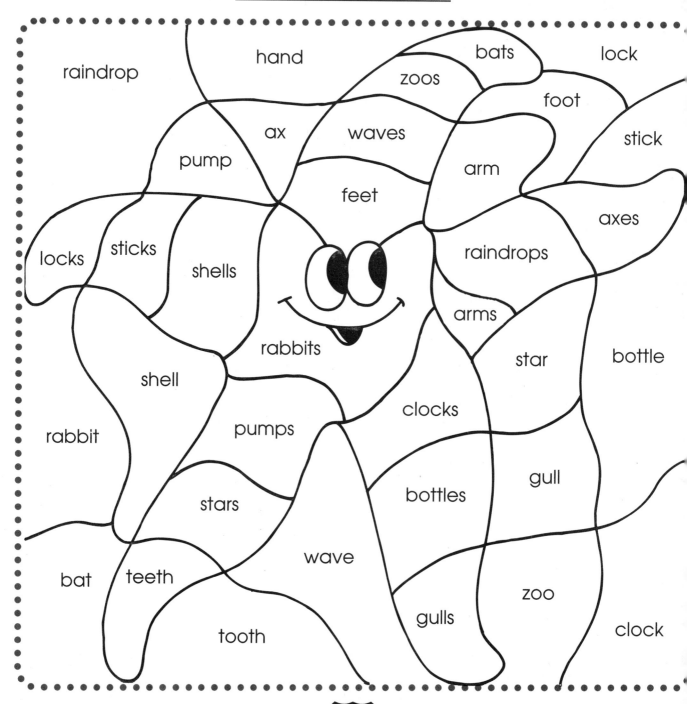

raindrop
hand
zoos
bats
lock
ax
waves
foot
pump
arm
stick
feet
locks
sticks
raindrops
axes
shells
arms
star
bottle
rabbits
shell
clocks
pumps
gull
rabbit
bottles
stars
wave
zoo
bat
teeth
gulls
clock
tooth

SUCH A FACE!

Color the space **green** if the word means only one.
Color the space **brown** if the word means more than one.

Who owns this face? _____

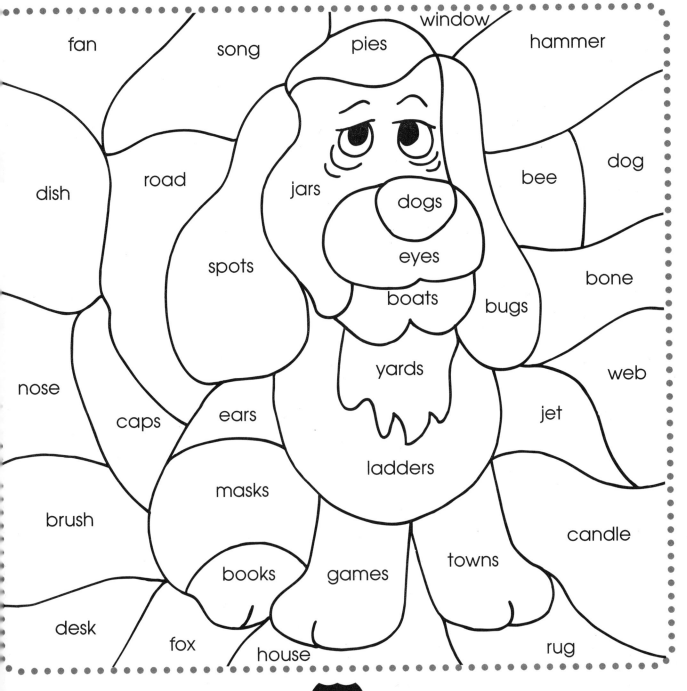

fan   song   pies   window   hammer

dish   road   jars   bee   dog

spots   dogs

eyes   bone

boats   bugs

nose   yards   web

caps   ears   jet

ladders

masks

brush   candle

books   games   towns

desk   fox   house   rug

A SIGN OF FALL

Color the space **yellow** if the word names a color.
Color the space **green** if the word names a number.

What is a sign of fall? _____

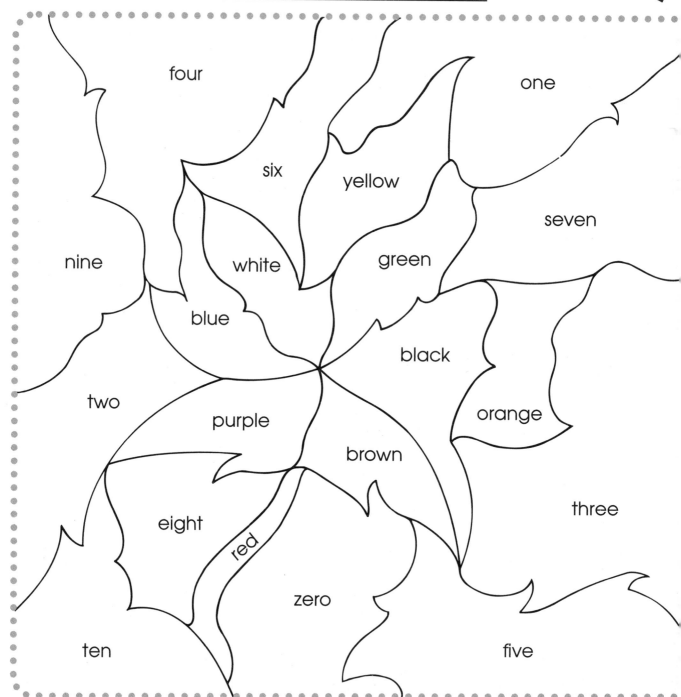

AS QUIET AS . . .

Color the space **brown** if the words mean the same.
Color the space **blue** if the words mean the opposite.

Who is quiet? _____

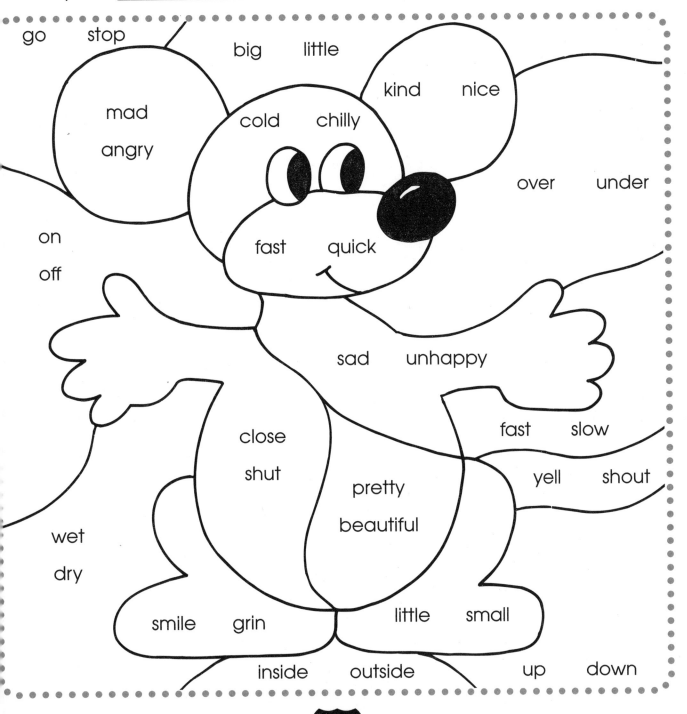

go   stop

big   little

mad
angry

kind   nice

cold   chilly

over   under

on
off

fast   quick

sad   unhappy

fast   slow

close
shut

yell   shout

pretty
beautiful

wet
dry

smile   grin

little   small

inside   outside

up   down

YUMMY!

Color the person words **red**.
Color the place words **blue**.
Color the things words **yellow**.
Color the action words **green**.
Color the when words **orange**.

What is this yummy treat? _____

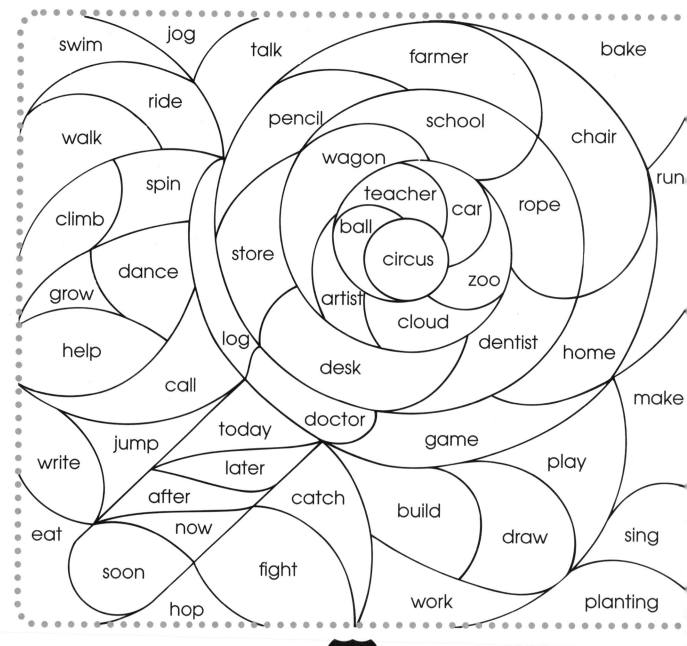

swim
jog
talk
farmer
bake
ride
pencil
school
chair
walk
wagon
run
spin
teacher
car
rope
climb
ball
store
circus
zoo
dance
artist
grow
cloud
help
dentist
home
log
desk
call
today
doctor
game
make
jump
later
play
write
after
catch
build
eat
now
draw
sing
soon
fight
work
planting
hop

BREEZING ALONG

Color the space **blue** if the words are opposites.
Color the space **yellow** if the words sound the same.
Color the space **red** if the words mean the same.

What is breezing along? _____

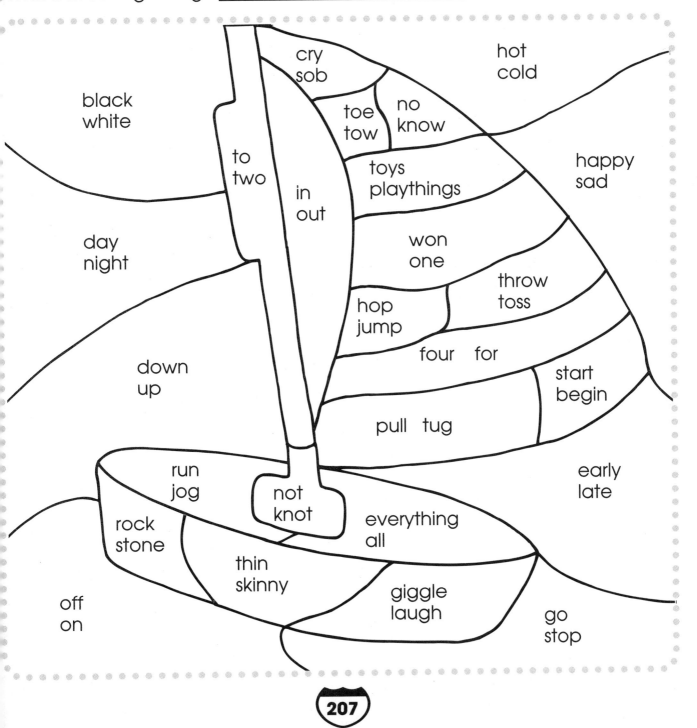

cry
sob

hot
cold

black
white

toe
tow

no
know

to
two

toys
playthings

happy
sad

in
out

won
one

day
night

throw
toss

hop
jump

down
up

four   for

start
begin

pull   tug

run
jog

early
late

not
knot

everything
all

rock
stone

thin
skinny

giggle
laugh

off
on

go
stop

ALL-TIME FAVORITE

Color the fruit words **orange**.
Color the vegetable words **green**.
Color the grain product words **red**.
Color the milk product words **blue**.
Color the meat product words **brown**.
Color the dinnertime words **yellow**.

What is the all-time favorite? _____

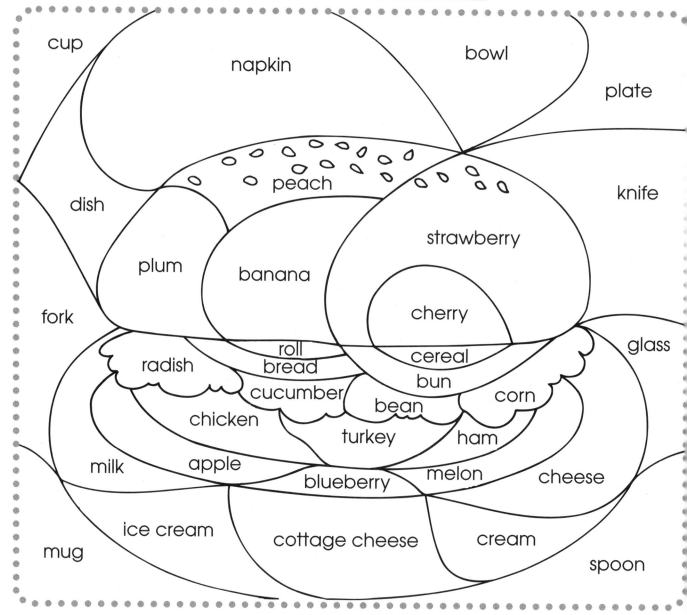

cup

napkin

bowl

plate

dish

peach

knife

strawberry

plum

banana

cherry

fork

roll
bread

cereal

glass

radish

bun

cucumber

corn

bean

chicken

turkey

ham

milk

apple

melon

cheese

blueberry

ice cream

cottage cheese

cream

mug

spoon

THE GOOD OLD DAYS

Color clothing words **red**.
Color weather words **yellow**.
Color toy words **black**.
Color food words **brown**.
Color animal words **green**.

Who battled dragons? _____

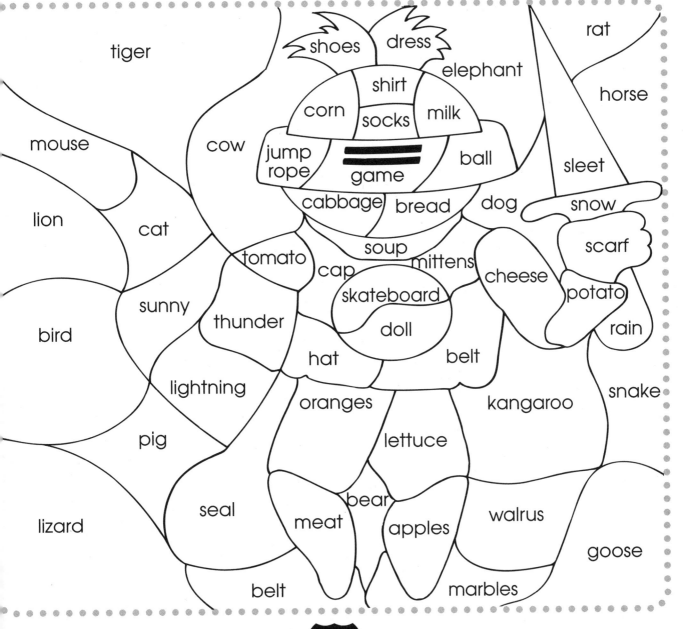

tiger

shoes   dress

rat

elephant

shirt

horse

corn   socks   milk

cow

jump rope   game   ball

sleet

mouse

cabbage   bread   dog

snow

lion

cat

soup

scarf

tomato   cap   mittens

cheese

potato

sunny

skateboard

thunder   doll

rain

bird

hat   belt

lightning

oranges   kangaroo

snake

pig

lettuce

seal   bear   walrus

lizard

meat   apples

goose

belt   marbles

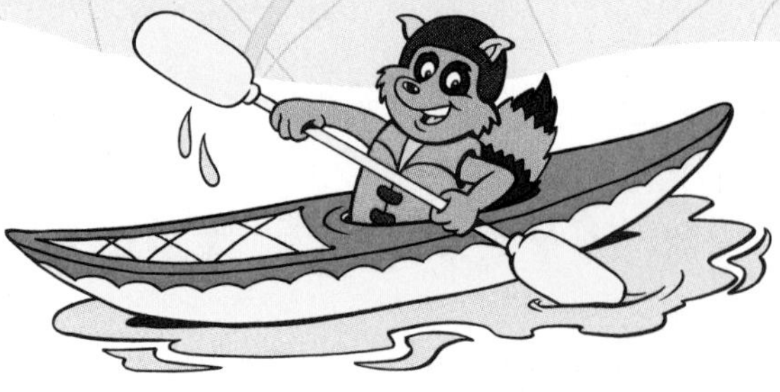

TREATS

Color the synonym pairs **blue**.
Color the antonym pairs **red**.
Color all single words **yellow**.

What treats are found in the picture? ________________

Synonyms are words that mean the same. **Antonyms** are words that are opposites.

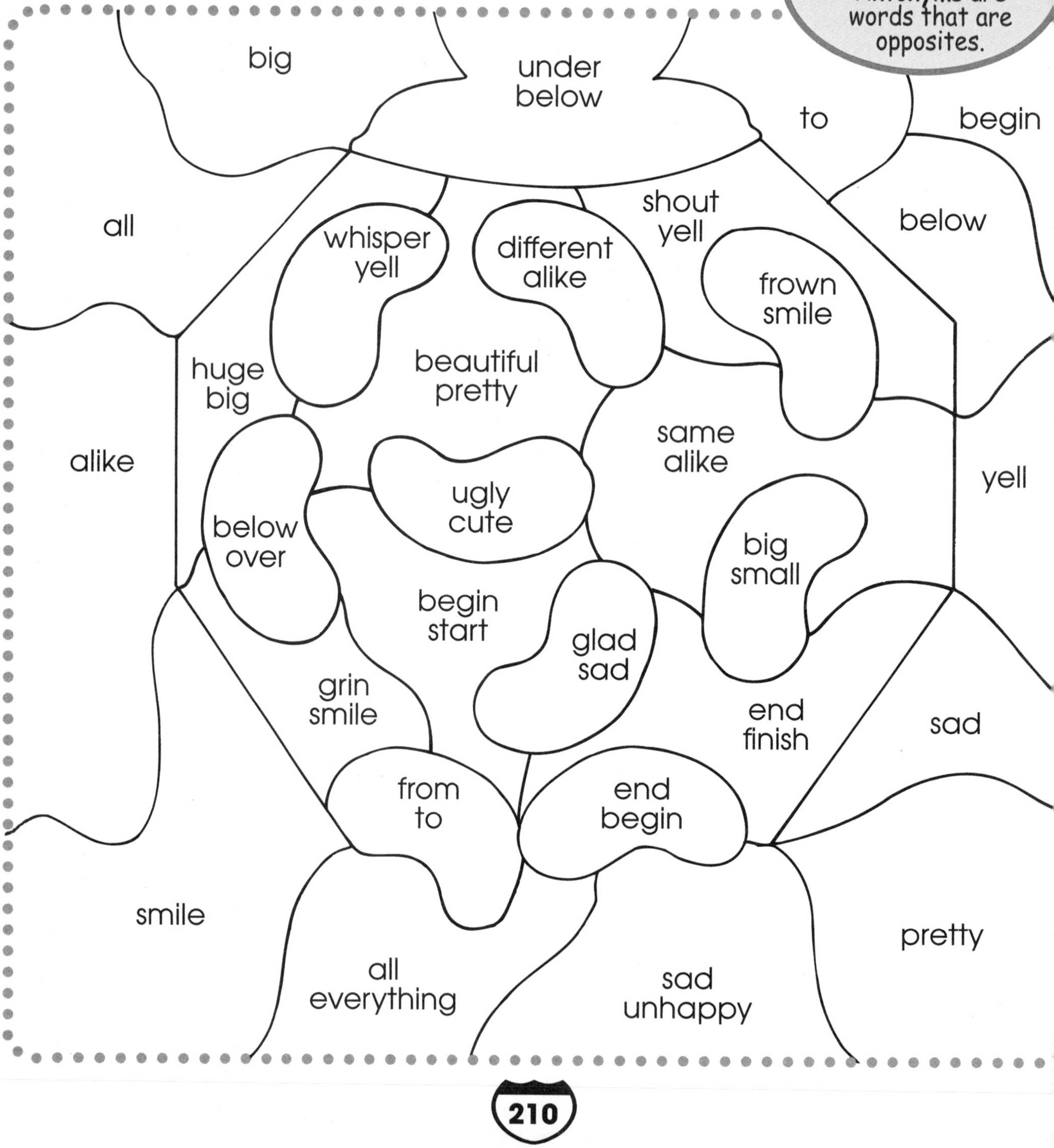

big
under below
to
begin
all
shout yell
below
whisper yell
different alike
frown smile
huge big
beautiful pretty
alike
same alike
yell
ugly cute
below over
big small
begin start
glad sad
grin smile
end finish
sad
from to
end begin
smile
all everything
sad unhappy
pretty

SOFT AND CUDDLY

Color the singular words **brown**.
Color the plural words **green**.

What is soft and cuddly? _____

Singular means only one.
Plural means more than one.

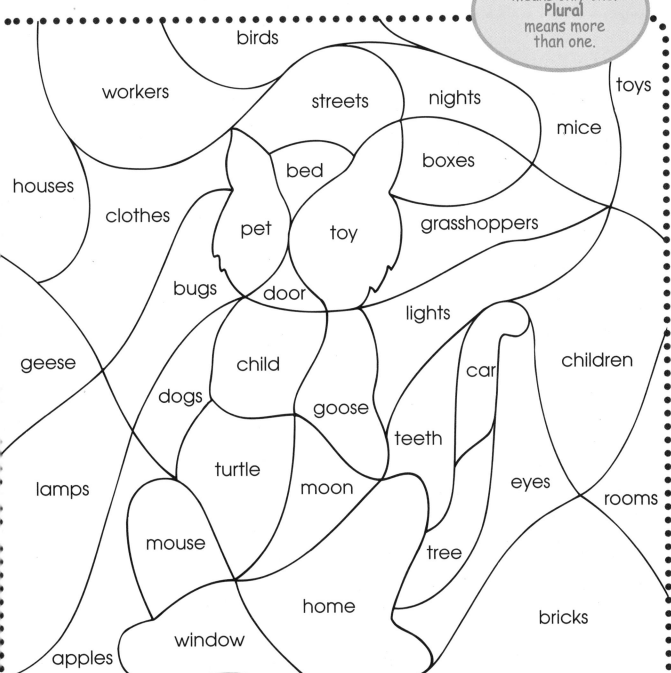

birds

workers

streets   nights   toys

mice

houses   bed   boxes

clothes   pet   toy   grasshoppers

bugs   door   lights

geese   child   car   children

dogs   goose

teeth

turtle   moon   eyes   rooms

lamps

mouse   tree

home   bricks

apples   window

ELECTRIFYING

Color the singular words **yellow**.
Color the plural words **blue**.

What is electrifying? _____

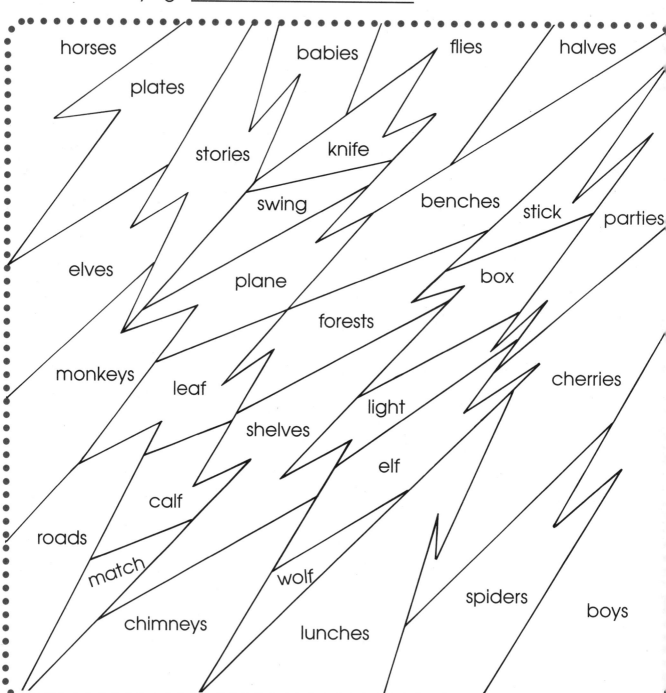

horses

plates

babies

flies

halves

stories

knife

swing

benches

stick

parties

elves

plane

box

forests

monkeys

leaf

cherries

light

shelves

elf

calf

roads

match

wolf

spiders

boys

chimneys

lunches

BRIGHT AND BEAUTIFUL

Color the space **yellow** if you have to only add an "s" to make the word plural.
Color the space **orange** if you have to add "es" to make the word plural.
Color the space **blue** if you have "to change the last letter" and then add "es"
to make the word plural.

What is this bright and beautiful sight? _____

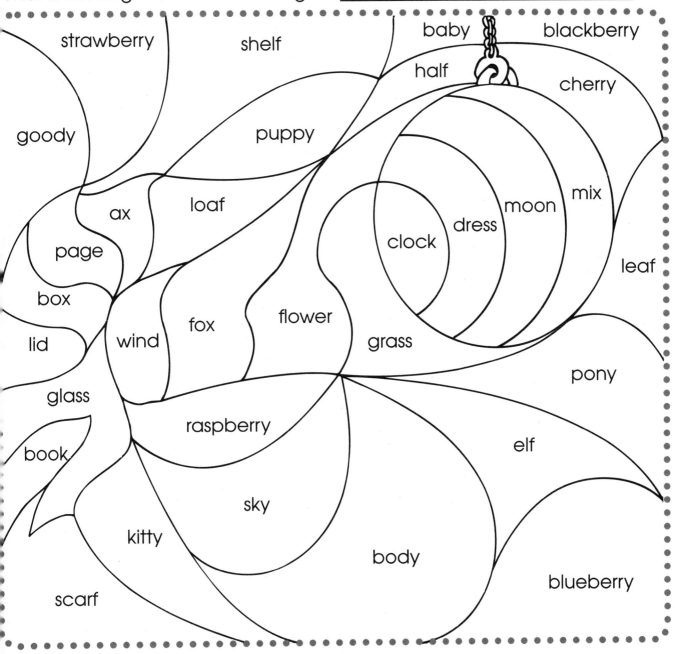

SUMMER TREAT

Color the plural words **green**.
Color the contractions **black**.
Color the compound words **red**.
Color the possessive words **blue**.

Name this summer treat. _____

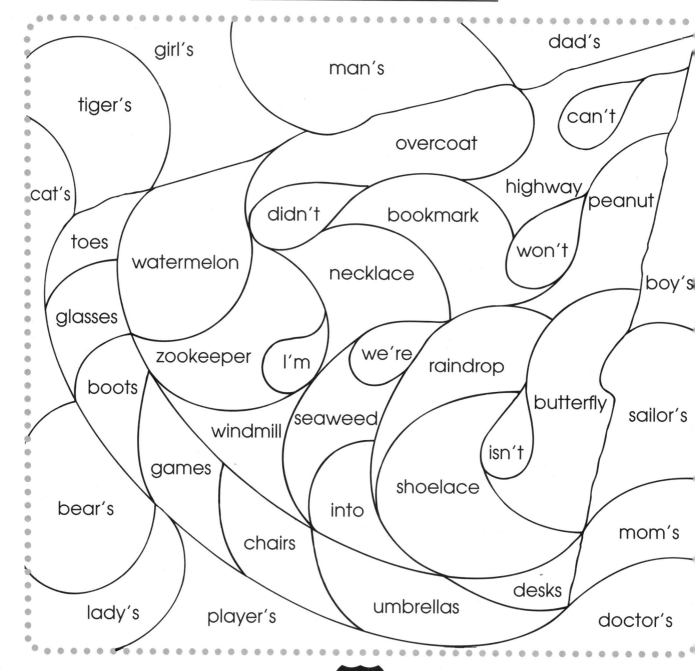

girl's

man's

dad's

tiger's

can't

overcoat

cat's

highway

peanut

didn't

bookmark

won't

toes

watermelon

necklace

boy's

glasses

zookeeper

I'm

we're

raindrop

boots

butterfly

sailor's

windmill

seaweed

isn't

games

shoelace

bear's

into

mom's

chairs

desks

lady's

player's

umbrellas

doctor's

OUCH!

Color the one-syllable words **orange**.
Color the two-syllable words **blue**.
Color the three-syllable words **black**.

What can make you say ouch? _____

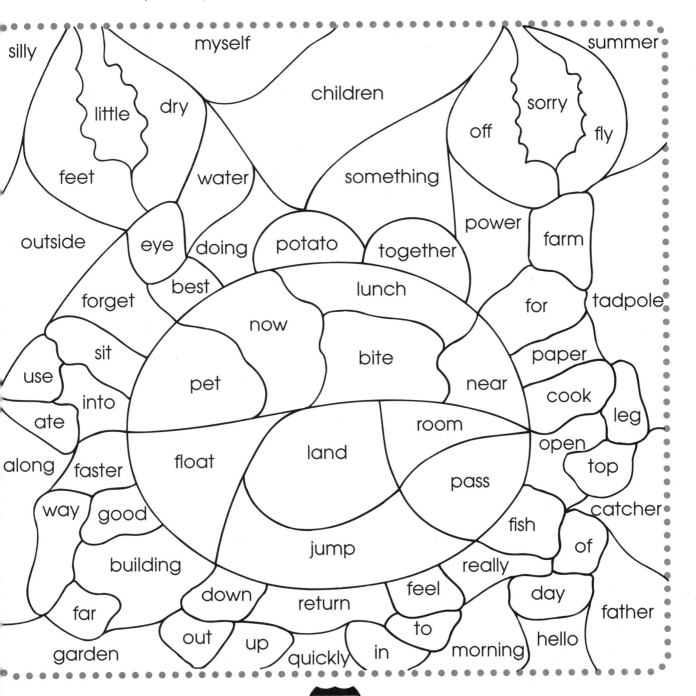

silly

myself

summer

little dry

children

sorry

off fly

feet water

something

power farm

outside eye doing potato together

best lunch for tadpole

forget now

sit bite paper

use pet near cook

into leg

ate room

along faster float land open

way good pass top

fish catcher

jump of

building really

down feel day

far return father

out up to hello

garden quickly in morning

215

TO THE COUNT

Color the one-syllable words **brown**.
Color the two-syllable words **green**.
Color the three-syllable words **blue**.

What animal is suited for boxing? _____

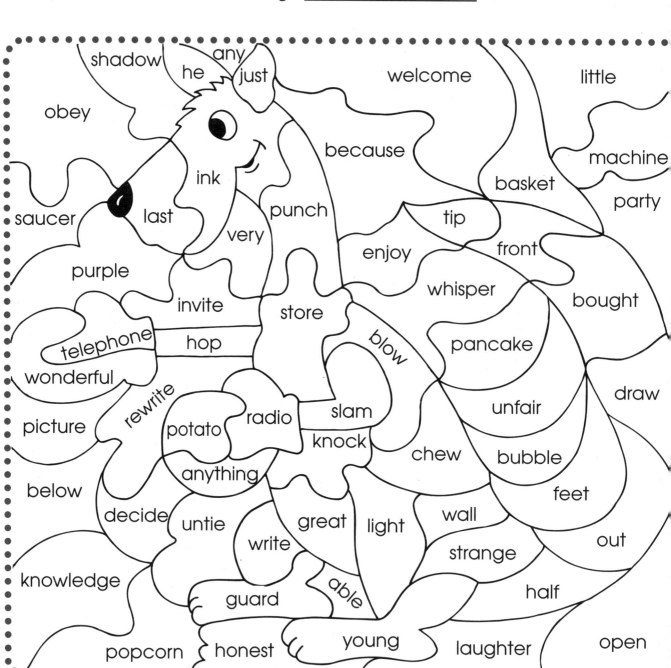

shadow any he just welcome little

obey

because

machine

ink basket party

saucer last punch tip front

very enjoy

purple whisper bought

invite store blow pancake

telephone hop

wonderful slam unfair draw

rewrite radio

picture potato knock chew bubble

anything feet

below wall

decide untie great light out

write strange

knowledge able half

guard

popcorn honest young laughter open

RIGHT OUT OF THE OVEN

Color the antonyms **blue**.
Color the synonyms **red**.
Color the homophones **brown**.

Name this oven-fresh treat? _____

Clues:
Antonyms are words that are opposites.
Synonyms are words that mean the same.
Homophones are words that sound alike but are spelled differently.

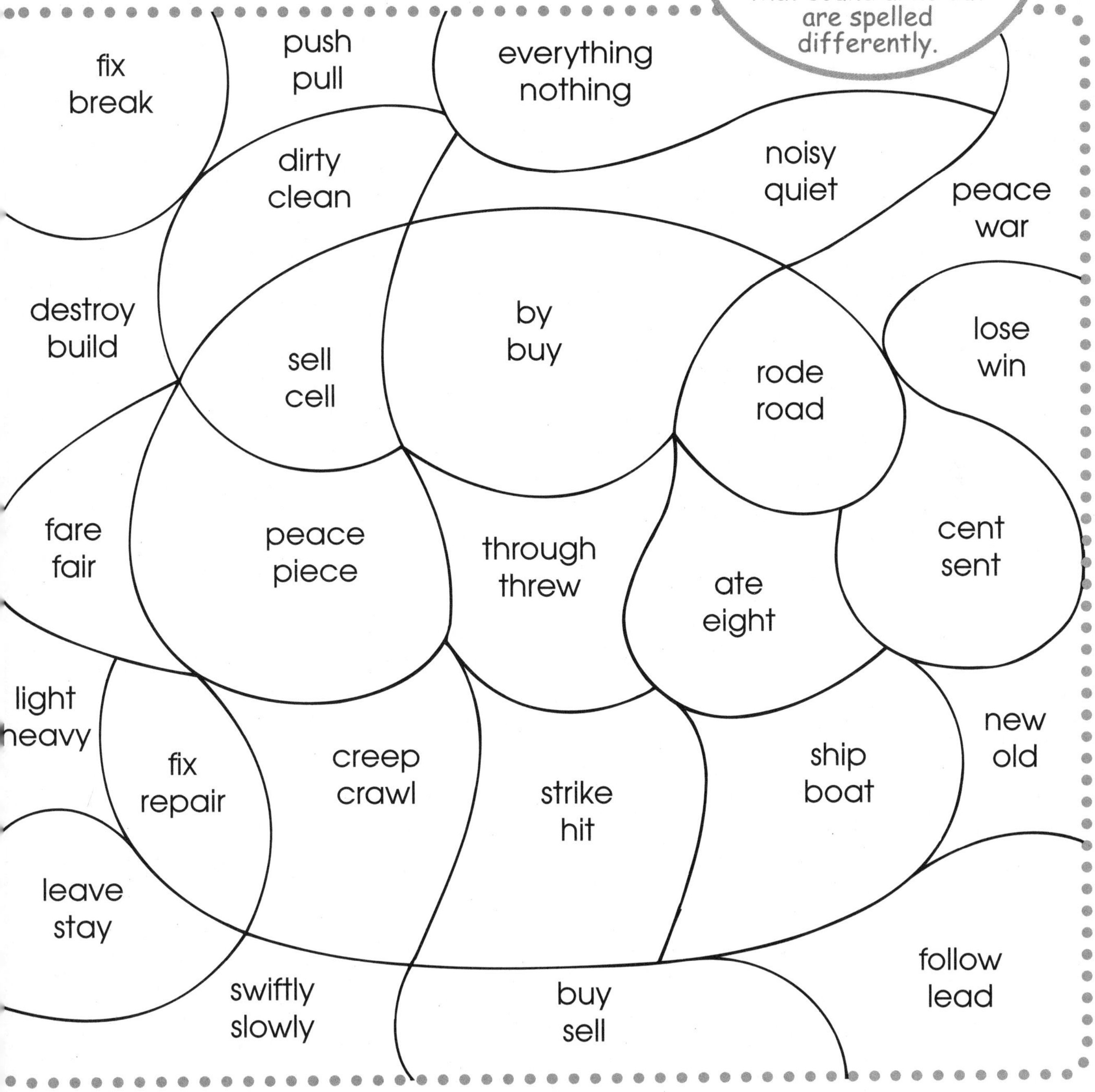

fix
break

push
pull

everything
nothing

noisy
quiet

peace
war

dirty
clean

destroy
build

sell
cell

by
buy

rode
road

lose
win

fare
fair

peace
piece

through
threw

ate
eight

cent
sent

light
heavy

fix
repair

creep
crawl

strike
hit

ship
boat

new
old

leave
stay

swiftly
slowly

buy
sell

follow
lead

SEE THE SEA

Color the synonyms **brown**.
Color the antonyms **blue**.
Color the homophones **green**.

What do you see? _____

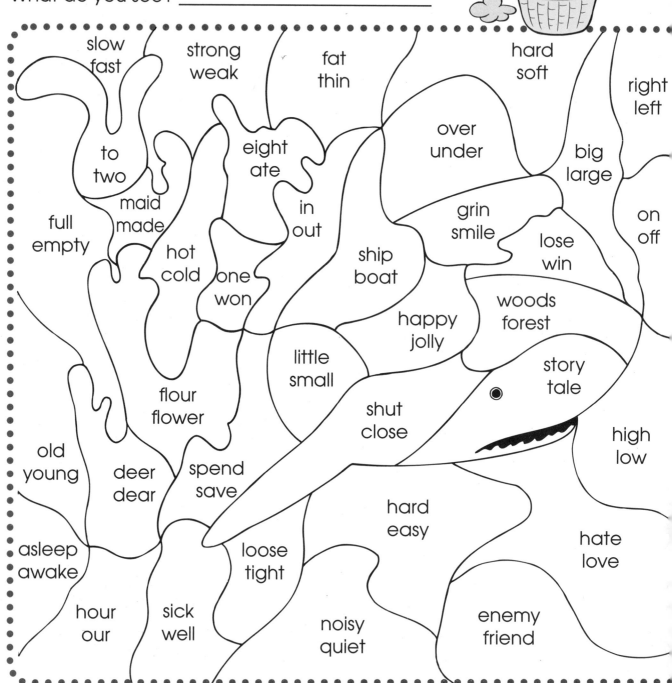

slow / fast

strong / weak

fat / thin

hard / soft

right / left

to / two

eight / ate

over / under

big / large

full / empty

maid / made

hot / cold

in / out

grin / smile

lose / win

on / off

one / won

ship / boat

happy / jolly

woods / forest

little / small

story / tale

flour / flower

shut / close

high / low

old / young

deer / dear

spend / save

hard / easy

hate / love

asleep / awake

loose / tight

hour / our

sick / well

noisy / quiet

enemy / friend

WORD CHALLENGE GAMES

Speak pig Latin, make up rhymes and more with these fun word games.

PIG LATIN, PLEASE

Have you ever spoken pig Latin? The rules are easy! Just take English words and do the following:

 Move a consonant or a consonant blend from the front of a word to the end of it and add "ay." For example, car becomes ar-cay and speak becomes eak-spay.

 Leave a word that begins with a vowel as is except add "ay" to the end. For example, open becomes open-ay.

Try speaking pig Latin with your family during part of your trip. *aybe-May ou'll-yay ind-fay it's-ay un-fay!*

RHYME TIME

See how long you can keep up a conversation in rhyme. Each time you speak, you have to include a pair of rhyming sentences. For example:

Let's play a game. Something different, not the same.

Okay. I'll play.

Shall we keep score? Hmm, let's not do that anymore.

No score this time is fine with me. Does everybody else agree?

SPOT AND SPELL

Use the signs you spot along the way for this super spelling game.

One player finds a road sign that displays the name of a street, city or landmark. The player calls out the name and the other players write on a sheet of paper. (If the sign is long, the player may call out only two of the words.)

Next, everyone tries to make words using only the letters in the name. For example, if the name is "Washington," a player can list words such as wash, ng and gas. After 3 minutes, the person with the most words wins.

WASHINGTON AVE 3 MILES

wash sing gas ton tan hang

A NAME CHAIN

One player begins the game by saying the first and last names of a person. he person may be real or make-believe and can be a celebrity, cartoon haracter, friend or family member.

The next player has to name a different person. The only restriction is that the person's name must begin with the first letter of the last name of the previous person. So, if the first player says "Sleeping Beauty," for example, the second player might say "Benjamin Franklin." The third player would then have to come up with a name that starts with "F." The game continues with the players making their "name chain" as long as possible.

CAN'T SAY IT

Everyone agrees not to say a certain word during a set time period. he word should be a common word such as yes, o, time or it. Then, whenever a person says the orbidden word, he or she gets 1 point. The person vith the least number of points at the end of the time eriod is the winner.

WHAT AM I SPELLING?

Player A thinks of a word and gives the first letter. The other players then guess what the word is. Player A gives the second letter and the other players guess. The game continues with the word being spelled one letter at a time and a guess being made after each letter. The person who is the first person to guess correctly chooses the next word.

V-A-C

VACATION!

DOUBLE-DUTY NAMES

To play the game, players have to write down people's names that can also mean something else. (Examples: Rose, Penny, Pat, Mark, Grant, Bill. Players can work individually or as a group to make a list as long as possible.

SALT AND PEPPER

In this game, players list names of people or objects that are usually paired together. After 5 minutes, the person with the greatest number of pairs wins. Here are some ideas:

- salt and pepper
- nuts and bolts
- Romeo and Juliet
- bread and butter
- pen and paper
- Batman and Robin
- meat and potatoes
- Stars and Stripes
- Lois and Clark

SILLY LANGUAGE

Make up your own silly language and use it for however long you like while you're traveling. Here are some ideas you can try.

Add a syllable to the end of every word. For example, *This-ee game-ee is-ee fun-ee* means *This game is fun.*

Move the last word in the sentence to the front. For example, *Snack I'd like a* means *I'd like a snack.*

Make every other word a color word. For example, *Look red at yellow that blue cat* means *Look at that cat.*

Replace real words with silly words. For example, you can use *gork* for *radio*, *meeble* for *car*, and so on.

ADD IT UP

In this game, someone chooses a category, such as animals, food or colors. Each player then writes a word that fits the category. Everyone adds up his or her points according to the values of the letters in the word. (Use page 224 to help you score this game.) The person with the most points wins.

Be careful—the longest word isn't necessarily the one that will score the most points. For example, "cheetah" scores 50 points but "skunk" scores 76 points.

ADD IT UP CHART

(Directions are found on page 223.)

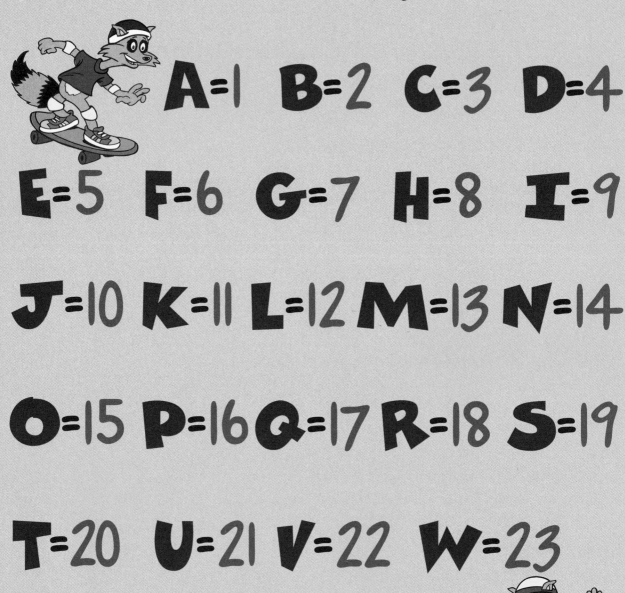

A=1 B=2 C=3 D=4

E=5 F=6 G=7 H=8 I=9

J=10 K=11 L=12 M=13 N=14

O=15 P=16 Q=17 R=18 S=19

T=20 U=21 V=22 W=23

X=24 Y=25 Z=26

CHALLENGE GAMES

Try these challenging games—fun for the entire family.

WORD SQUARES

EXAMPLE:

Word squares spell the same word both down and across. Fill in the word squares using the letters above each square.

AAACCEEEE
HHHNSTT

S	E	A	T
E	A	C	H
A	C	H	E
T	H	E	N

VTMMEETE
ACSANNOQ

AACCCEEIH
HKKLPPT

COMA

KEPT

AKLLSAEES
SEEHLSS

ACCEEL
MNOOR
RSSTT

ELSE

LNAM

WORD SQUARES

EXAMPLE:

Word squares spell the same word both down and across. Fill in the word squares using the letters above each square.

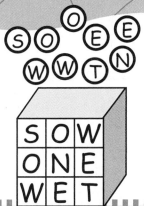

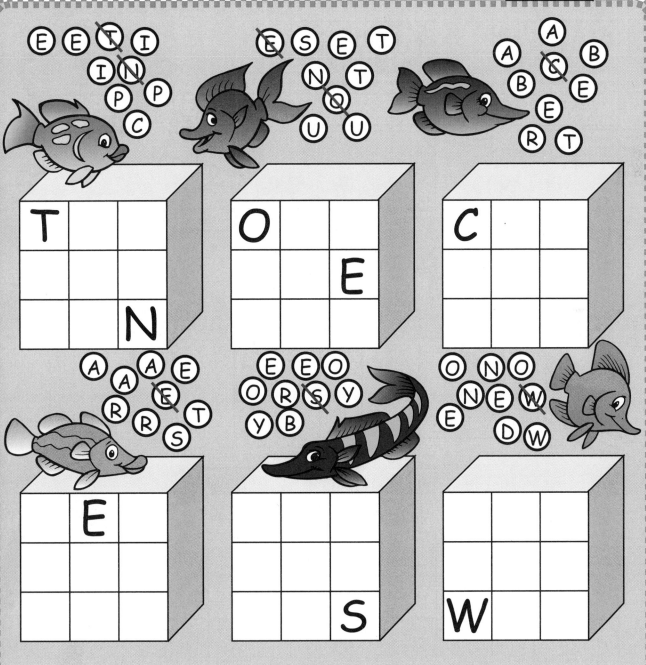

WORD SQUARES

EXAMPLE:

Word squares spell the same word both down and across. Fill in the word squares using the letters above each square.

Example:

S	O	E	E	N
W	O	W	T	

S	O	W
O	N	E
W	E	T

A A B C D E E R R

B E D D E R R R Y

G E E N O O P P T

L L P T R E E A A

A S A E E T A W T

N E E P U T U S T

A R R T A S A E E

L W W W O H H O O

228

WORD STEPS

Begin climbing the stairs with the word on the bottom step. Remove the letter that is on the side of the step and rearrange the remaining letters to form a new word. Keep going until you reach the top.

EXAMPLE:

BE

BET **T**

BEST **S**

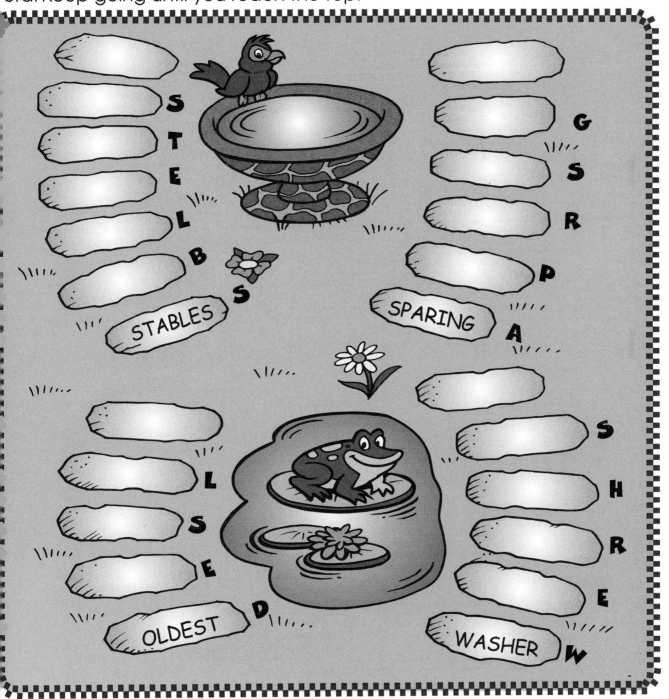

S

T

E

L

B

S

STABLES

G

S

R

P

SPARING

A

S

H

R

E

WASHER **W**

L

S

E

OLDEST **D**

WORD STEPS

Begin climbing the stairs with the word on the bottom step. Remove the letter that is on the side of the step and rearrange the remaining letters to form a new word. Keep going until you reach the top.

EXAMPLE:

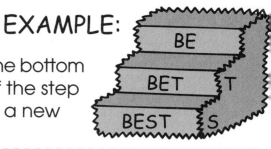

BE

BET | T

BEST | S

T

E

R

W

WINTER | N

G

I

R

D

READING | E

N

E

D

DONATE | A

S

D

I

L

SHIELD | L

FORMING WORDS GAME

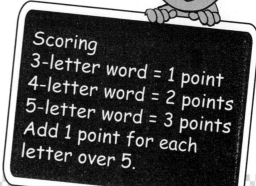

Make 30 new words from the letters in READING and write them on the lines below or use another sheet of paper. Use the scoring table to help you figure your points for each word.

WORDS   **PTS**.

1. _____ ____
2. _____ ____
3. _____ ____
4. _____ ____
5. _____ ____
6. _____ ____
7. _____ ____
8. _____ ____
9. _____ ____
10. _____ ____
11. _____ ____
12. _____ ____
13. _____ ____
14. _____ ____
15. _____ ____

16. _____ ____
17. _____ ____
18. _____ ____
19. _____ ____
20. _____ ____
21. _____ ____
22. _____ ____
23. _____ ____
24. _____ ____
25. _____ ____
26. _____ ____
27. _____ ____
28. _____ ____
29. _____ ____
30. _____ ____

YOUR SCORE _____

How do you rate?
over 60 = Excellent
50-60 = Good
40-49 = Fair
under 40 = Try Again

HIDDEN WORDS

Write the sentence hidden in the table on the lines below.
Hint: The sentence begins with "Dinnertime" and has 9 words.

Sentence: ____

____

____

Write other hidden words on the plates.

W E C A L P R E H T A E

A S A L W A Y S S H (left column, top to bottom)

M I T R E N N I D S (right column, top to bottom)

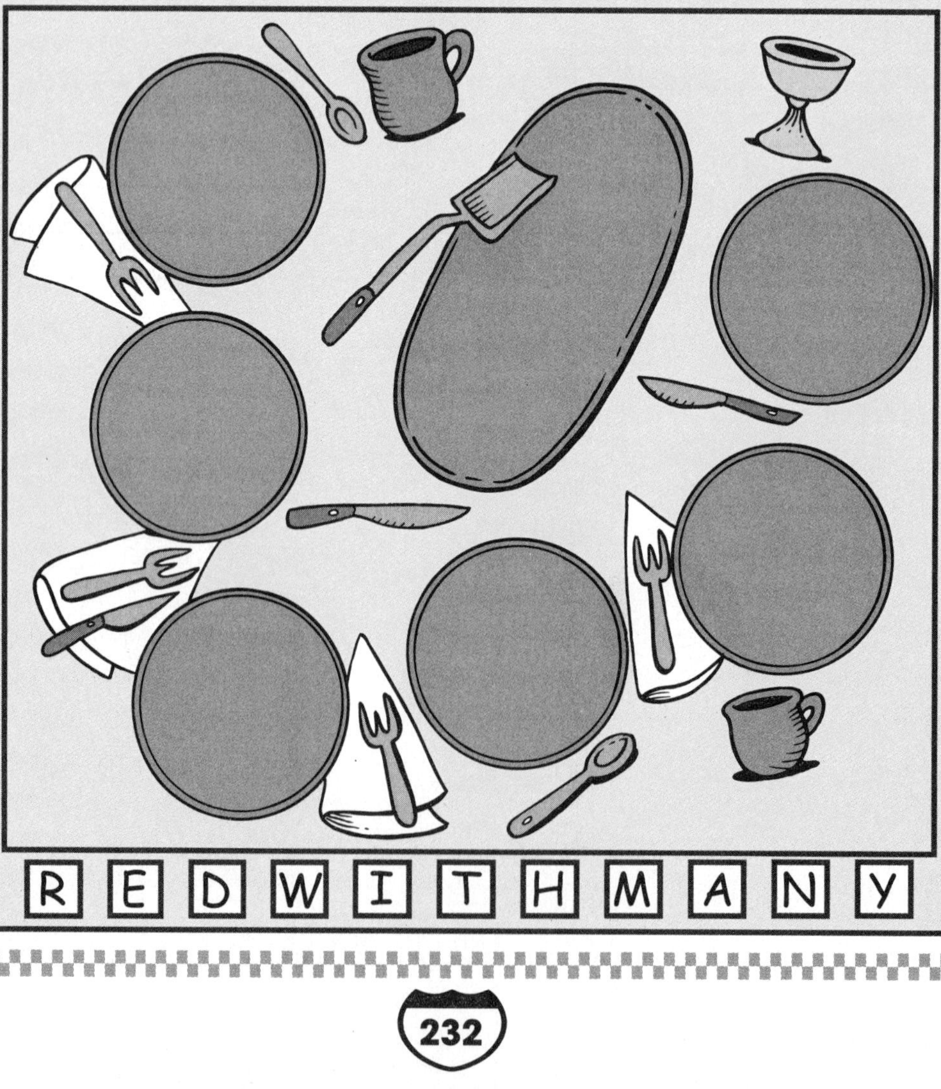

A R E D W I T H M A N Y O

HIDDEN WORDS

Write the sentence hidden in the ice-cream cone on the lines below. **Hint:** The sentence begins with "Beat."

Sentence: _____

_____

HIDDEN WORDS

Write the sentence hidden in the boat on the lines below.
Hint: The sentence begins with the word "It" and has 17 words.

Sentence: _____

_____

_____

WORD LADDERS

EXAMPLE:

Change the word at the bottom of each ladder to the word at the top by changing one letter at a time. Begin with the word at the bottom. Use the letters on the right or left to make a new word at each step.

Rules:

1. If the letter is on the right, remove it from the word and put another letter in its place.
2. If the letter is on the left, add it to the word after you remove the letter that is in its place.

TAIL
-L
TALL
+A
TOLL
-D
TOLD
+T
HOLD
-E
HELD
+L
HEAD

JILL
-P
+L
-A
+L
-K
+P
JACK

DIME
+M
-L
+E
-E
+L
CENT

MOM
-P
+O
-D
+M
DAD

LIVE
-D
+V
-S
+M
DIES

WORD LADDERS

EXAMPLE:

Change the word at the bottom to the word at the top by changing one letter at a time. Begin with the word at the bottom. Use the letters on the right or left to make a new word at each step.

Rules:

1. If the letter is on the right of the step, remove it from the word and put another letter in its place.
2. If the letter is on the left, add it to the word after you remove the letter that is in its place.

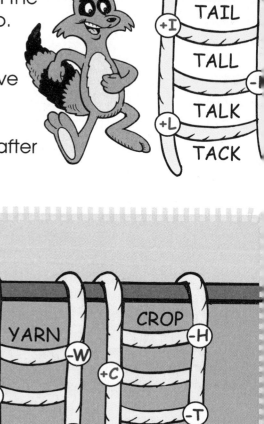

NAIL
+I — TAIL
TALL
+L — TALK
TACK

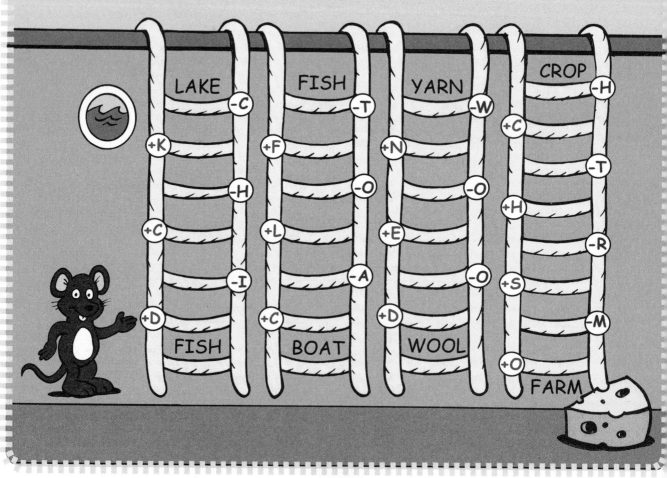

LAKE
-C
+K
-H
+C
-I
+D
FISH

FISH
-T
+F
-O
+L
-A
+C
BOAT

YARN
-W
+N
-O
+E
-O
+D
WOOL

CROP
-H
+C
-T
+H
-R
+S
-M
+O
FARM

236

WORD LADDERS

EXAMPLE:

Change the word at the bottom to the word at the top by changing one letter at a time. Begin with the word at the bottom. Use the letters on the right or the left to make a new word at each step.

Rules:

1. If the letter is on the right, remove it from the word and put another letter in its place.
2. If the letter is on the left, add it to the word after you remove the letter that is in its place.

DOG
+G
DOT
-P
POT
+O
PET

HILL
+I
-E
+H
VALE

KID
-L
+D
-O
+L
TOT

SKY
+K
-B
+y
-U
+B
SUN

SHEEP
-R
+E
SHEAR

GRAPH

Graph each point. First, locate the letter on the graph, then the number. Follow those lines until they meet. Put a dot at that point. Connect the dots as you go along.

Example: G15 has been done for you.

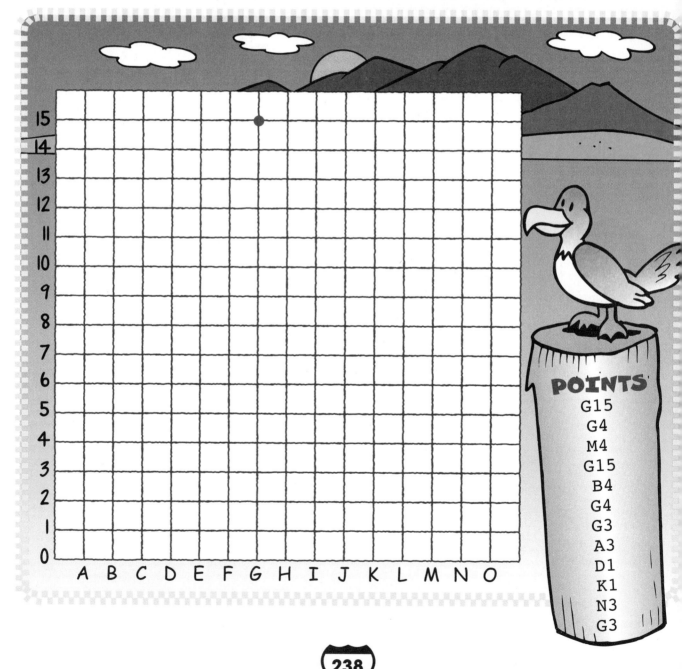

POINTS

G15
G4
M4
G15
B4
G4
G3
A3
D1
K1
N3
G3

MAZE

Mazes can help you learn to think ahead. Can you think far enough ahead to get through this maze from "start" to "finish"? Try it with a pencil.

GRAPH

Graph each point. First, locate the letter on the graph, then the number. Follow those lines until they meet. Put a dot at that point. Connect the dots as you go along. When you come to the word "lift," do not connect the dots at that point; begin at the next dot.

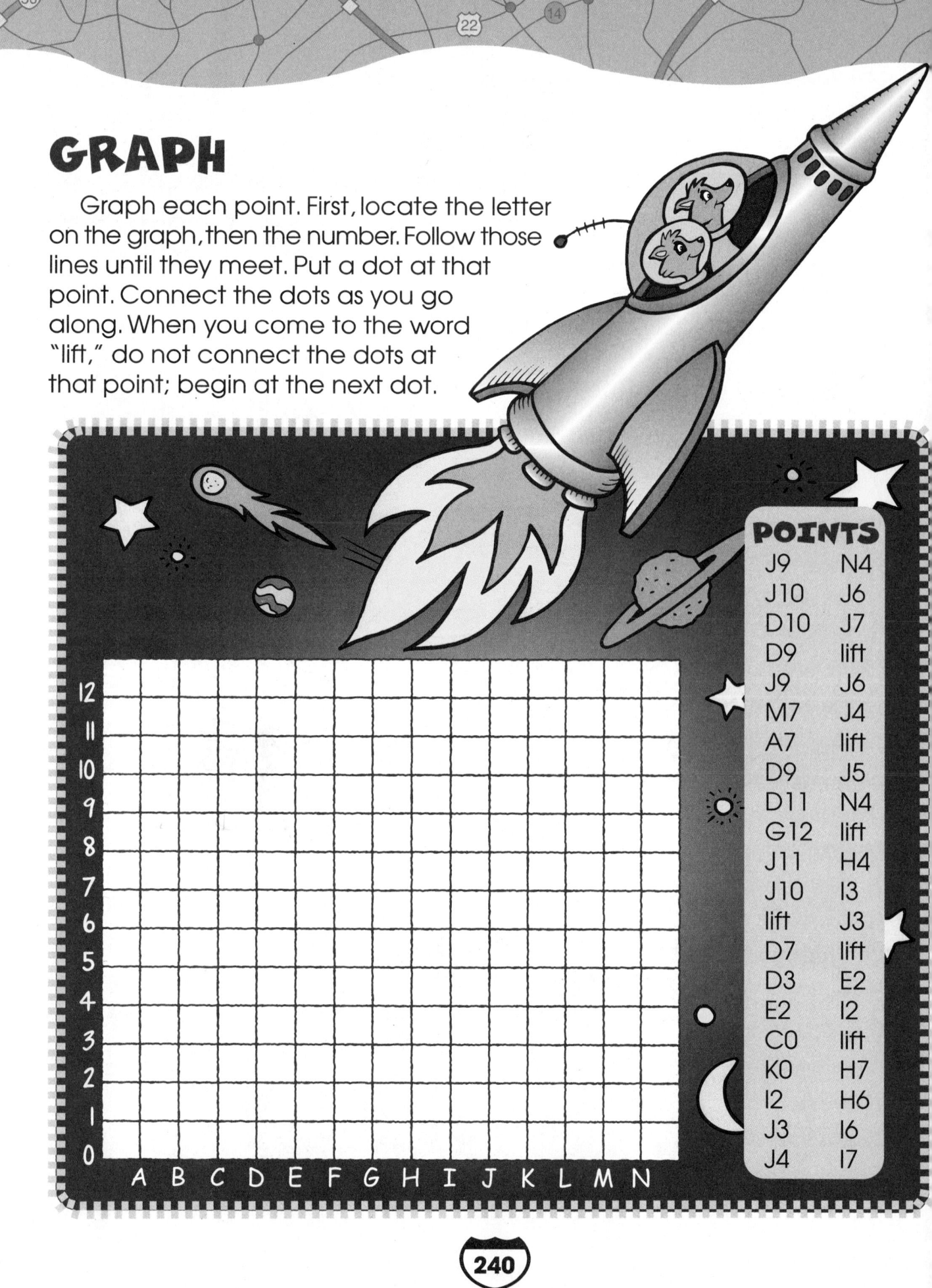

POINTS

J9	N4
J10	J6
D10	J7
D9	lift
J9	J6
M7	J4
A7	lift
D9	J5
D11	N4
G12	lift
J11	H4
J10	I3
lift	J3
D7	lift
D3	E2
E2	I2
C0	lift
K0	H7
I2	H6
J3	I6
J4	I7

CODES

Break the code to find the names of fruits. Each number stands for a different letter of the alphabet.

Hint: Each **9** stands for a **U**.
　　　Each **6** stands for a **P**.

1. __ __ __ __ __
   3　8　12　6　5

2. __ __ __ __
   6　1　9　14

3. __ __ __ __ __ __
   2　12　4　12　4　12

4. __ __ __ __ __ __
   21　8　12　4　3　5

5. __ __ __ __ __ __ __ __
   7　21　4　5　16　18　5　13

6. __ __ __ __ __ __ __ __ __
   8　12　20　6　2　5　8　8　16

7. __ __ __ __ __ __ __ __ __
   17　12　4　3　5　8　15　4　5

8. __ __ __ __ __ __ __ __ __ __
   3　8　12　6　5　19　8　9　15　17

9. __ __ __ __ __ __ __ __ __
   2　1　9　5　2　5　8　8　16

10. __ __ __ __ __ __ __ __ __ __
    11　12　4　17　12　1　21　9　6　5

11. __ __ __ __ __ __ __ __ __ __
    20　17　8　12　13　2　5　8　8　16

12. __ __ __ __ __ __ __ __ __
    4　5　11　17　12　8　15　4　5

13. __ __ __ __ __
    12　6　6　1　5

14. __ __ __ __
    10　15　13　15

15. __ __ __ __ __
    6　5　12　11　7

DOT-TO-DOT & MAZES

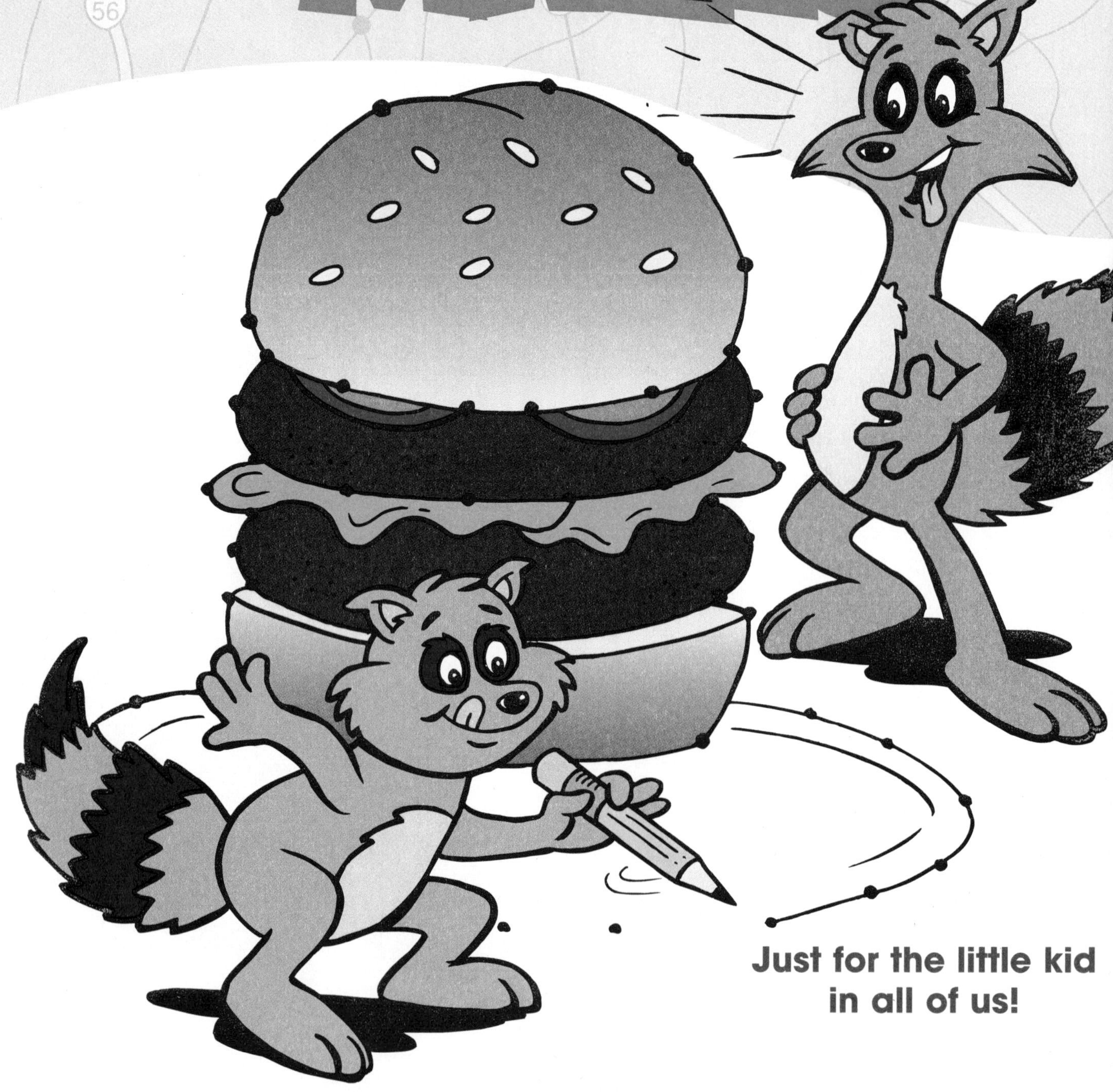

Just for the little kid in all of us!

WHAT IS HATCHING?

Draw a line to connect the dots in 1, 2, 3 order.

WHAT IS HIDING IN THE SNOW?

Draw a line to connect the dots in ABC order.

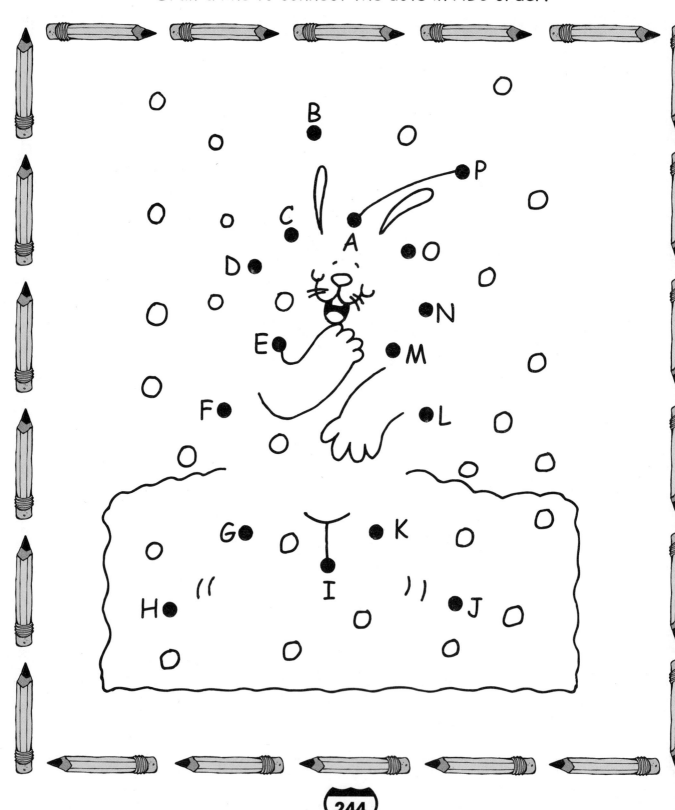

WHAT IS ON TOP OF THE PACKAGE?

Draw a line to connect the dots in 1, 2, 3 order.

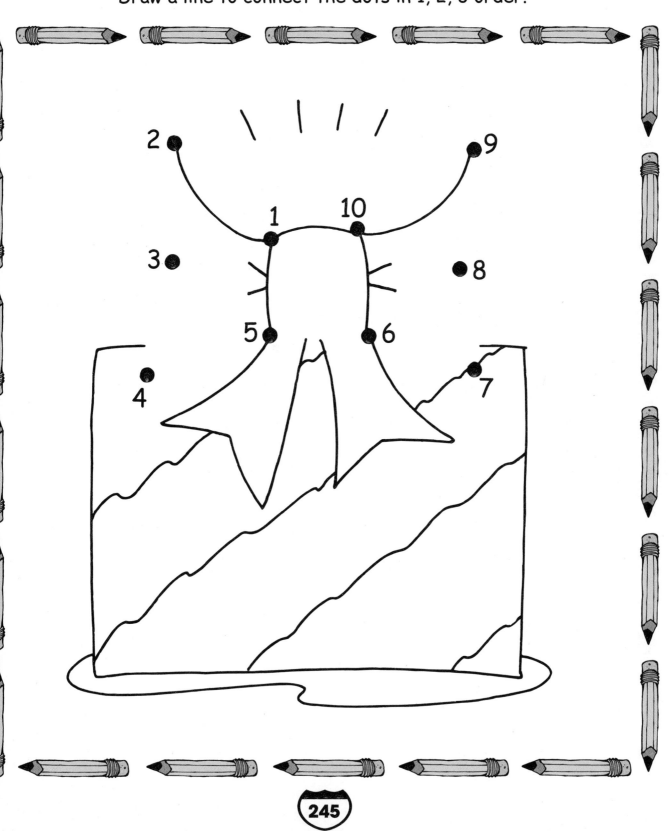

WHAT IS HIDING IN THE DESERT?

Draw a line to connect the dots in ABC order.

WHAT IS ON THE BREAKFAST TABLE?

Draw a line to connect the dots in 1, 2, 3 order.

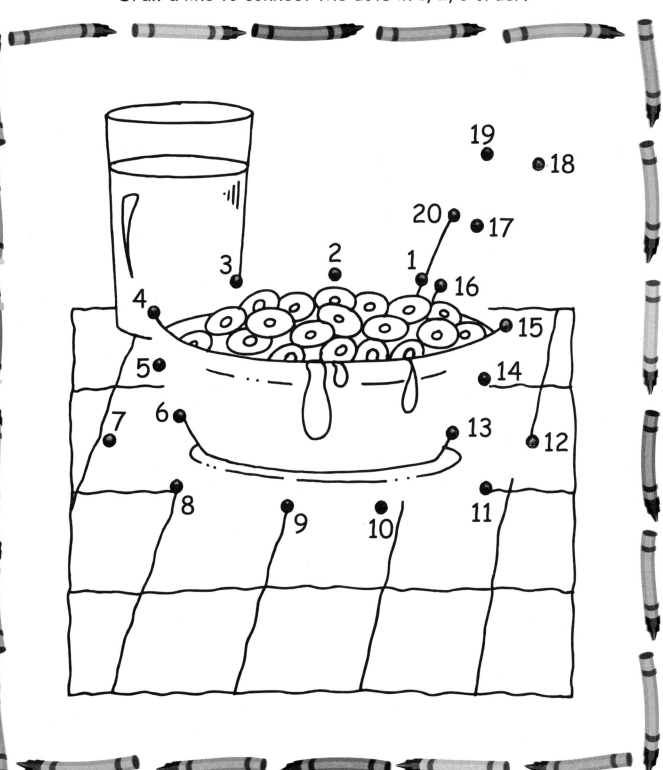

WHAT IS HIDING IN THE MEADOW?

Draw a line to connect the dots in ABC order.

WHICH WAY TO THE LODGE?

Help the lost skier find her way to the ski lodge.

WHAT IS FLOATING IN THE BATHTUB?

Draw a line to connect the dots in 1, 2, 3 order.

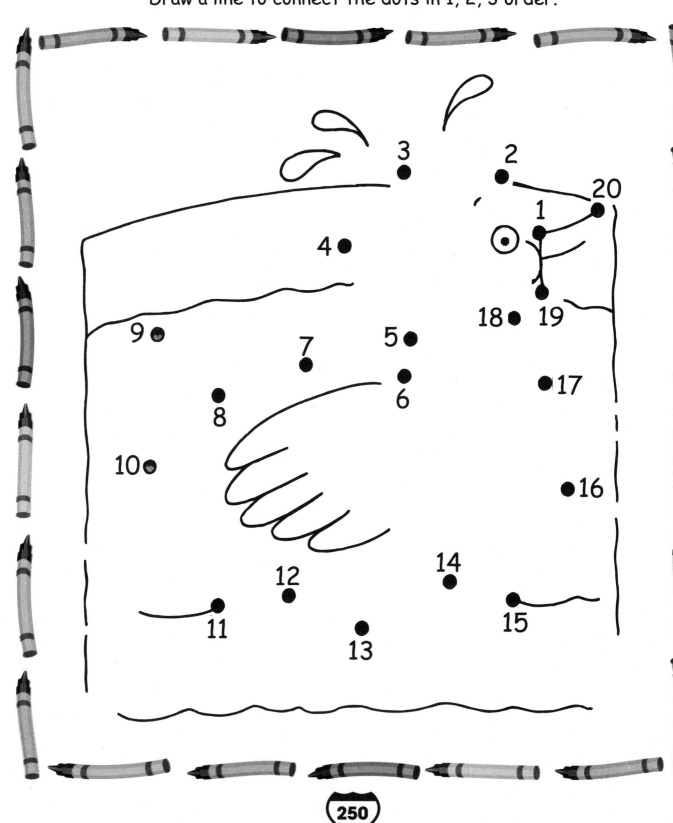

WHAT IS HIDING IN THE RAIN?

Draw a line to connect the dots in ABC order.

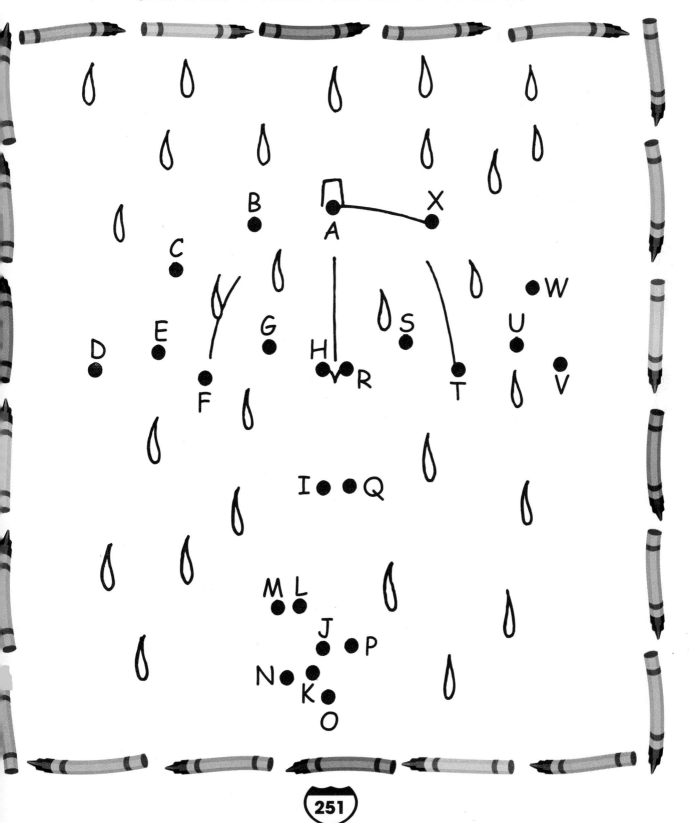

WHAT IS ON THE LEAF?

Draw a line to connect the dots in 1, 2, 3 order.

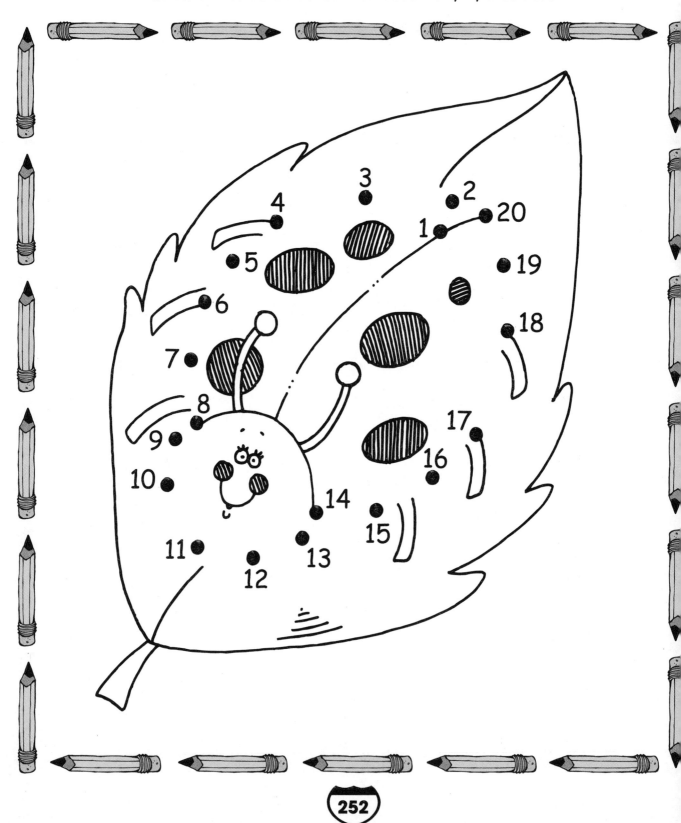

WHAT IS HIDING IN THE MUD?

Draw a line to connect the dots in ABC order.

WHICH WAY TO THE DOCK?

Help the sailboat find its way to the dock.

WHAT IS ON THE BEACH?

Draw a line to connect the dots in 1, 2, 3 order.

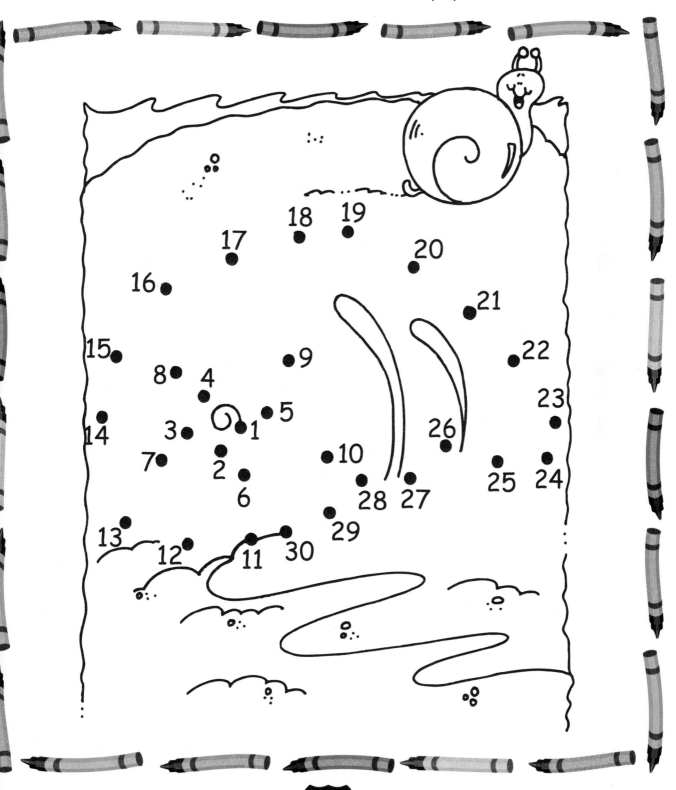

WHICH WAY TO SCHOOL?

Help the girl find the schoolhouse.

WHICH WAY TO THE AIRPORT?

Help the lost airplane find the airport.

WHAT IS HIDING IN THE OCEAN?

Draw a line to connect the dots in ABC order.

WHAT IS ON TOP OF THE QUEEN'S HEAD?

Draw a line to connect the dots in 1, 2, 3 order.

WHAT IS HIDING IN THE WOODS?

Draw a line to connect the dots in ABC order.

WHICH WAY TO THE CASTLE?

Help the prince find his way to the castle.

WHAT IS IN THE TREE?

Draw a line to connect the dots in 1, 2, 3 order.

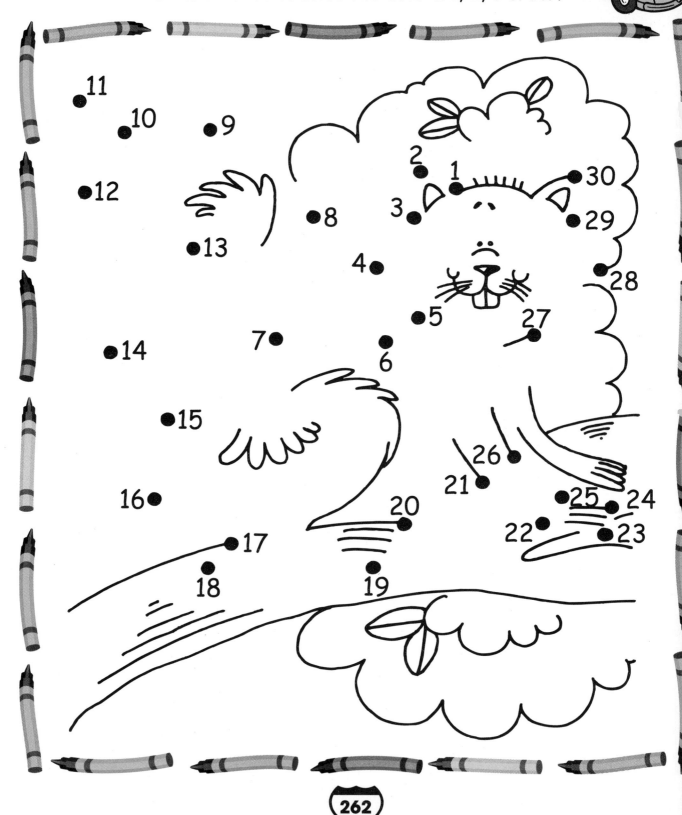

WHICH WAY TO THE TOY?

Help the baby find her pull toy.

WHAT IS HIDING IN THE SWAMP?

Draw a line to connect the dots in ABC order.

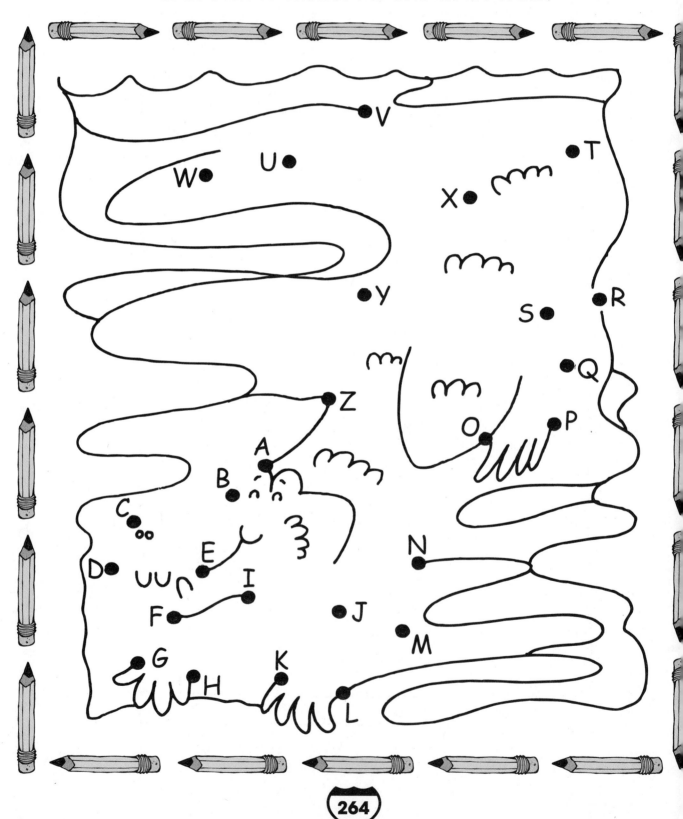

AROUND WE GO

One person begins telling a story. After a minute, the person points to someone else who must continue the story. The story keeps growing with everyone adding sentences. The game ends when a person finishes the story or when everyone has had a few turns adding to the plot.

WHO HAS THE LAST WORD?

In this game, a story grows with the help of all the players but with a twist. The first person begins the story with one sentence. The next person adds another line but must use the last word in the previous sentence as the first word in his or her new sentence. For example:

First person: A long time ago a giant lived in the forest.

Second person: Forest rangers used to go and visit the giant every day.

The game continues with each person adding a sentence based on the last word in the previous sentence. The story keeps growing for a certain number of minutes or until everyone has had a chance to add two or three sentences to the tale.

ADD A WORD

This game requires group effort and a lot of concentration.

One person begins a story by saying one word. Then, another person quickly adds another word. Everyone takes turns adding one word at a time until the story is complete or until someone takes too long trying to think of a word to add.

HIDDEN NAMES

Here's a fun challenge for storytellers.

Each person takes a turn telling a story. One person must begin a story with a phrase made up of words that start with the first three letters in his or her name. If possible, the storyteller continues adding other phrases. Everyone can pitch in with suggestions to help add to the story. Example: beginning of a story "Matthew" might use:

Many **a**lien **t**ourists parachuted down from the sky. **M**eg's **A**untie **T**illy saw the tourists first. She ran to **M**r. **A**llen's **t**ravel agency and knocked madly at the door.

WHAT IF?

Choose a fairy tale and retell it by mixing in characters from other fairy tales. For example, you might tell a story describing what could happen if the Three Bears found Sleeping Beauty in a deep sleep in their bedroom. Would the bears try to find the prince to help them get rid of their unexpected guest? What if they can't find the prince? Could the Frog Prince in the neighboring forest substitute for him?

Everyone can help make the story as silly as possible. If you like, have a contest to see who can create the most outrageous tale!

WHAT AN IMAGINATION!

Let your imaginatio soar with these creative activities.

SQUIGGLE ART

Can you make a work of art out of a squiggle line? If you use your imagination, you can!

Play this game with another person. Use the space below and another sheet of paper. Both of you will draw a squiggle line on your paper. Then, trade papers and make an interesting picture using the squiggle as part of the drawing. You're sure to be impressed by the results!

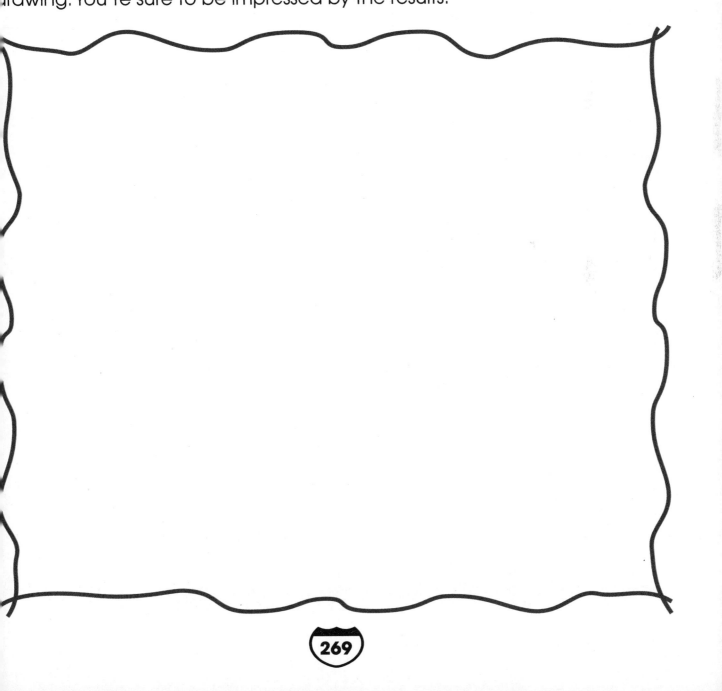

FANCY NAMES

Use the space below or another sheet of paper to try printing or writing your name in different ways. Add dots and fancy strokes to make your name look interesting. How many different looks can you create?

CLOUD PICTURES

Have you ever seen faces, animals and other pictures in the clouds? You can also try making pictures from trees, mountains and other things you see, too. Look at colors, textures and shapes. Look at the outlines of things on the horizon. You just might be surprised by what you "see."

Use this space or another sheet of paper for your cloud pictures.

BUILD A CHARACTER

In this drawing game, everyone works together to build a character.

One player starts by drawing a head on a sheet of paper. The head can look like a person, a robot, an animal or any other thing. The paper is passed on to the next player, who adds a body. The paper is passed on from one person to the next with various body parts being added each time. (Examples: hair, legs, feet, arms, hands.)

For added fun, have each person help build a name for the character as well. The first player chooses the first letter, the second player chooses the second letter, and so on.

Variation: Fold the paper on this page and on pages 273–276 into thirds so that the first third is on top. The first player draws a head on that section of the paper, then folds the paper so the middle section is on top. The second player draws a body on this third of the paper, then folds the paper so the bottom section is on top. The third player draws the legs and feet. When the drawings are completed, unfold the paper to reveal an unusual character!

TOP

- - - - - - FOLD - - - - -

- - - - - - FOLD - - - - -

BOTTOM

BUILD A CHARACTER

(Directions are found on page 272.)

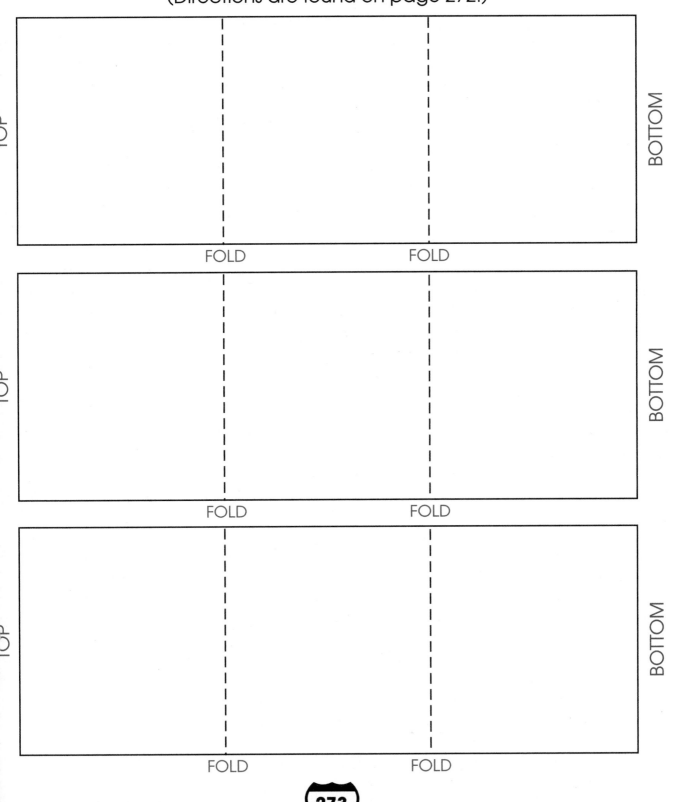

BUILD A CHARACTER

(Directions are found on page 272.)

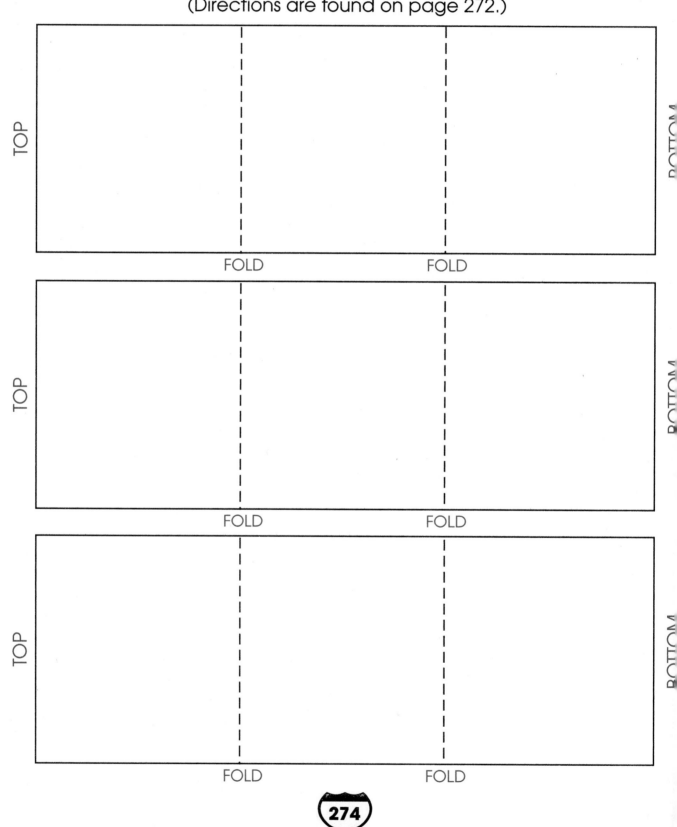

BUILD A CHARACTER

(Directions are found on page 272.)

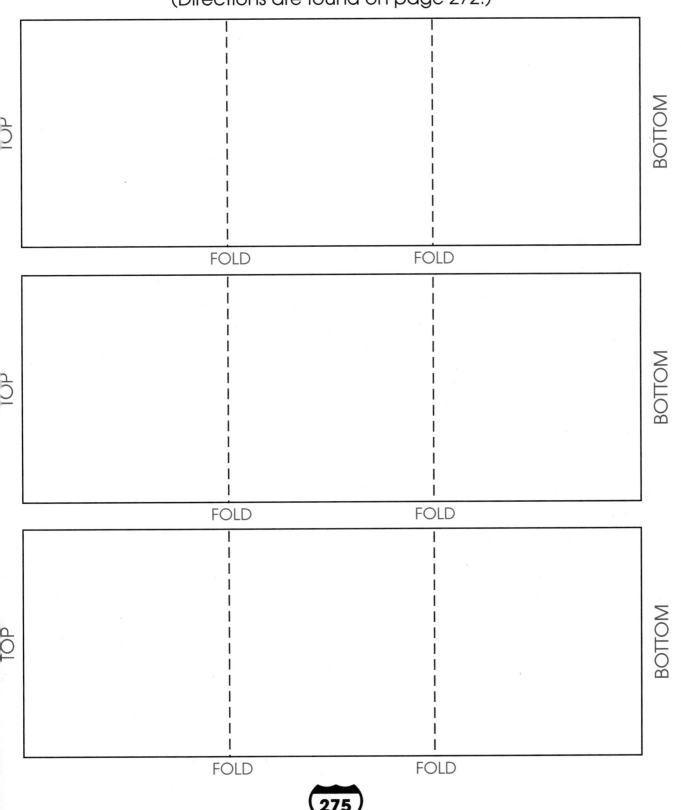

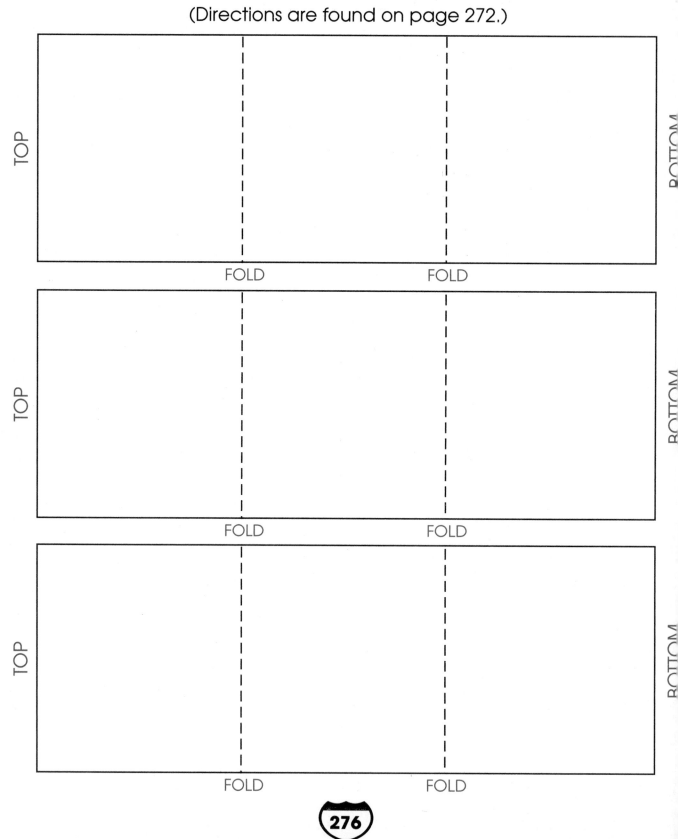

TOP

FOLD   FOLD

BOTTOM

TOP

FOLD   FOLD

BOTTOM

TOP

FOLD   FOLD

BOTTOM

CREATE A HAND ANIMAL

Arrange your hands to form the shape of an animal or move your hands to suggest an animal's movements. Here are some you can try:

Butterfly

Cross one thumb over the other and spread out the rest of your fingers. Wave your fingers to suggest wings fluttering.

Rabbit

Form a fist and hold up your index and middle fingers to make a rabbit with one hand. Can you think of another way to make a rabbit?

Swan

Form a swan's beak with one hand. Move your wrist and arm gracefully back and forth.

Take turns showing your hand animals to one another. Can the others guess your animal?

GAMES GALORE

Here is a
mixed bag of game
that will help keep
you entertained
on your trip.

BOXED IN

Use the gameboard on this page and on pages 280–285.

Two people can play this strategy game. Each player takes a turn drawing a line to connect a pair of dots either horizontally or vertically. When a line is drawn so that a box is made, that player writes the first letter of his or her name inside the box and claims it. After all the dots have been connected, the players count how many boxes each has made. The one with the most boxes wins.

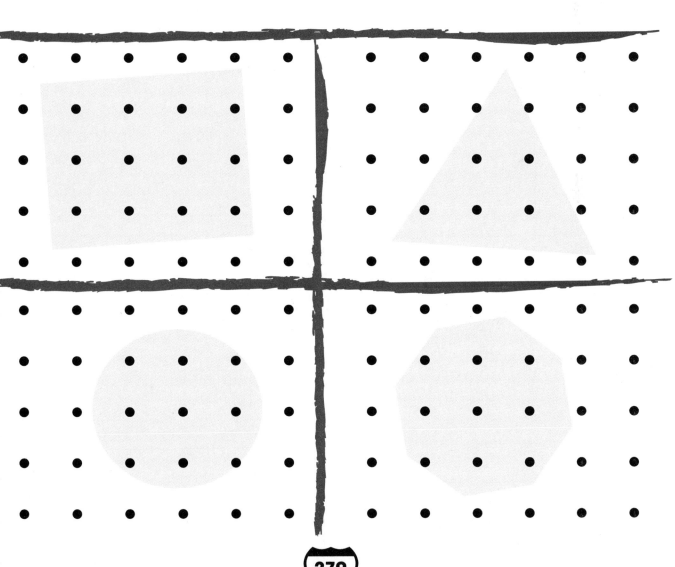

BOXED IN

(Directions are found on page 279.)

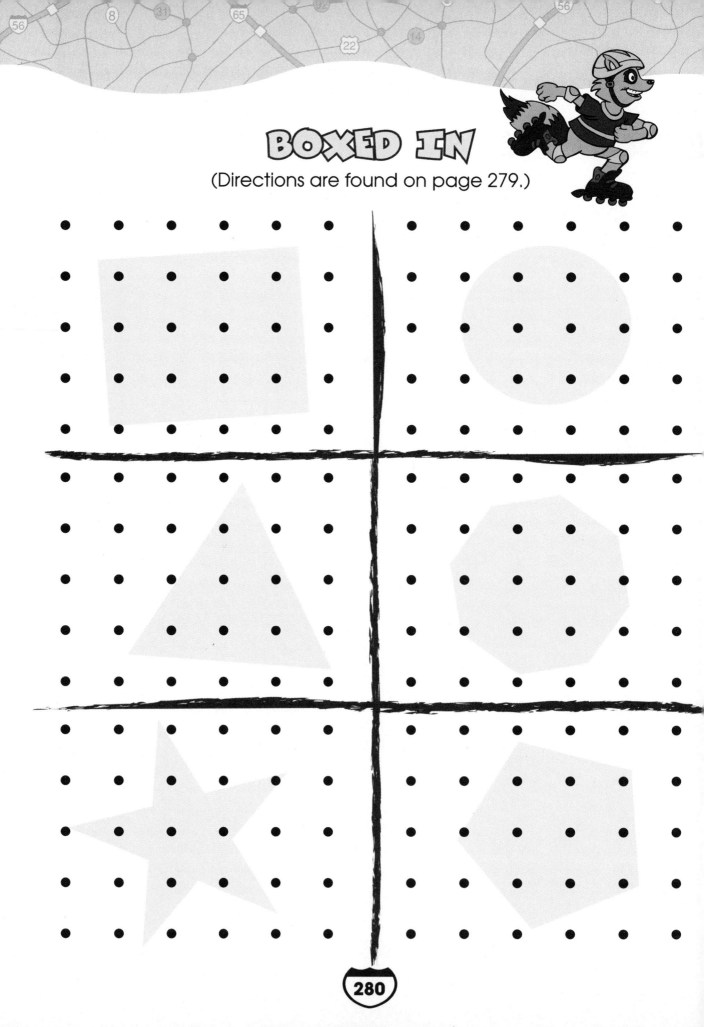

BOXED IN

(Directions are found on page 279.)

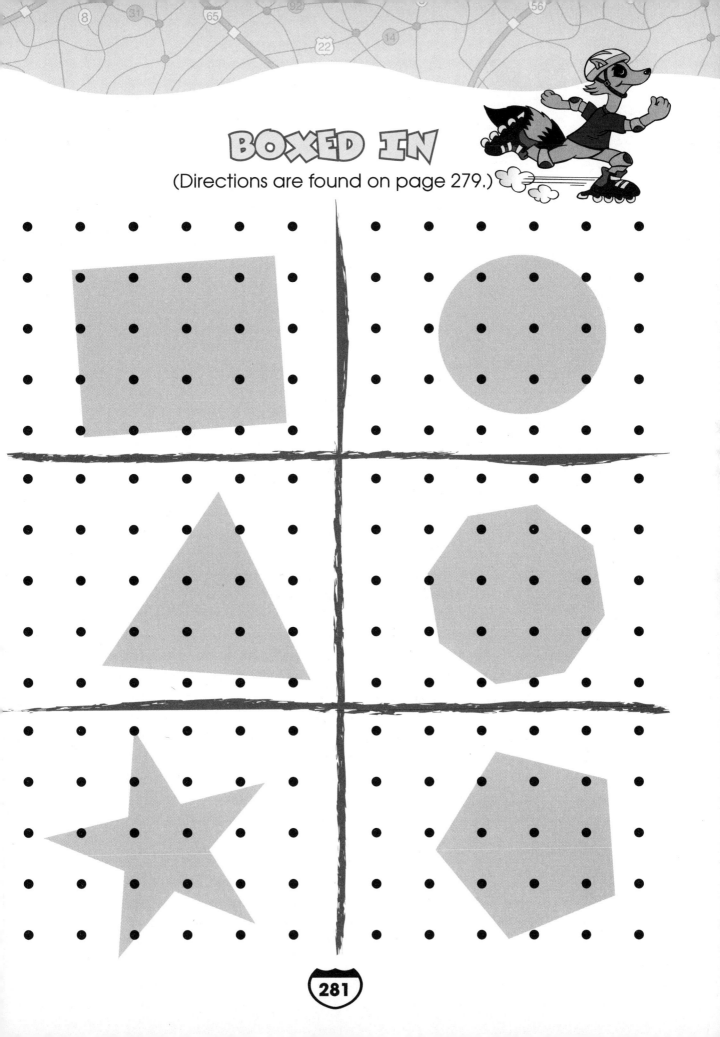

BOXED IN

(Directions are found on page 279.)

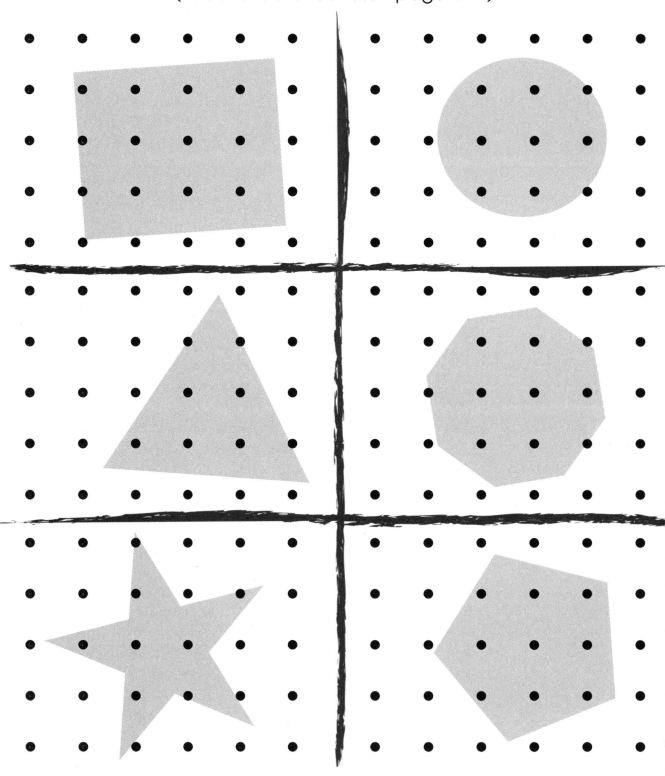

BOXED IN

(Directions are found on page 279.)

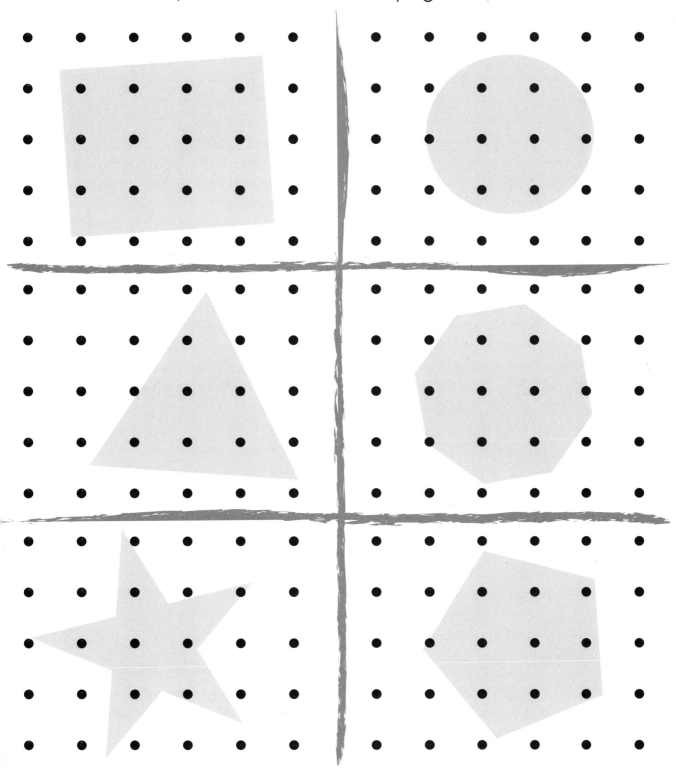

BOXED IN

(Directions are found on page 279.)

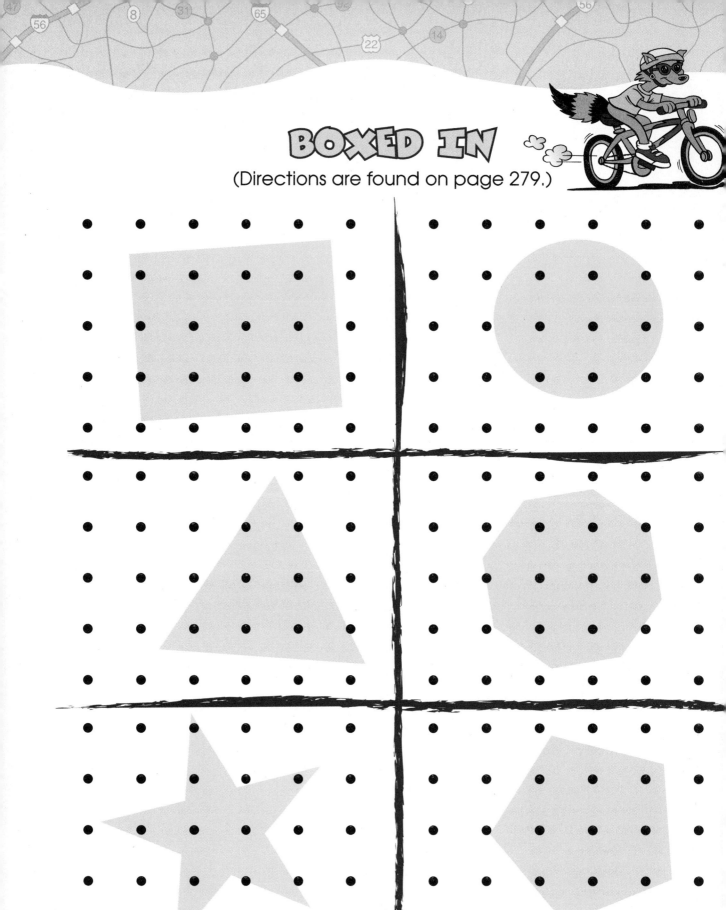

BOXED IN

(Directions are found on page 279.)

DON'T LAUGH

Each player tries to make the others laugh by making funny faces, telling a joke, singing in a crazy way, and so on. Tickling is not allowed, though! A person who laughs is out of the game. The last one left is, of course, the winner!

DRAW SOME FUNNY FACES

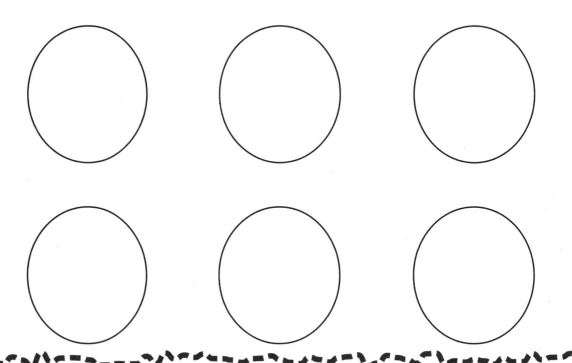

DRAW SOME FUNNY FACES

DRAW SOME FUNNY FACES

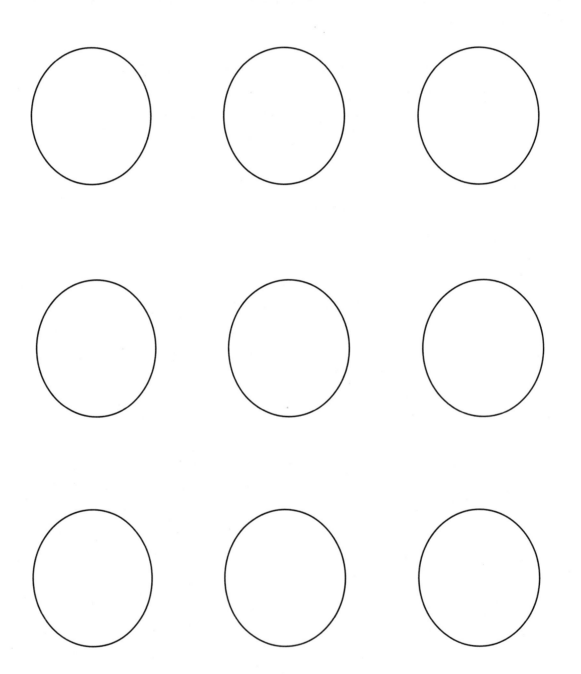

ROCK, PAPER, SCISSORS

This traditional game is played in many different cultures. Players each make a fist and together move their fists up and down three times as they count, "One, Two, Three!" At the count of three, each player forms a rock, paper or scissors.

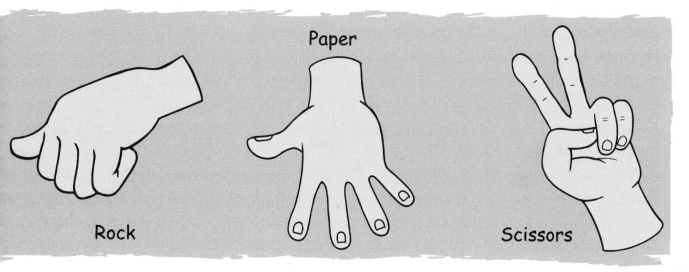

Rock

Paper

Scissors

To score, one player has to beat the others:

Rock wins over Scissors since a pair of scissors cannot cut a rock.
Scissors wins over Paper since paper can be cut.
Paper wins over Rock since a rock can be covered up by paper.

If there are only two players, one person will always score a point unless both players display the same symbol. In that case, no one scores. If there are more than two players, a person scores if only two or more winning symbols are displayed and he or she has the winning hand. For example, with three players, Player A scores a point in Example 1, Players A and B each score a point in Example 2, and no one scores in Example 3. See who scores 20 points first!

Example 1:	Player A-rock	Player B-scissors	Player C-scissors
Example 2:	Player A-rock	Player B-rock	Player C-scissors
Example 3:	Player A-rock	Player B-scissors	Player C-paper

SCRAMBLED WORDS

Cut 20 slips of paper and write an interesting word on each one. Then, place the paper slips in a paper bag. Each person takes a turn drawing four slips out of the bag and making a sentence containing all four words. The sentence has to make sense, but it can be silly! When each person has had a turn saying a sentence, the words can be used again or replaced by other words.

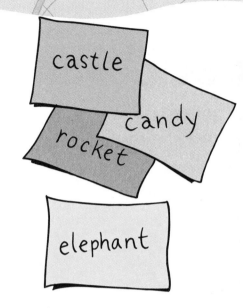

CLAP, SLAP AND SNAP

Player A is the leader and starts off by creating a rhythm either by clapping hands, slapping thighs or snapping fingers. The other players have to follow along by copying the action. Player A then picks up the pace and changes the actions. For example, if Player A started off by clapping, he or she can now alternate clapping and snapping:

Clap, clap, snap! Clap, clap, snap!

The action can change as many times as Player A wishes. The other players have to follow along without losing the rhythm. After a few minutes, another player becomes the leader.

HEADS OR TAILS

Here's a fun version of a familiar game. Place six pennies in a shoebox and close the lid. Designate one player as "Heads" and the other as "Tails." The first player ("Heads") shakes the box for a few seconds, then looks in the box. He or she scores 1 point for each penny facing heads up. The second player then takes a turn shaking the box and scoring points for every penny facing tails up. Continue the game for several rounds and keep track of the score. The player with the most points wins.

DON'T GET SHORTY

You need at least as many straws as you have players for this game.

Cut about one-quarter inch off the end of one straw. Then put all the straws in a lunch bag. Each player draws a straw from the bag. When all the straws have been drawn, the players look to see who has the short straw. That player scores 1 point. Play the game for several rounds. The winner is the player with the least number of points.

RED OR BLACK?

You'll need a deck of cards for this game of chance.

First, each player predicts whether he or she will have more red cards or black cards. Then, one person deals out all the cards until there are none left. (It doesn't matter if the cards are not dealt out evenly.)

Everyone counts how many red and black cards there are. Players with correct predictions score 1 point.

Start each round with new predictions. The player who reaches 10 points first wins.

READ MY LIPS

How well can you read lips? Maybe better than you think! One player begins by mouthing a short sentence. The other players watch carefully and try to guess the sentence. The one who guesses correctly makes up a new sentence for the game.

CALCULATOR PUZZLES

Directions:

1. Begin by reading the phrase.

2. Next, load the number given or calculated in the "Enter" section.

3. Now, press each operation button shown in the boxes and the numbers that follow. If the operation box is shaded in, simply do what the directions tell you to do. (With some calculators, you may need to press the equal sign after each operation.)

4. When you get to the equal sign, press it and flip the calculator upside down to read the answer.

A really large oinker
is a . . . .

ENTER: 2,159

x	twenty
+	seven
x	fourteen
=	

Babies have to be fed
very carefully when they
are . . . .

ENTER: 173

x	160
+	nine
x	200
+	eighteen
=	

ANSWER:

Playing the piano and building model planes are two great . . . .

ENTER: 443

x	thirty
+	seven
x	400
+	four
=	

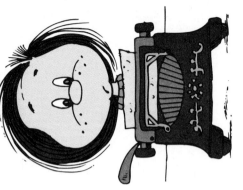

The name for a beautiful southern girl is . . . .

ENTER: 377

x	100
+	thirty
■	add (4 + 4)
=	

ANSWER:

ANSWER:

294

This girl's name starts and ends with "e."

ENTER: 650

x	54
+	seven
x	ten
+	three
=	

Having a best friend is true . . . .

ENTER: 788

x	35
+	nine
x	two
=	

ANSWER:

A watermelon as large as
a bath-tub is a real . . . .

ENTER: 1,583

×	100
+	nine
×	two
=	

Telephone poles are
made from . . . .

 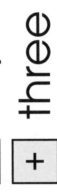 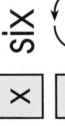

ENTER: 934

×	five
+	three
×	four
×	fifty
+	three
×	six
=	

Messy eaters need a . . . .

ENTER: 8,000

÷	two
+	ninety-three
×	200
■	add (9 + 9)
=	↺

ANSWER:

This African bird's beak looks almost like a shoe.

ENTER: 3,859

×	twenty
+	three
×	1,000
+	forty-five
=	↺

ANSWER:

What you get when you fall down.

ENTER: 1,000,000

x	five
+	8,000
■	add (2 x 4)
=	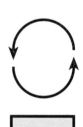

The polished table had a . . . .

ENTER: 56.2

x	twenty
x	seven
x	seven
=	

298

Something kids like to do.

ENTER: 10 less than 100

x	523
+	seven
x	eight
=	

Some rides at a fair can make you . . . .

ENTER: 1 x 1

+	ten
x	seventy
+	one
=	

When you have lots and lots, you have . . .

ENTER: 10 − 5

×	580
+	three
×	two
=	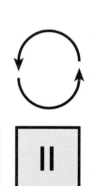

The best place to lean on a window is the . . .

ENTER: the missing number:

43, ____ , 45

×	five
×	seven
+	three
×	five
=	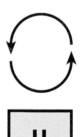

When you can't stop
laughing, you have a bad
case of the . . . .

ENTER: 50 + 50

×	531
+	seventy-seven
×	100
+	fifteen
=	

ANSWER:

The story of David and
Goliath is in the . . . .

ENTER: 2 less than 10

×	500
×	ten
−	2,182
=	

ANSWER:

301

Let's go "dashing through the snow in a one horse open . . . "

ENTER: 5 less than 50

x	eighty-two
+	the number of people it takes to ride a unicycle
x	125
=	

A girl's name with two l's and two e's.

ENTER: half of 1,000

x	640
−	63
−	2,400
=	

When animals get thorns
in their paws they . . . .

ENTER: the number of letters
in "ocean"

$\times$	eighty
$\times$	947
$+$	four
$=$	

The first name of someone
who lost her sheep.

ENTER: the number of letters
in "baa"

$-$	two
$+$	6.2
$\div$	nine
$=$	

Very light brown is . . . .

ENTER: the number of letters in "magenta"

add (2 + 3)

	÷ two
	× 6,023
	= 

This belongs with "Old MacDonald's farm."

ENTER: the number of letters in "Moo Moo"

+ four
− nine
− .8687
=

To move up and down in water is to . . . .

ENTER: the number word that sounds the same as "for"

× twenty-five

+ one

× eight

=

When you put too much peanut butter and jelly between your bread, it _____ out!

ENTER: the number of letters in "Mississippi"

+ twenty-two

+ 100

× 400

=

George Washington said
"I cannot tell a . . . ."

ENTER: the number of pennies in a quarter

x	two
x	6.2
+	seven
=	

What you might say if your dog grabs your hamburger.

ENTER: the number of pennies in a nickel

÷	five
−	.75952
÷	six
=	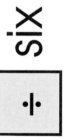

The person who gives orders is the . . . .

ENTER: the number of pennies in a dollar

+	two
x	three
x	eighteen
=	

ANSWER:

A nickname for Gilbert is . . . .

ENTER: the value of six nickels

+	5.8
x	five
x	four
=	

ANSWER:

A large hermit crab's home is a . . .

ENTER: the number of pennies in two dollars

- − 39
- × 300
- + 41
- × two
- × 800
- + eighteen
- =

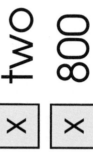

ANSWER:

The Spanish word "hola" means . . .

ENTER: the number of quarters in a dollar

- × two hundred thirty-two
- ÷ fifty-eight
- − 15.2266
- =

ANSWER:

Your sense of direction is something you never want to . . . .

ENTER: the number of dimes in a dollar

×	fifty
×	seven
+	seven
=	

In order for one person to buy, another must . . . .

ENTER: the number of quarters in a dollar

+	three
×	221
×	five
=	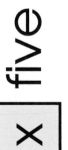

A model of the Earth is a . . . .

ENTER: the number of nickels in a dollar

÷	.8
−	thirteen
×	3,173
=	

Bacon on a hot griddle might . . . .

ENTER: the number of pennies in four dimes

    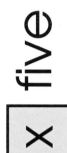  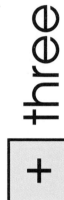

×	1,861
+	three
×	five
=	

A fish that looks like a snake is an . . . .

ENTER: the number of dimes in a dollar

x seventy

+ thirty-five

− two

=

The ears on an African elephant are real . . . .

ENTER: the number of pennies that equals two dimes

x 443

+ one

x 600

+ eighteen

=

311

The contraction for "I will" is . . . .

ENTER: the number of numerals on a clock face

+

ENTER: the number of months in 2 years

twelve

÷

three

+

12.85

×

=

If centipedes needed these, they would go broke!

ENTER: the number of seconds in one minute

fifteen

÷

one

+

10,609

×

=

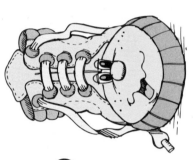

A boy's name that rhymes with "rely."

ENTER: the number on a clock face that stands for twenty minutes after the hour

×	two
−	three
×	34.6
=	

When our ice-cream cone falls on the ground, we . . . .

ENTER: the number of hours between noon and 4 P.M.

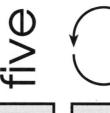

×	(25 + 25)
−	thirty-nine
×	five
=	

The opposite of "she."

ENTER: the number of days in a week

+	eight
x	two
■	add (2 + 2)
=	

When you hear this ring, school is over.

ENTER: the number on the clock that represents 5 minutes before the hour

+	nineteen
x	258
−	two
=	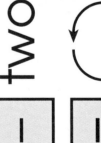

A baby might say . . .

ENTER: the number of people it takes to play on a seesaw

add (3 + 3)

 ÷ two

- three

- .93994

=

ANSWER:

What Saint Nicholas loves to say before "Merry Christmas."

ENTER: the number of reindeer named Rudolph pulling Santa's sleigh

- .79798

÷ two

x four

=

ANSWER:

The tall, round structure on a farm where grain is stored is called a . . . .

ENTER: the number of wheels on a tractor

+	. 10
+	. 19
÷	six
=	

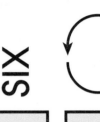

A good thing to teach your dog to do is . . . .

ENTER: the number of wheels on a pair of in-line skates

×	400
+	467
×	two
=	

When the villain enters, the audience . . . .

ENTER: the number of months old you are on your first birthday

÷ two

+ ten

× 313

= ⟳

ANSWER:

A dog can easily make a cat . . . .

ENTER: the number of fingers you have

÷ two

+ one

× 919

= ⟳

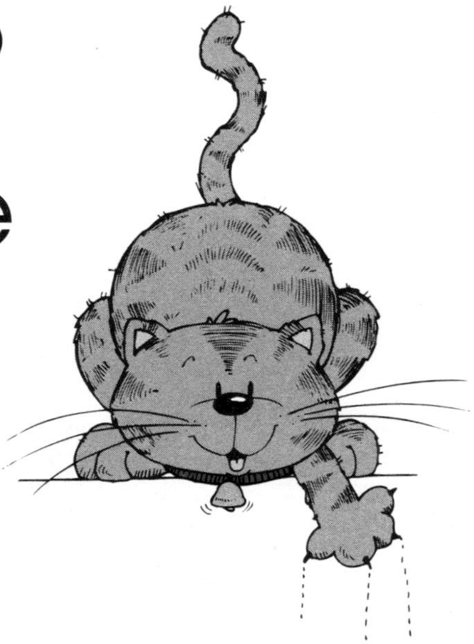

ANSWER:

Add this to "zag" to describe a crooked line.

ENTER: the number of wheels on an in-line skate

+ 4.5

× eight

× nine

=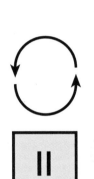

ANSWER:

A great tool for gardening is a . . .

ENTER: the number of toes on your left foot

× sixty

add (5 + 5)

subtract (3 + 3)

=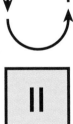

ANSWER:

The capital of Idaho is . . . .

ENTER: the number of minutes
in 1 hour

×	145
+	77
×	four
=	

The universal distress
signal is . . . .

ENTER: the number you dial in
an emergency

÷	two
–	.5
+	fifty
=	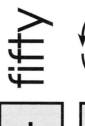

ANSWER:

A June bug is often
mistaken for a . . . .

ENTER: the number of days in
a school week

x	80.6
x	sixty
+	seven
x	fourteen
=	

Where can you find
elephants and penguins?

ENTER: the number of legs on a
horse + 3

+	ninety-three
÷	five
■	divide by 1,000
=	

ANSWER:

The year both Alaska and Hawaii became part of the United States.

ENTER: the number of stripes on the American flag

+ twenty-eight

× 160

+ one

= ⟳

A name for a boy or girl that rhymes with see.

ENTER: the number of moons revolving around our planet

+ the number of days in the month of May

+ twenty-six

− fifty-five

× seven

+ ⟳

=

ANSWER:

The policeman will
_____ the stolen money.

ENTER: the number of legs
on an octopus

 × 800

 + twenty-seven

× five

 =

These help you see in
the water.

ENTER: the number of ounces
in 1 pound

+ 584

× 8,961

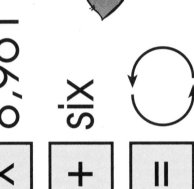 + six

=

ANSWER:

ANSWER:

When we think of nursery rhymes, we think of Mother . . .

ENTER: the number of days in the month of January

−	six
×	two
×	seven hundred
■	add six
=	↻

What you tell a fly when you want it to go away.

ENTER: the number of feet in a yard

the number of toes on both your feet

+	two
+	five
÷	two
−	.64
−	eight
÷	↻
=	

A famous bear's best
friend is named . . . .

ENTER: the number for the
Spanish number "dos"

x	ten
−	twelve
x	.101
=	

The contraction for
"he is."

ENTER: the number of days in
February in a leap year

−	five
÷	four
x	.89
=	

Who sells sea shells by the sea shore?

ENTER YOUR RESPONSE: If kitty was given three pieces of tuna for breakfast and for dinner, how many pieces did she have in all?

÷	two
×	one before six
×	twenty-three
=	

I want a big hug or . . . .

ENTER YOUR RESPONSE: Your pet Mittens had five kittens. How many tiny paws are scrambling over your kitchen floor?

−	ten
×	four hundred
−	427
=	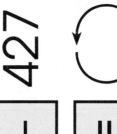

TRAVEL MEMORIES

Here are some fun ideas for capturing the memorable moments of your trip.

TRAVEL LOG

While traveling, write down any details about your trip that you'd like to remember. For example, you could write about fascinating sights, interesting people or memorable incidents. If you prefer, use a portable tape recorder to record information about your trip. You might also want to interview different members of your family to get their views and feelings as the trip is in progress. Add sound effects (such as a beeping watch or a small bell), musical numbers and "commercials" to make your recording more lively and interesting.

VACATION REVIEW QUIZ

After your trip is over, plan to give your family a quiz that reviews the highlights of your trip. To prepare the quiz, you'll need to take notes during your vacation. Write down details that can be used in your quiz at a later date. For example, your quiz might contain a question about who ate what at a certain restaurant or the time you left a particular hotel. After your family takes the quiz, go over the answers and make a "Vacation Quiz Whiz" award for the person with the highest score.

MAP IT OUT

Before your trip, look at a map to see where you will be going. Then, afte your trip, look at the map again and see if you can retrace the various route: you took. Use removable stickers to mark the different places you stopped to rest or to view interesting sights.

SOUVENIR COLLECTION

How many free souvenirs can you get on your trip? While traveling, collect business cards, restaurant menus, place mats, paper napkins, hotel brochures and other souvenirs. Every item collected counts as 1 point. Make sure you don't take anything that is not meant to be given away (such as cutlery or towels), and don't count items that were paid for.

After your trip, see how many points you and your family "scored." Then, work with your family to make a great souvenir scrapbook or album with all the items you collected.

SOUVENIR FASHION

As you're traveling, pick up souvenirs you can attach to a baseball cap or a jacket. Pins, buttons, stickers, badges, clip-on pens and other small items are perfect for creating an eye-catching souvenir outfit. Later, when you get home from your trip, wear your souvenirs as a way of sharing your vacation memories with your friends.

HOW HIGH CAN WE GO?

Look across and down to find the words from the Word Bank in the puzzle. Circle them.

```
f i n d l d
h t r e y p u f
e w u z o l f o
r o n d u a u r
e c o m e y n w
s k m a k e n e
o j u m p p y o
e h e l p a
```

WORD BANK

here	come
find	funny	for	jump
two	so	play	run
we	make	help	

23

I CAN READ IT!

Look across to find the words from the Word Bank in the puzzle. Circle them.

```
a n d b u p
s e e k a t
c i s p w r
t o d n o t
e r u n h f
j i n t h e
i t m v g o
```

WORD BANK

and	to	at	go
in	is	it	not
run	see	the	up

24

LOOK WHAT I SEE!

Look down to find the words from the Word Bank in the puzzle. Circle them.

```
d b u m w i a y
o d l u e m w o
w a i s n l a u
n f t a t o y b
a t t i e o c i
m e l d m k a g
y r e o e s n r
```

WORD BANK

down	after	away	big
little	said	went	my
look	you	me	can

25

CAREFUL!

Circle the words from the Word Bank in the puzzle. Color the spaces you circled blue. What did you find? __a car__

```
d i o e c r b z w c n p q t e a
b h j e c a r r o t c o r f g i
m r m c c l o c k c o f d u w j
s i n x c h a i r o b c s c r h
a c c c c a k e c t c c o l o r
v o a l c h o p u t i c l e a n
p o s a c o s t p o t c h e s t
t k t m c r a s h n y c l o u d
m n b c o t f h g o t c a t m s
c b r c a n j i e c t c u t o e
```

WORD BANK

cot	clam	cast
cat	color	chest
carrot	cook	cob
chair	can	cup
clean	cloud	chop
city	cost	crash
cake	clock	cut
	cotton	

26

TRUCKIN' ALONG

Circle the words from the Word Bank in the puzzle. Color the spaces that you circled green. What did you find? __a jeep__

```
p t n d f h j u i v j d o l e
x r e j k e i s t y a o u z a
e o o j a d e p t u b c d j j
w a j u n g l e j u m p j j k
i c j o l l y j e e p s a o t
e d f j e l l y j o k e m g s
j f s g j e t j o k j a r r v
k g t h j o b k j l j u g t u
b a s d f j g h i l o p s y z
```

WORD BANK

jump	jug	jolly
jade	jet	jog
joke	jungle	job
jelly	jar	jeeps
jab	jam	

27

WHAT'S THE WORD?

Circle the words from the Word Bank in the puzzle. Color the squares you circled red. What did you find? __yes__

```
y g h u p y t i d r e o n m t c
d y c y i b y y i w g y u l l
b o t a s r e y e t n m a o m f
c w s r j f l a d g h o w s e c
x l y n l k l y e s t y n y a
d y e h u p o y o u i m t a y
v p a g e o w u n m j l u b
h k s o m p y o k e k m v c p
g m t c s y a r d c z y a p
i l u r f k g u l f d u x o r e
```

WORD BANK

yak	yawn	yes
yams	yeast	yet
yap	yell	yip
yard	yellow	yoke
yarn	yowl	yule
you		

28

CREATIVE COLORS

Find and circle the color words from the Word Bank in the puzzle. Look across and down. Color the squares you circled blue. What did you find? __art__

```
o r a n g e b d c a e g i k r z t
p x h o e b u n w n f a d f e q x
i l m n b l v c x z a s f g d h a
n y u i o u r e w q t p w h i t e
k g r a y e x p b n v m x k y u p
b u d r u g t u b r o w n m e n o
l a s d m r r r v n e t y w l l h
a b d f g e h p j k m u z m l n a
c g h k o e i l e w n l v f o g n
k s d u e n l e j o m c s x w y w
```

WORD BANK

blue	black
brown	yellow
red	pink
orange	gray
green	purple
white	

29

TICKET, PLEASE!

Find and circle the number words from the Word Bank in the puzzle. Look across and down. Color the squares you circled black. What did you find? __a train__

```
a l m j e f o p q d g u i
c f h i k f f c e b m n p
b e r t y s e v e n z c b
h o e r s j t e n l h n g
u x e t c d o n e t h i k
w f l n y x f e z h d i o
p i e i s t o i e r a u p
a s n i w u g r n k l
a e n e x e y o r h e f h
b c n d f g i t j l m n o
```

WORD BANK

zero	four	eight
one	five	nine
two	six	ten
three	seven	eleven

30

A GENTLE BREEZE

Find the words from the Word Bank in the puzzle. Color the squares you circled red. What did you find? __sailboat__

WORD BANK

grin	yell
shut	street
fast	unhappy
steps	beautiful
starts	go
cap	talk
same	small

```
t w p x m a u o g r a t a k g a
n s r e p g h b a r v r h i o l
v w b n s f p r m d u d t e f m
b o t m f d g i e n h r p o q c
a b z p c i e s s k c f h c t m e
j l t e a y m i u q w b o l t
e g f d r t u s d s t a r t s
h r y c f m o t w f y e b h j e
k j p g i e q a l s o f m l p n i
s h u t b e a u t i f u l l y
f a s t s t r e e t u n h a p p
c m a s t e p s t a l k g o g a t
```

31

WHAT WILL I BE?

...nd and circle the words Word Bank in the puzzle. Look across and down.
...the squares you circled black. What did you find? __a question mark__

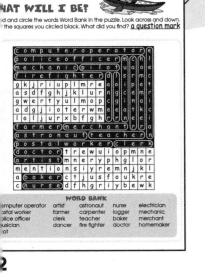

WORD BANK

...computer operator · artist · astronaut · nurse · electrician
...postal worker · farmer · carpenter · logger · mechanic
...police officer · clerk · teacher · baker · merchant
...musician · dancer · fire fighter · doctor · homemaker

WAY TO GO!

Find and circle the words from the Word Bank in the puzzle.
Look across and down. Color the squares you circled yellow.
What did you find? __a bus__

WORD BANK

monorail · trains · cable cars · schoolbus · tram
airplane · bus · elevator · ship · truck
boat · cab · escalator · subway · van
car · · helicopter · taxi · jet

A MAJESTIC VIEW

Find and circle the words from the Word Bank in the puzzle.
Look across and down. Color the squares you circled green.
What did you find? __a tree__

WORD BANK

age · fir · moss · plant · seedlings · sun · water
bark · forests · needles · rings · seeds · trees · woods
cones · leaves · pine · roots · soil · trunk

REFRESHING DIP

...nd and circle the words from the Word Bank in the puzzle.
...across and diagonally. Color the squares you circled orange.
...t did you find? __a fish__

WORD BANK

...at · fins
...lear · breathe
...umps · scales
...ye · aquariums
...n · plants
...ubbles · water
...ill · air
...wim · tall
...are · rocks

HEADING FOR THE SLOPES

Find and circle the words from the Word Bank in the puzzle. Color the
squares you circled one color. What did you find? __a ski__

WORD BANK

shell · should · shallow · sharp
shouts · sheep · shares · shirts
she · short · shape · show
shine

WHAT A RECIPE

...ead the clues. Write the words that mean the same. Find and circle
...answers in the puzzle.
...nt: All words start with the prefixes "un," "dis" or "re."

CLUES

Not happy __unhappy__   11. To stop appearing __disappear__
Not true __untrue__   12. To write again __rewrite__
To not obey __disobey__   13. Wash again __rewash__
Not hurt __unhurt__   14. Not tied __untied__
To not like __dislike__   15. Not folded __unfolded__
Not safe __unsafe__   16. To not agree __disagree__
To fill again __refill__ 17. To do again __redo__
Not fair __unfair__   18. To open again __reopen__
To wrap again __rewrap__ 19. Not friendly __unfriendly__
Not seen __unseen__   20. To build again __rebuild__

TAGALONG WORD SEARCH

Antonyms are words that have opposite meanings.

Draw a line through the words in the word search that are antonyms of
the words in the Word Bank. In tagalong, use the words in the order they are
listed. The last letter of the word just found will be the first letter of the next
word to be found.

Attract/repel has been done for you.

TAGALONG WORD SEARCH

Draw a line through the words in the word search that
are antonyms of the words in the Word Bank. In tagalong,
use the words in the order they are listed. The last letter of the
word just found will be the first letter of the next word to be found.

Shy/bold has been done
for you.

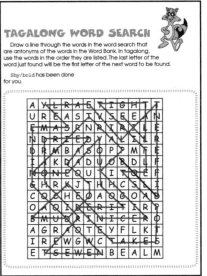

33 **34** **36** **38** **39**

TAGALONG WORD SEARCH

Homophones are words that sound alike but are spelled differently and have different meanings.

Draw a line through the word in the word search that is a homophone of the word in the Word Bank. In tagalong, use the words in the order they are listed. The last letter of the word just found will be the first letter of the next word to be found.

Fur/fir has been done for you.

40

TAGALONG WORD SEARCH

A synonym is a word that means about the same as another word.

Draw a line through the word in the word search that is a synonym of the word in the Word Bank. In tagalong, use the words in the order they are listed. The last letter of the word just found will be the first letter of the next word to be found.

Rank/rate has been done for you.

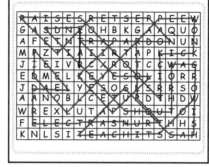

41

WHAT A PACE!

Number the pictures 1, 2, 3, 4 to show the order from fastest to slowest.

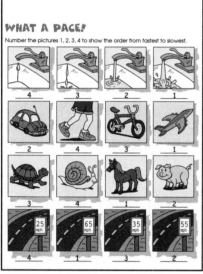

80

PLEASE HELP ME FIND MY OWNER

Help each pet find its owner. Start at the picture of each animal. Follow the directions at the bottom to find each pet's owner.

Example: S4 means to go south 4 spaces.

Cat E4 · S3 · W3 · S3 · E6 · S4 · W4 · S1 · E8 · N7 · W2

Dog S6 · W3 · N5 · W3 · S6 · E6 · S2 · W5

The cat's owner is __John__. The dog's owner is __Lynn__.

81

ON THE WAY TO THE BIG GAME

Jan and Jeff are meeting at the baseball field. Start at the picture of each child. Follow the directions at the bottom to find out how each one entered the field.

Example: S4 means to go south 4 spaces.

Jan E2 · S1 · E6 · S1 · W7 · S4 · E6 · S3 · E3 · N1

Jeff W8 · N3 · E9 · N7 · W2 · S6 · W2 · N2 · W3

Who entered the field from the south? __Jan__

82

GOING FOR REPAIRS

Your bike needs to go to the repair shop. Your parents' car needs to go to a garage for new tires. Follow the lines to see how the bike and the car reached the correct repair shops.

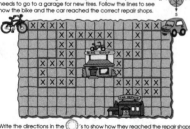

Write the directions in the ○'s to show how they reached the repair shops. The first ones have been done for you.

Example: 4 spaces to the west is written W4.

🚲 E4 · S4 · W2 · S2 · E3 · N5 · E4 · S1

🚗 W3 · S3 · W2 · S3 · E4 · S1 · W3

How many spaces was the bike from the repair shop? __25__
How many spaces was the car from the garage? __19__
Which repair shop was farthest away? __bike shop__

83

ISLAND-HOPPING HELICOPTER RIDE

Hawaii, our 50th state, is really a group of islands in the Pacific Ocean. Many people like to island-hop, which means traveling from one island to another. One way to island-hop is to fly in a helicopter.

Look at the map. Starting at Hilo, follow the route shown by the dashed line. Write the names of the islands in the order of the route.

1. Hawaii
2. Maui
3. Kahoolawe
4. Lanai
5. Molokai
6. Oahu
7. Kauai
8. Niihau

Honolulu is the capital of Hawaii. On what island will we find Honolulu?
__Oahu__

On which side of the island is Honolulu located? __south__

84

PONY EXPRESS

The "pony express" carried the mail across our country between April 3, 1860 and October 28, 1861. A young man would ride a horse from one station to the next, changing horses at each station. It was a very dangerous ride. The trip went from Sacramento, California to St. Joseph, Missouri.

Look at the map. Write the names of the states in the order the pony express rider traveled through them while carrying the mail from California to Missouri.

1. California   4. Wyoming   7. Nebraska
2. Nevada   5. Nebraska   8. Kansas
3. Utah   6. Colorado   9. Missouri

Which state did you write two times? __Nebraska__

How long did the pony express deliver mail? __April 3, 1860 to October 28, 1861; 19 months; 574 days__

85

OLD-TIME STAGECOACH RIDE

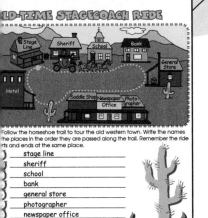

Follow the horseshoe trail to tour the old western town. Write the names of the places in the order they are passed along the trail. Remember the ride starts and ends at the same place.

1. stage line
2. sheriff
3. school
4. bank
5. general store
6. photographer
7. newspaper office
8. saddle shop
9. hotel
10. stage line

6

HELPING A LOST STUDENT

Recess is over. A first grade student cannot find her way to Room 1. Can you help her? Look at the map. The dotted line shows the way from the playground to Room 1.

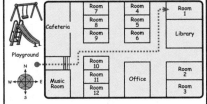
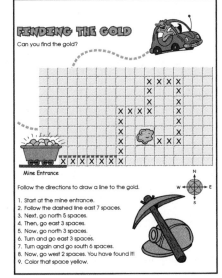

Number the directions by following the path of the dotted line.

- 4 Turn north at the bottom of the steps.
- 1 First, you open the door and come into the school.
- 6 Continue walking down the long hall past the office.
- 7 Turn north when you reach the library.
- 2 Walk by the music room.
- 8 Keep walking until you come to Room 1.
- 3 Go down three steps.
- 5 Turn east and walk down the hall between Rooms 9 and 10.

How does it feel to be lost? _____ Answers will vary.

87

PLAN A ROUTE

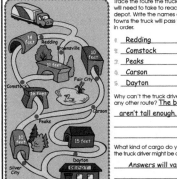

A truck driver has to decide which roads he will use to deliver his cargo to the depot. He has to be sure his truck will go under the bridges and through the tunnels. His truck is 12 feet high. The heights of the bridges and tunnels are marked on the map.

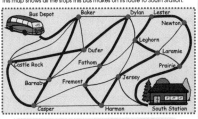

Trace the route the truck driver will need to take to reach the depot. Write the names of the towns the truck will pass through in order.

1. Redding
2. Comstock
3. Peaks
4. Carson
5. Dayton

Why can't the truck driver take any other route? The bridges aren't tall enough.

What kind of cargo do you think the truck driver might be carrying?

Answers will vary.

88

ARRIVING ON TIME

There are TV monitors at the airport that show when planes are arriving and departing. Here is one showing arrivals.

Flight Number	Arriving From	Arrival Time	Gate Number
562	Detroit	1:45 P.M.	B-56
497	San Francisco	2:06 P.M.	E-42
612	Denver	3:18 P.M.	A-12
724	Miami	3:35 P.M.	M-53
906	Honolulu	4:10 P.M.	C-34
893	Boston	5:20 P.M.	L-26

Use the information on the monitor to answer the questions. What is the . . .

city listed before Denver? San Francisco
flight number listed before 906. 724
gate number listed before M-53? A-12
arrival time listed before 4:10 P.M.? 3:35 P.M.
flight number listed after 562? 497
gate number listed after C-34. L-26
city listed after Miami? Honolulu
arrival time listed after 2:06 P.M. 3:18 P.M.
city listed before San Francisco? Detroit
arrival time listed after 4:10 P.M.? 5:20 P.M.

9

FINDING THE GOLD

Can you find the gold?

Mine Entrance

Follow the directions to draw a line to the gold.

1. Start at the mine entrance.
2. Follow the dashed line east 7 spaces.
3. Next, go north 5 spaces.
4. Then, go east 3 spaces.
5. Now, go north 3 spaces.
6. Turn and go east 3 spaces.
7. Turn again and go south 6 spaces.
8. Now, go west 2 spaces. You have found it!
9. Color that space yellow.

90

THE BUS ROUTE

This map shows all the stops this bus makes on its route to South Station.

Write the names of the stops in alphabetical order to show the bus route.

1. Baker
2. Barnaby
3. Casper
4. Castle Rock
5. Dufer
6. Dylan
7. Fathom
8. Fremont
9. Harmon
10. Jersey
11. Laramie
12. Leghorn
13. Lester
14. Newton
15. Prairie

Use a crayon to connect the stops in the order of the bus route.

91

CRUISING

There are many islands in the Caribbean Sea. These islands are favorite vacation spots for many people. Cruise ships take several different routes to the different islands.

Legend
X where cruise stops
--- Vacation Cruise Line
--- Sea Cruise Line
--- Sail Away Cruise Line

Write in order the names of the islands where each cruise ship stops. Be sure to include where each cruise line begins and ends.

Vacation Cruise Line	Sea Cruise Line	Sail Away Cruise Line
1. Miami	1. Miami	1. Miami
2. Nassau	2. Puerto Rico	2. Barbados
3. Jamaica	3. Martinique	3. Antigua
4. Grand Cayman	4. Trinidad	4. St. Martin
5. Cozumel	5. Nassau	5. St. Thomas
6. Miami	6. Miami	6. Miami

If your ship left port without you, what would you do? _____
Answers will vary.

2

THEY SHOWED THE WAY

Meriwether Lewis and William Clark were chosen by President Jefferson to find a route to the Pacific Ocean. They had to draw maps of the land, record weather conditions and write about the plants and animals they found along the way. People wanted to know what it was like west of the Mississippi River. On May 14, 1804, they started their expedition. They arrived at the Pacific Ocean in the winter of 1805. They set up a camp which they named Fort Clatsop.

Write the names of the states in the order Lewis and Clark traveled through them on their expedition from St. Louis, Missouri to Fort Clatsop, Oregon.

1. Missouri
2. Kansas
3. Iowa
4. Nebraska
5. South Dakota
6. North Dakota
7. Montana
8. Idaho
9. Washington
10. Oregon

93

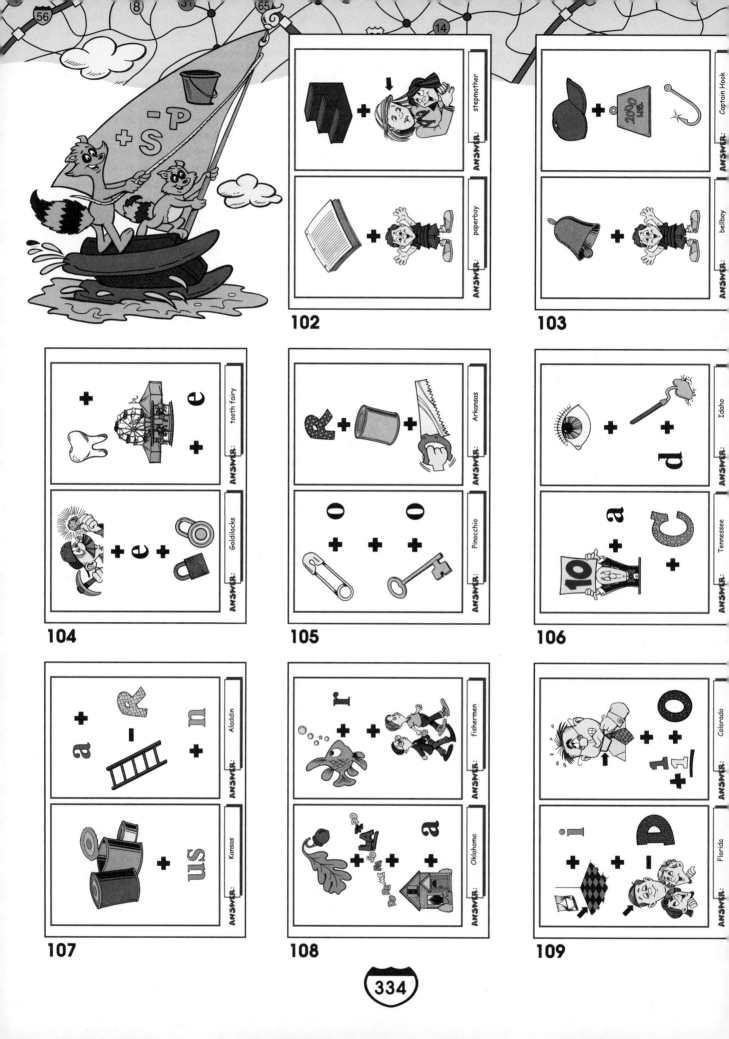

102

ANSWER: stepmother

ANSWER: paperboy

103

ANSWER: Captain Hook

ANSWER: bellboy

104

ANSWER: tooth fairy

ANSWER: Goldilocks

105

ANSWER: Arkansas

ANSWER: Pinocchio

106

ANSWER: Idaho

ANSWER: Tennessee

107

ANSWER: Aladdin

ANSWER: Kansas

108

ANSWER: fishermen

ANSWER: Oklahoma

109

ANSWER: Colorado

ANSWER: Florida

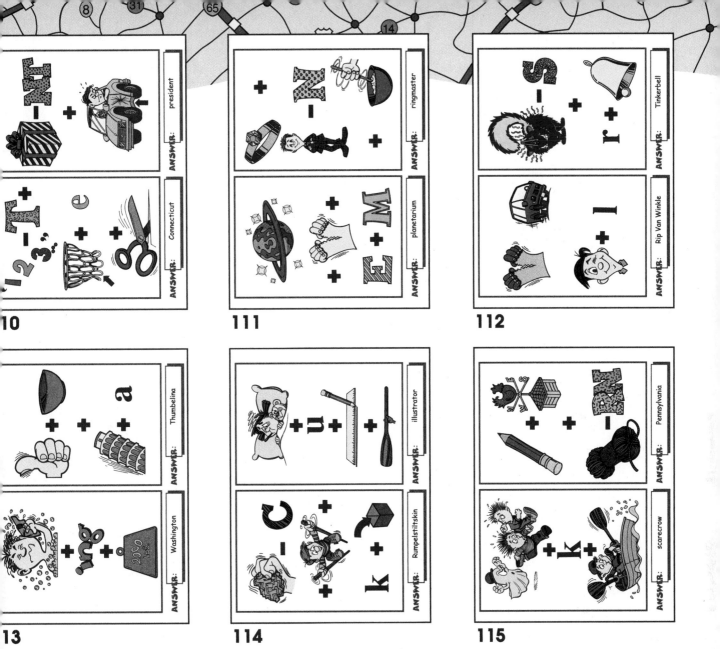

ANSWER: president

ANSWER: Connecticut

10

ANSWER: ringmaster

ANSWER: planetarium

111

ANSWER: Tinkerbell

ANSWER: Rip Van Winkle

112

ANSWER: Thumbelina

ANSWER: Washington

13

ANSWER: illustrator

ANSWER: Rumpelstiltskin

114

ANSWER: Pennsylvania

ANSWER: scarecrow

115

ANSWER: Montana

ANSWER: Nebraska

16

ANSWER: Japan

ANSWER: gentlemen

117

ANSWER: Nairobi

ANSWER: Marie Curie

118

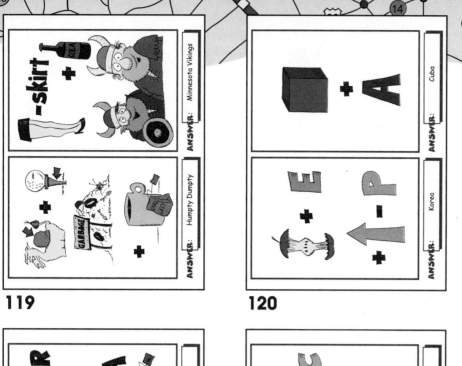

119
ANSWER: Minnesota Vikings
ANSWER: Humpty Dumpty

120
ANSWER: Cuba
ANSWER: Korea

121
ANSWER: Teen of Age
ANSWER: Alberta

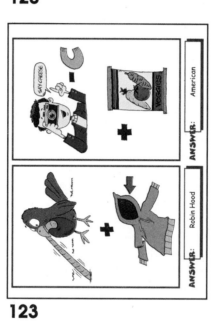

122
ANSWER: Cincinnati
ANSWER: Sherlock Holmes

123
ANSWER: American
ANSWER: Robin Hood

124
ANSWER: Old Mother Hubbard
ANSWER: Antarctica

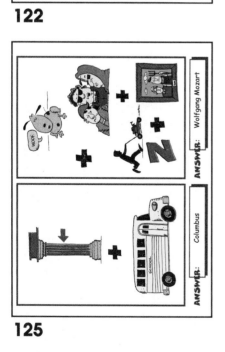

125
ANSWER: Wolfgang Mozart
ANSWER: Columbus

126
ANSWER: Moscow
ANSWER: Calcutta

127
ANSWER: Erie Canal
ANSWER: Pocahontas

128

ANSWER: Harpo Marx

ANSWER: Jackie Robinson

129

ANSWER: Shaquille O'Neal

ANSWER: Boyz II Men

130

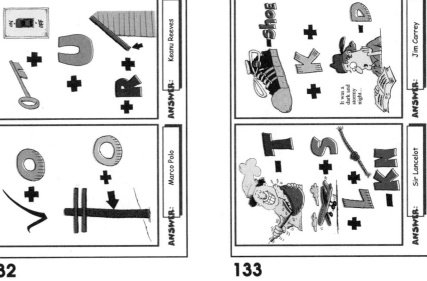

ANSWER: Europe

ANSWER: Annie Oakley

131

ANSWER: Wizard of Oz

ANSWER: Italy

132

ANSWER: Keanu Reeves

ANSWER: Marco Polo

133

ANSWER: Jim Carrey

ANSWER: Sir Lancelot

134

ANSWER: Mississippi

ANSWER: Beethoven

135

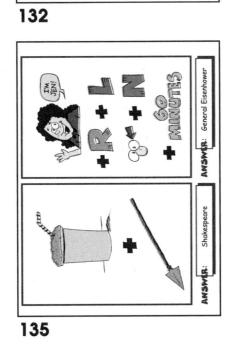

ANSWER: General Eisenhower

ANSWER: Shakespeare

136

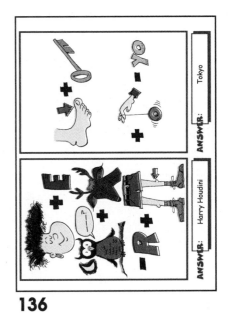

ANSWER: Tokyo

ANSWER: Harry Houdini

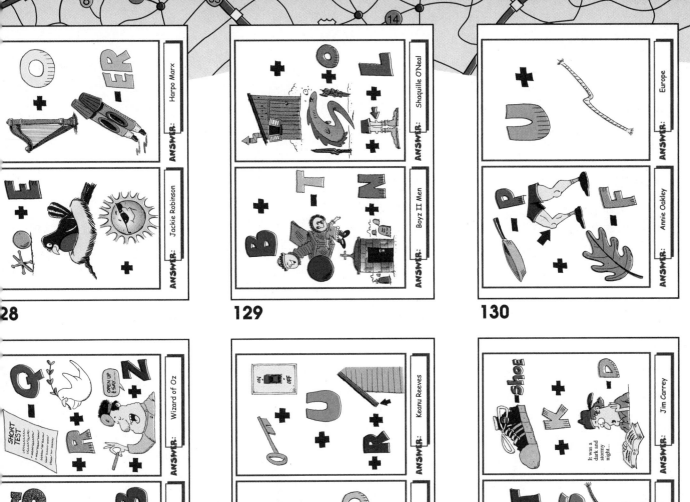

137

ANSWER: Paul Bunyan

ANSWER: Beirut

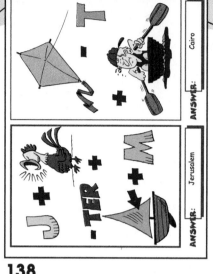

138

ANSWER: Cairo

ANSWER: Jerusalem

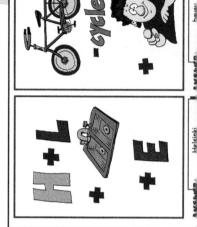

139

ANSWER: Helsinki

CAPITAL CITIES

STATE	CITY	STATE	CITY
Alabama	Montgomery	Montana	Helena
Alaska	Juneau	Nebraska	Lincoln
Arizona	Phoenix	Nevada	Carson City
Arkansas	Little Rock	New Hampshire	Concord
California	Sacramento	New Jersey	Trenton
Colorado	Denver	New Mexico	Santa Fe
Connecticut	Hartford	New York	Albany
Delaware	Dover	North Carolina	Raleigh
Florida	Tallahassee	North Dakota	Bismarck
Georgia	Atlanta	Ohio	Columbus
Hawaii	Honolulu	Oklahoma	Oklahoma City
Idaho	Boise	Oregon	Salem
Illinois	Springfield	Pennsylvania	Harrisburg
Indiana	Indianapolis	Rhode Island	Providence
Iowa	Des Moines	South Carolina	Columbia
Kansas	Topeka	South Dakota	Pierre
Kentucky	Frankfort	Tennessee	Nashville
Louisiana	Baton Rouge	Texas	Austin
Maine	Augusta	Utah	Salt Lake City
Maryland	Annapolis	Vermont	Montpelier
Massachusetts	Boston	Virginia	Richmond
Michigan	Lansing	Washington	Olympia
Minnesota	St. Paul	West Virginia	Charleston
Mississippi	Jackson	Wisconsin	Madison
Missouri	Jefferson City	Wyoming	Cheyenne

152

SCHOOL SPIRIT

Count the items. Use the Word Bank to help you write the number words in the puzzles.

Word Bank
seven eight one
two four five

161

OOPS!

Use the Word Bank to help you find answers to the clues. Write them in the puzzles.

Across
1. A _____ is _____ ORANGE

Down
2. An _____

2. PURPLE

Across
2. _____ are _____

Down
1. An _____ is _____

Across
2. A _____ is _____ GREEN

Down
1. A _____ is _____

Word Bank
brown orange purple green red gray

162

ASTRO ADVENTURE

Use the Word Bank to help you find words that match the pictures. Write them in the puzzle.

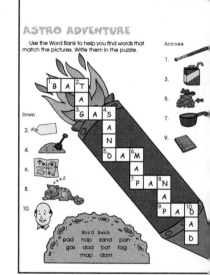

Across
1.
3.
5.
7.
9.

Down
2.
4.
6.
8.
10.

Word Bank
pad nap sand pan
gas dad bat tag
map dam

163

MBRELLAS UP!

Word Bank to help you find
that match the pictures.
them in the puzzle.

Down words / puzzle grid:
- 1. BUS
- 2. SUU / SUB
- 3. BUG / GU
- 5. HUMP
- 7. NUTS SUN
- 9. PLUM
- 8. SUN
- MUG

Word Bank
mug   bus   sun   pup   hut
gum   hump   bug   sub   plum
nuts

4

DON'T JUST SIT THERE!

Use the Word Bank to help you find words that match
the pictures. Write them in the puzzle.

Across
1. 10¢
7. (car)
8. (donkey)
6. (bench)

Puzzle grid:
- D R U M
- D E E R
- D I M E
- D R E S S
- D U S T
- D O W N
- D O C K
- D E N T
- D O N K E Y

Word Bank
dinner   dime   desk
dock   dust   donkey
deer   dent   down
drum   dress

Down
1. 2. 3. 4. 5. 7.

165

HIT THE HAY!

Use the Word Bank to help you find words
that match the pictures. Write them in the puzzle.

Across
1. (hat)
6. (broom)
3. (thumb)
4. (hammer)
5. (rabbit)
6. (hay)
7. (hand)

Puzzle grid:
- HAT
- HOLE
- HELL / HELMET
- HAMMER
- HAPPY
- HOP
- HAY
- HAND
- HUT

Word Bank
hop   hole   hill
happy   helmet
hen   hose
hut   hay   hand
hammer   hat

Down
1. 2. 3.
4. 5. 6.

166

MBING KOALA

e the Word Bank to help
nd words that match the
res. Write them in the puzzle.

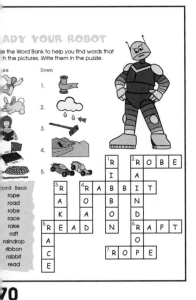

Puzzle grid:
- KETTLE
- KIN
- KANGAROO
- KITE
- KITE
- KIND
- KEYS

Word Bank
king   keys   kite   kettle
kangaroo   kits   koala bear
kick   kitten   kind

67

IS IT REALLY MAGIC?

Use the Word Bank to help you
find words that match the pictures.
Write them in the puzzle.

Across
1.
2.
3.
5.
5.
8.

Puzzle grid:
- MAIL
- MATCH
- MOP
- MONSTER
- MITTENS
- MUG
- MOUSE
- MASK

Word Bank
mittens   melt
map   mitt
mug   mop
mail   moon
mask   match
monster   mouse

Down
1. 4.
2. 5.
3. 7.

168

NAP TIME IN THE NEST

Use the Word Bank to help you find words that match the
pictures. Write them in the puzzle.

Across
2.
4.
5.
6.

Puzzle grid:
- NAIL
- NINE
- NUMBERS
- NOTE
- NEEDLE
- NEST

Word Bank
note nose numbers needle
net nail nine nurse nest

Down
1.
2. 1, 2, 3, 4, ...
3.
5.
6.

169

ADY YOUR ROBOT

e the Word Bank to help you find words that
he pictures. Write them in the puzzle.

Down
1.
2.
3.
4.

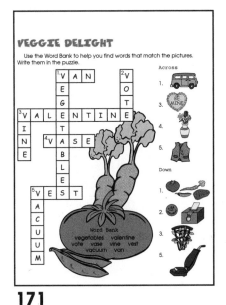

Puzzle grid:
- ROBE
- RAIN
- RABBIT
- RAKE
- ROBOT
- READ
- RAFT
- ROPE
- RACE

Word Bank
rope
road
robe
race
rake
raft
raindrop
ribbon
rabbit
read

70

VEGGIE DELIGHT

Use the Word Bank to help you find words that match the pictures.
Write them in the puzzle.

Across
1.
3.
4.

Puzzle grid:
- VAN
- VOTE
- VEGGIE
- VALENTINE
- VASE
- VEST
- VACUUM

Word Bank
vegetables   valentine
vote   vase   vine   vest
vacuum   van

Down
1.
2.
3.
5.

171

JUST CLOWNING AROUND

Count the ⚾'s. Write the
number words in the puzzle.
Use the Word Bank to help you.

Word Bank
three   eight
one   six   zero   ten
five   nine   four
seven   two

Across
2.
3.
6.
8.

Puzzle grid:
- ZERO
- FOUR
- FIVE
- THREE
- TWO
- EIGHT
- ONE
- TEN
- NINE
- SEVEN
- SIX

Down
1.
2.
3.
4.
7.
8.

172

FACING THE SUN

Use the Word Bank to help you find words that match the clues. Write them in the puzzle.

Across
1. A farm animal
2. A buzzing bug
4. A fruit
6. A very tall plant
7. The color of grass
8. A big bird

Down
1. At night you . . .
3. A mouse eats . . .
5. You _____ food.
6. 2 + 1 = _____
9. A part of a plant

Word Bank
bee   cheese   eat
sheep   green   peach   tree
sleep   eagle   leaf   three

Crossword answers: SHEEP, BEE, EACH, TREE, GREEN, EAGLE

173

SOOOO . . . COZY

Use the Word Bank to help you find words that match the clues. Write them in the puzzle.

Word Bank
stone   open   home
bones   toes   road
doe   hole   notes
rope   soap   boat
pole   globe   stove
toad

Crossword answers: BONES, ROAD, STONE, DOE, TOES, GLOBE, POLE

Across
3. Not shut
5. Dogs like these
7. A street
10. These are on your feet
12. A rock
13. A mother deer
14. A long, rounded piece of wood

Down
1. Your house
2. A mole digs this
4. Musical
5. A ship
6. You cook on this
7. You can jump with this
8. A round map
9. Like a frog
11. You wash with this

174

PLACES, EVERYONE!

Use the Word Bank and the pictures below to help you fill in the puzzle.

Word Bank
first   second   third   fourth   fifth
sixth   seventh   eighth   ninth   tenth

Crossword answers: FIFTH, SIXTH, FIRST, NINTH

Across
2. frog
4. flower
6. tree
9. sun

Down
1. snake
3. bear
5. rain
6. bird
7. squirrel
8. butterfly

175

NICE HAT!

Use the Word Bank to help you fill in the puzzle.

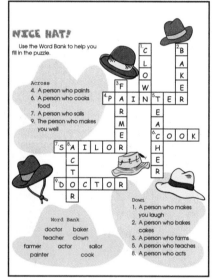

Across
4. A person who paints
6. A person who cooks food
7. A person who sails
9. The person who makes you well

Down
1. A person who makes you laugh
2. A person who bakes cakes
3. A person who farms
5. A person who teaches
8. A person who acts

Crossword answers: PAINTER, COOK, SAILOR, DOCTOR, CLOWN, FARMER

Word Bank
doctor   baker
teacher   clown
farmer   actor   sailor
painter   cook

176

HELPFUL FRIENDS

Use the Word Bank to help you fill in the puzzle.

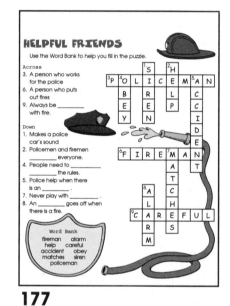

Across
3. A person who works for the police
6. A person who puts out fires
9. Always be _____ with fire.

Down
1. Makes a police car's sound
2. Policemen and firemen _____ everyone.
4. People need to _____ the rules.
5. Police help when there is an _____ .
7. Never play with _____ .
8. An _____ goes off when there is a fire.

Crossword answers: POLICEMAN, FIREMAN, CAREFUL

Word Bank
fireman   alarm
help   careful
accident   obey
matches   siren
policeman

177

AN ATTACK OF THE MUNCHIES

Use the Word Bank to help you fill in the puzzle.

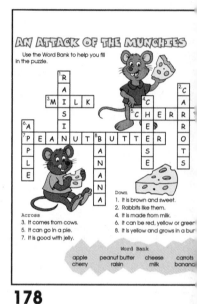

Crossword answers: MILK, CHERRY, PEANUT BUTTER

Down
1. It is brown and sweet.
2. Rabbits like them.
4. It is made from milk.
6. It can be red, yellow or green.
8. It is yellow and grows in a bunch.

Across
3. It comes from cows.
5. It can go in a pie.
7. It is good with jelly.

Word Bank
apple   peanut butter   cheese   carrots
cherry   raisin   milk   banana

178

A GOOD SCOUT

Use the Word Bank to help you fill in the puzzle.

Across
1. A word you say when you get hurt
3. The shape of a circle
5. The opposite of quiet
7. To find out how many, you must . . .
9. The opposite of north
11. The opposite of in
12. Animal like a rat
14. A very high land form

Down
2. Fluffy white object in the sky
4. Ground wheat that is used in making bread
6. Not having something
7. A sofa
8. A fish
10. A home
12. A part of your face
13. To make a ball go down and up

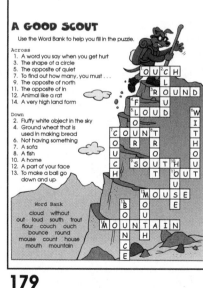

Crossword answers: OUCH, ROUND, LOUD, COUNT, SOUTH, WITHOUT, MOUSE, BOUNCE, MOUTH, MOUNTAIN

Word Bank
cloud   without
out   loud   south   trout
flour   couch   ouch
bounce   round
mouse   count   house
mouth   mountain

179

SLUMBERING SLIPPERS

Use the Word Bank to help you fill in the puzzle.

Across
4. Opposite of frown
5. A small, slow-moving creature
6. Opposite of rough
9. Resting
10. To slant or lean
11. What your nose does
13. Intelligent
14. Ah . . . choo!

Down
1. To shut with a bang
2. A smooth, layered rock
3. A cracking sound
4. Very clever, like a fox
6. To trip
7. A kind of shoe
8. Reptiles
11. Frozen white flakes
12. Something burning gives off

Crossword answers: SMILE, SNAIL, SMOOTH, SLEEPING, SLOPE, SMART, SNEEZE, SLAM, SMELL, SNOW

Word Bank
smooth   snail   sly
slam   smart   slip
slipper   snow   smile
slope   slate   smoke
snakes   smells   sneeze
snap   sleeping

180

STRETCH!

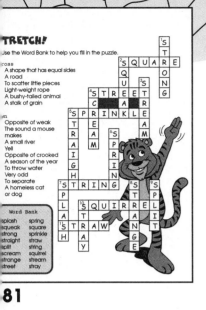

Use the Word Bank to help you fill in the puzzle.

Across
- A shape that has equal sides
- A road
- To scatter little pieces
- Light-weight rope
- A bushy-tailed animal
- A stalk of grain

Down
- Opposite of weak
- The sound a mouse makes
- A small river
- Yell
- Opposite of crooked
- A season of the year
- To throw water
- Very odd
- To separate
- A homeless cat or dog

Word Bank
splash, spring, squeak, square, strong, sprinkle, straight, straw, split, string, scream, squirrel, strange, stream, street, stray

---

READ ALL ABOUT IT

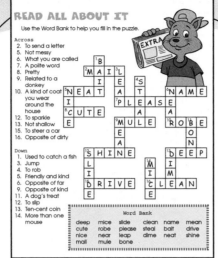

Use the Word Bank to help you fill in the puzzle.

Across
2. To send a letter
5. Not messy
6. What you are called
7. A polite word
8. Pretty
9. Related to a donkey
10. A kind of coat you wear around the house
12. To sparkle
13. Not shallow
15. To steer a car
16. Opposite of dirty

Down
1. Used to catch a fish
2. Jump
3. To rob
4. Friendly and kind
5. Opposite of far
6. Opposite of kind
11. A dog's treat
12. To slip
13. Ten-cent coin
14. More than one mouse

Word Bank

deep	mice	slide	clean	name	mean
cute	robe	please	steal	bait	drive
nice	near	leap	dime	neat	shine
mail	mule	bone			

COOL CIDER

Use the Word Bank to help you fill in the puzzle.

Across
3. A baby's bed
5. The cost of something
7. A castle
8. A yellow vegetable
9. You can mold things with this
10. A very small house

Down
1. Something to drink
2. Frozen water
4. A cold dessert that comes in a cone
7. A very large town
8. A desert animal with a humped back
9. A line that goes around

Word Bank
city, ice, ice cream, corn, circle, palace, cabin, clay, camel, price, crib, juice

---

IT'S A SNAP FOR A GIRAFFE!

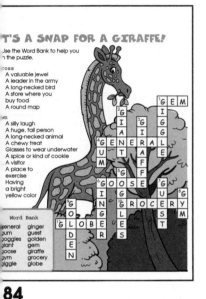

Use the Word Bank to help you fill in the puzzle.

Across
- A valuable jewel
- A leader in the army
- A long-necked bird
- A store where you buy food
- A round map

Down
- A silly laugh
- A huge, tall person
- A long-necked animal
- A chewy treat
- Glasses to wear underwater
- A spice or kind of cookie
- A visitor
- A place to exercise
- Having a bright yellow color

Word Bank
general, ginger, gum, guest, goggles, golden, giant, gem, goose, giraffe, gym, grocery, giggle, globe

---

LAUGHABLE FELLOW

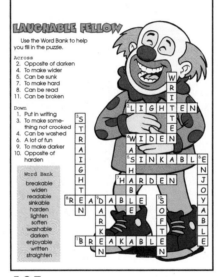

Use the Word Bank to help you fill in the puzzle.

Across
2. Opposite of darken
4. To make wider
5. Can be sunk
7. To make hard
8. Can be read
11. Can be broken

Down
1. Put in writing
3. To make something not crooked
4. Can be washed
6. A lot of fun
9. To make darker
10. Opposite of harden

Word Bank
breakable, widen, readable, sinkable, harden, lighten, soften, washable, darken, enjoyable, written, straighten

---

LIGHTHOUSE

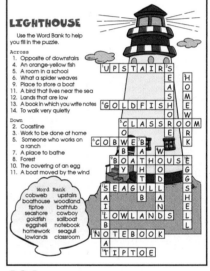

Use the Word Bank to help you fill in the puzzle.

Across
1. Opposite of downstairs
3. An orange-yellow fish
5. A room in a school
7. What a spider weaves
9. Place to store a boat
11. A bird that lives near the sea
12. Lands that are low
13. A book in which you write notes
14. To walk very quietly

Down
2. Coastline
3. Work to be done at home
5. Someone who works on a ranch
7. A place to bathe
8. Forest
10. The covering of an egg
11. A boat moved by the wind

Word Bank
cobweb, upstairs, boathouse, woodland, tiptoe, bathtub, seashore, cowboy, goldfish, sailboat, eggshell, notebook, homework, seagull, lowlands, classroom

---

HOMOPHONE CROSSWORD

Homophones are words that sound alike but are spelled differently and have different meanings. Fill in the blanks to form homophones for the words listed below. To help, some of the letters have been given.

Across
1. tows
9. hairs
fryer
bee
too
wore
wear
break
lead
19. hew
20. rows
22. cents
25. feat
26. wring
29. here
31. troop
32. kneads
34. you're
35. not
37. peeks
39. gait
40. lei
41. oh
42. serf
43. seem

Down
2. oar
3. steak
4. heal
5. rode
6. sew
7. fleas
8. write
9. bear
11. or
12. waist
14. peal
15. bred
16. row
18. ate
21. mite
22. sleigh
23. know
24. air
27. loot
28. nay
30. role
31. trey
33. new
36. four
38. some

SYNONYM CROSSWORD

Synonyms are words that mean about the same as another word. Fill in the blanks to form synonyms for the words listed below. To help, some of the letters have been given.

Across
2. easy
9. drenched
9. damp
11. beautiful
13. quiet
14. hurried
15. blazing
16. strange
17. enjoyable
18. annual
21. unusual
22. mad
24. final
25. alike
26. ruddy
28. mended
32. uncovered
33. independent
34. extreme
37. sick
39. arid
40. naughty
41. feminine
42. mild
43. happy
44. ordinary
45. curved

Down
1. dull
2. sturdy
3. untidy
4. older
5. all
6. entire
7. broad
8. secure
9. insane
10. aged
12. youthful
13. rough
17. less
19. simpler
20. misplaced
22. plentiful
23. tidy
24. high
26. lifted
27. lifeless
29. reliable
30. peaceful
31. proper
35. speechless
36. just
38. tardy
41. plump

PALINDROME CROSSWORD

Palindromes are words that are spelled the same both forward and backward. Examples: tat, Bob.
Use the clues below to help you fill in the crossword. Hint: Two words you may have trouble finding include ABBA and CIVIC.

Across
1. More red
4. Short for statistics
6. Paper showing land ownership
8. Sound a chick makes
10. Aramaic name for father
11. Flies alone
12. Day before a holiday
14. A prank
17. Even
18. Midday
20. Past tense of do
22. Short for chrysanthemum
23. Sound of a horn
26. Title of respect for a lady
27. A napkin tied under the chin
28. A little dog

Down
1. It detects airplanes
2. Common name for father
3. A blade on a helicopter
4. Watches
5. An Eskimo's canoe
7. A female sheep
8. A soda
9. Energy
13. A seeing organ
15. Short for mother
16. Describes a citizen's duties
19. A religious sister
21. Expression of surprise
24. A small child
25. A failure

NOT JUST ANY STAR

Color the space blue if the word means only one.
Color the space red if the word means more than one.

What kind of star is this? __a starfish__

202

SUCH A FACE!

Color the space green if the word means only one.
Color the space brown if the word means more than one.

Who owns this face? __a dog__

203

A SIGN OF FALL

Color the space yellow if the word names a color.
Color the space green if the word names a number.

What is a sign of fall? __colorful leaves__

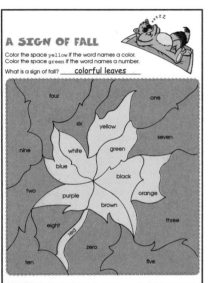

204

AS QUIET AS . . .

Color the space brown if the words mean the same.
Color the space blue if the words mean the opposite.

Who is quiet? __a mouse__

205

YUMMY!

Color the person words red.
Color the place words blue.
Color the things words yellow.
Color the action words green.
Color the when words orange.

What is this yummy treat? __a lollypop__

206

BREEZING ALONG

Color the space blue if the words are opposites.
Color the space yellow if the words sound the same.
Color the space red if the words mean the same.

What is breezing along? __a sailboat__

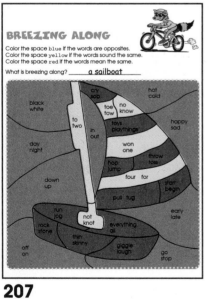

207

ALL-TIME FAVORITE

Color the fruit words orange.
Color the vegetable words green.
Color the grain product words red.
Color the milk product words blue.
Color the meat product words brown.
Color the dinnertime words yellow.

What is the all-time favorite? __a hamburger__

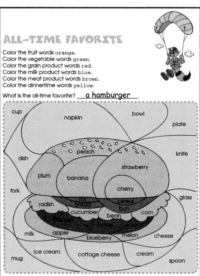

208

THE GOOD OLD DAYS

Color clothing words red.
Color weather words yellow.
Color toy words black.
Color food words brown.
Color animal words green.

Who battled dragons? __a knight__

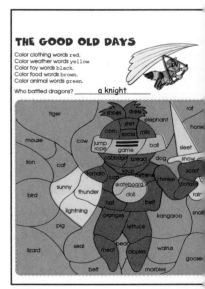

209

Top Left — TREATS (210)

...REATS

...or the synonym pairs blue.
...or the antonym pairs red.
...or all single words yellow.

...at treats are found in the picture? __jelly beans__

Synonyms are words that mean the same. Antonyms are words that are opposites.

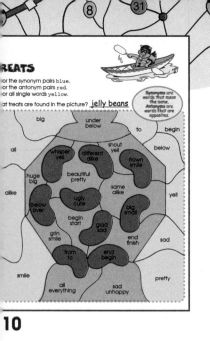

big / under below / to / begin
all / below
whisper yell / different alike / frown smile
huge big / beautiful pretty / same alike / yell
alike / ugly cute / big small
below over / begin start / glad sad / end finish / sad
grin smile / from to / end begin
smile / pretty
all everything / sad unhappy / pretty

10

Top Middle — SOFT AND CUDDLY (211)

Color the singular words brown.
Color the plural words green.

What is soft and cuddly? __a cat__

Singular means only one. Plural means more than one.

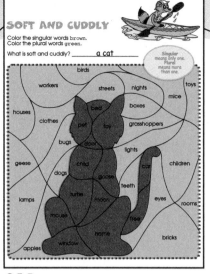

birds / workers / streets / nights / toys
houses / bed / boxes / mice
clothes / pet / toy / grasshoppers
bugs / door / lights
geese / child / car / children
dogs / goose / teeth
lamps / turtle / moon / eyes / rooms
mouse / tree
apples / home / bricks
window

211

Top Right — ELECTRIFYING (212)

Color the singular words yellow.
Color the plural words blue.

What is electrifying? __lightning__

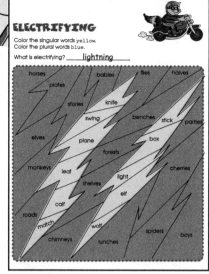

horses / babies / flies / halves
plates
stories / knife
swing / benches / stick / parties
elves / plane / box
monkeys / leaf / forests
shelves / light / cherries
calf / elf
roads
match / wolf
chimneys / lunches / spiders / boys

212

Middle Left — BRIGHT AND BEAUTIFUL (213)

...or the space yellow if you have to only add an "s" to make the word plural.
...or the space orange if you have to add "es" to make the word plural.
...or the space blue if you have "to change the last letter" and then add "es" ...make the word plural.

...at is this bright and beautiful sight? __a wind sock__

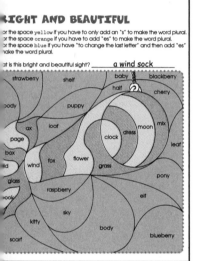

strawberry / shelf / baby / blackberry
half / cherry
...body / puppy
ax / loaf / moon / mix
page / clock / dress / leaf
box / wind / fox / flower / grass
...glass / pony
...ook / raspberry / elf
sky / kitty / body
scarf / blueberry

13

Middle Middle — SUMMER TREAT (214)

Color the plural words green.
Color the contractions black.
Color the compound words red.
Color the possessive words blue.

Name this summer treat. __watermelon__

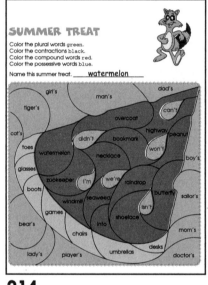

girl's / man's / dad's
tiger's / can't
overcoat / highway / peanut
cat's / didn't / bookmark / won't
toes / watermelon / necklace / boy's
glasses / zookeeper / i'm / we're / raindrop
boots / windmill / seaweed / butterfly / sailor's
games / isn't
bear's / into / shoelace
chairs / mom's
lady's / player's / umbrellas / desks
doctor's

214

Middle Right — OUCH! (215)

Color the one-syllable words orange.
Color the two-syllable words blue.
Color the three-syllable words black.

What can make you say ouch? __a crab__

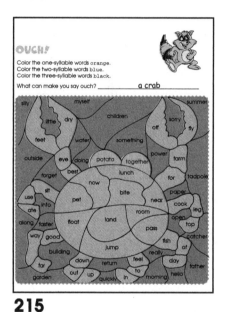

silly / myself / summer
little / dry / children / sorry
feet / water / off / fly
outside / eye / doing / potato / together / power / farm
best / lunch / for / tadpole
forget / now / bite / paper
sit / near / cook
use / into / pet / leg
ate / room / open / top
along / faster / float / land / pass / catcher
way / good / fish / of
building / jump / really
far / down / return / feel / day / father
garden / out / up / quickly / in / to / morning / hello

215

Bottom Left — ...THE COUNT (216)

...or the one-syllable words brown.
...or the two-syllable words green.
...or the three-syllable words blue.

...t animal is suited for boxing? __a kangaroo__

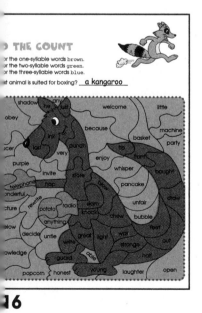

shadow / pony / just / welcome / little
obey / he / because / machine
ink / basket / party
...cer / ax / very / punch / tip / front
purple / enjoy / whisper / bought
invite / store / pancake / draw
telephone / hop
...onderful / rewrite / unfair
...ture / potato / radio / earn / knock / chew / bubble
...low / anything / feet / out
decide / untie / great / war / strange
...owledge / write / guard / axle / half
popcorn / honest / young / laughter / open

16

Bottom Middle — RIGHT OUT OF THE OVEN (217)

Color the antonyms blue.
Color the synonyms red.
Color the homophones brown.

Name this oven-fresh treat? __bread__

*Clues:
Antonyms are words that are opposites.
Synonyms are words that mean the same.
Homophones are words that sound alike but are spelled differently.*

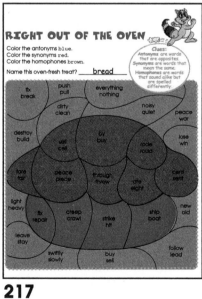

push pull / everything nothing
fix break / dirty clean / noisy quiet / peace war
destroy build / by buy / lose win
tore fair / rode road
use cell / peace piece / through threw / ate eight / cant sent
light heavy / fix repair / creep crawl / strike hit / ship boat / new old
leave stay / swiftly slowly / buy sell / follow lead

217

Bottom Right — SEE THE SEA (218)

Color the synonyms brown.
Color the antonyms blue.
Color the homophones green.

What do you see? __a shark__

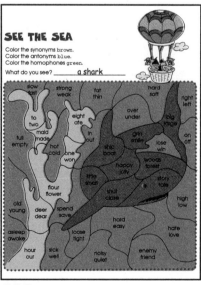

slow fast / strong weak / fat thin / hard soft / right left
to two / eight ate / over under / big large
maid made / grin smile / on off
full empty / hot cold / one won / ship boat / lose win
happy jolly / woods forest
flour flower / little small / story tale
old young / deer dear / shut close / high low
asleep awake / spend save / hard easy / hate love
hour our / sick well / loose tight / noisy quiet / enemy friend

218

WORD SQUARES

EXAMPLE:

AAACCEEEE
HHHNSTT

S	E	A	T
E	A	C	H
A	C	H	E
T	H	E	N

Word squares spell the same word both down and across. Fill in the word squares using the letters above each square.

VTMMEETE ACSANNOQ

C	O	M	A
O	V	E	N
M	E	E	T
A	N	T	S

AACCCKEIH HAKLAPK

L	A	C	K
A	C	H	E
C	H	I	P
K	E	P	T

AKLLSAEES SSEHLSS

H	E	A	L
E	L	S	E
A	S	K	S
L	E	S	S

ACCEEL MNOOR RSSTT

L	O	S	T
O	N	C	E
S	C	A	R
T	E	R	M

226

WORD SQUARES

EXAMPLE:

SOOEE
WMWTN

S	O	W
O	N	E
W	E	T

Word squares spell the same word both down and across. Fill in the word squares using the letters above each square.

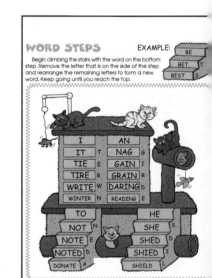

T	I	P
I	C	E
P	E	N

O	U	T
U	S	E
T	E	N

C	A	B
A	R	E
B	E	T

S	E	A
E	A	R
A	R	T

B	O	Y
O	R	E
Y	E	S

N	O	W
O	N	E
W	E	D

227

WORD SQUARES

EXAMPLE:

SOEEN
WOWT

S	O	W
O	N	E
W	E	T

Word squares spell the same word both down and across. Fill in the word squares using the letters above each square.

AABCD EERR

B	A	R
A	C	E
R	E	D

BEDDE RRRY

B	E	D
E	R	R
D	R	Y

GEENO OPPT

T	O	P
O	N	E
P	E	T

LLPTR EEAA

P	A	L
A	R	E
L	E	T

ASAEE TAWT

S	A	T
A	W	E
T	E	A

NEEPU TUST

P	U	T
U	S	E
T	E	N

ARRTA SAEE

S	E	A
E	A	R
A	R	T

LWWWO HHOO

W	H	O
H	O	W
O	W	L

228

WORD STEPS

EXAMPLE:
BE
BET T
BEST S

Begin climbing the stairs with the word on the bottom step. Remove the letter that is on the side of the step and rearrange the remaining letters to form a new word. Keep going until you reach the top.

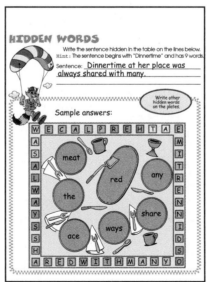

A
AS S
SAT T
SEAT E
TALES L
TABLES B
STABLES

IN
GIN G
SING S
RINGS R
SPRING P
SPARING A

TO
LOT L
LOST S
STOLE E
OLDEST

A
AS S
ASH H
RASH R
SHARE E
WASHER

229

WORD STEPS

EXAMPLE:
BE
BET T
BEST S

Begin climbing the stairs with the word on the bottom step. Remove the letter that is on the side of the step and rearrange the remaining letters to form a new word. Keep going until you reach the top.

I
IT T
TIE E
TIRE R
WRITE W
WINTER N

AN
NAG G
GAIN I
GRAIN R
DARING D
READING

TO
NOT N
NOTE E
NOTED D
DONATE A

HE
SHE S
SHED D
SHIED I
SHIELD

230

FORMING WORDS GAME

Make 30 new words from the letters in READING and write them on the lines below or use another sheet of paper. Use the scoring table to help you figure your points for each word.

Scoring
3-letter word = 1 point
4-letter word = 2 points
5-letter word = 3 points
Add 1 point for each letter over 5.

Sample answers:

WORDS		PTS				
1.	grain	3	16.	read	2	
2.	grade	3	17.	rind	2	
3.	ring	2	18.	dire	2	
4.	rang	2	19.	ding	2	
5.	dare	2	20.	red	1	
6.	gear	2	21.	rage	2	
7.	dear	2	22.	age	1	
8.	raid	2	23.	grin	2	
9.	rain	2	24.	rear	2	
10.	range	3	25.	daring	4	
11.	near	2	26.	earn	2	
12.	ear	1	27.	diner	3	
13.	dine	2	28.	danger	4	
14.	die	1	29.	anger	3	
15.	gain	2	30.	aged	2	

YOUR SCORE 64

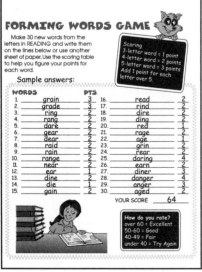

How do you rate?
over 60 = Excellent
50-60 = Good
40-49 = Fair
under 40 = Try Again

231

HIDDEN WORDS

Write the sentence hidden in the table on the lines below.
Hint: The sentence begins with "Dinnertime" and has 9 words.

Sentence: Dinnertime at her place was always shared with many.

Write other hidden words on the plates.

Sample answers:

W E C A L P R E H T A E — M I T R E N N I D S O

A L W A Y S

A R E D W I T H M A N Y O

meat
red
any
the
share
ace
ways

232

HIDDEN WORDS

Write the sentence hidden in the ice-cream cone on the lines below. Hint: The sentence begins with "Beat."

Sentence: Beat these western nights of heat with ice-cream cones and sundaes.

How many ice-cream cups can you fill with other hidden words?

Sample answers:

eat
west
sun
sand

233

HIDDEN WORDS

...te the sentence hidden in the boat on the lines below.
...he sentence begins with the word "It" and has 17 words.

...nce: It is fun to fish with my father and friends
... a big lake off our sailboat.

...mple answers:

Write other hidden words in the clouds.

four
sit
our
of
fun

WORD LADDERS

Change the word at the bottom of each ladder to the word at the top by changing one letter at a time. Begin with the word at the bottom. Use the letters on the right or left to make a new word at each step.

Rules:
1. If the letter is on the right, remove it from the word and put another letter in its place.
2. If the letter is on the left, add it to the word after you remove the letter that is in its place.

EXAMPLE:

TAIL
TALL
TOLL
TOLD
HOLD
HELD
HEAD

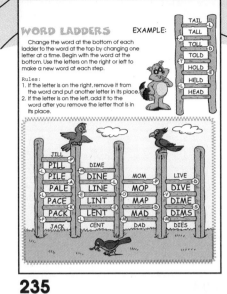

JILL
PILL
PILE
PALE
PACE
PACK
JACK

DIME
DINE
LINE
LINT
LENT
CENT

MOM
MOP
MAP
MAD
DAD

LIVE
DIVE
DIME
DIMS
DIES

WORD LADDERS

Change the word at the bottom to the word at the top by changing one letter at a time. Begin with the word at the bottom. Use the letters on the right or left to make a new word at each step.

Rules:
1. If the letter is on the right of the step, remove it from the word and put another letter in its place.
2. If the letter is on the left, add it to the word after you remove the letter that is in its place.

EXAMPLE:

NAIL
TAIL
TALL
TALK
TACK

LAKE
CAKE
CASE
CASH
DASH
DISH
FISH

FISH
FIST
LIST
LOST
COST
COAT
BOAT

YARN
WARN
WARE
WORE
WORD
WOOD
WOOL

CROP
CHOP
SHOP
SHOT
SOOT
SORT
FORT
FORM
FARM

WORD LADDERS

...ange the word at the bottom to the word at the top by changing one letter at a time. Begin with the word at the bottom. ...he letters on the right or the left to make ...w word at each step.

...s:
...he letter is on the right, remove it ...m the word and put another letter ...s place.
...he letter is on the left, add it to the word ...er you remove the letter that is in its place.

EXAMPLE:

DOG
DOT
POT
PET

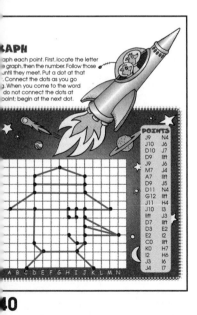

HILL
HALL
HALE
VALE

KID
LID
LIT
LOT
TOT

SKY
SAY
BAY
BAN
BUN
SUN

SHEEP
SHEER
SHEAR

GRAPH

Graph each point. First, locate the letter on the graph, then the number. Follow those lines until they meet. Put a dot at that point. Connect the dots as you go along.

Example: G15 has been done for you.

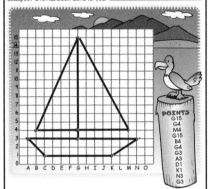

POINTS
G15
G4
M4
G15
B4
G4
G3
A3
D1
K1
N3
G3

MAZE

Mazes can help you learn to think ahead. Can you think far enough ahead to get through this maze from "start" to "finish"? Try it with a pencil.

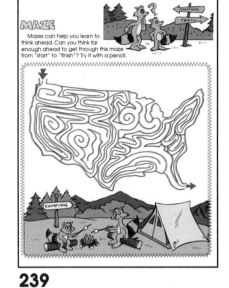

CAMPING

GRAPH

...aph each point. First, locate the letter ...e graph, then the number. Follow those ...until they meet. Put a dot at that ...Connect the dots as you go ...do not connect the dots at ...point; begin at the next dot.

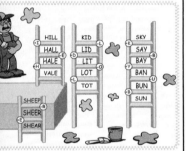

POINTS
J9   N4
J10   J6
D10   J7
J9   lift
M7   J6
A7   lift
D9   J5
D11   N4
G12   lift
J11   H4
J10   J3
lift H3
D7   lift
D3   E2
E2   C0
C0   H7
K0   H7
J3   I6
J4   I7

CODES

Break the code to find the names of fruits. Each number stands for a different letter of the alphabet.

Hint: Each 9 stands for a U.
Each 6 stands for a P.

1. G R A P E
   3 12 8 6 5
2. P L U M
   6 1 9 14
3. B A N A N A
   2 8 4 8 4 8
4. O R A N G E
   7 12 8 4 3 5
5. H O N E Y D E W
   10 7 4 5 13 11 5 16
6. R A S P B E R R Y
   12 8 15 6 2 5 12 12 16
7. T A N G E R I N E
   17 8 4 3 5 12 18 4 5
8. G R A P E F R U I T
   3 12 8 6 5 3 12 9 18 17
9. B L U E B E R R Y
   2 1 9 5 2 5 12 12 16
10. C A N T A L O U P E
    20 8 4 17 8 1 7 9 6 5
11. S T R A W B E R R Y
    15 17 12 8 21 2 5 12 12 16
12. N E C T A R I N E
    4 5 20 17 8 12 18 4 5
13. A P P L E
    8 6 6 1 5
14. K I W I
    10 18 22 18
15. P E A C H
    6 5 8 20 10

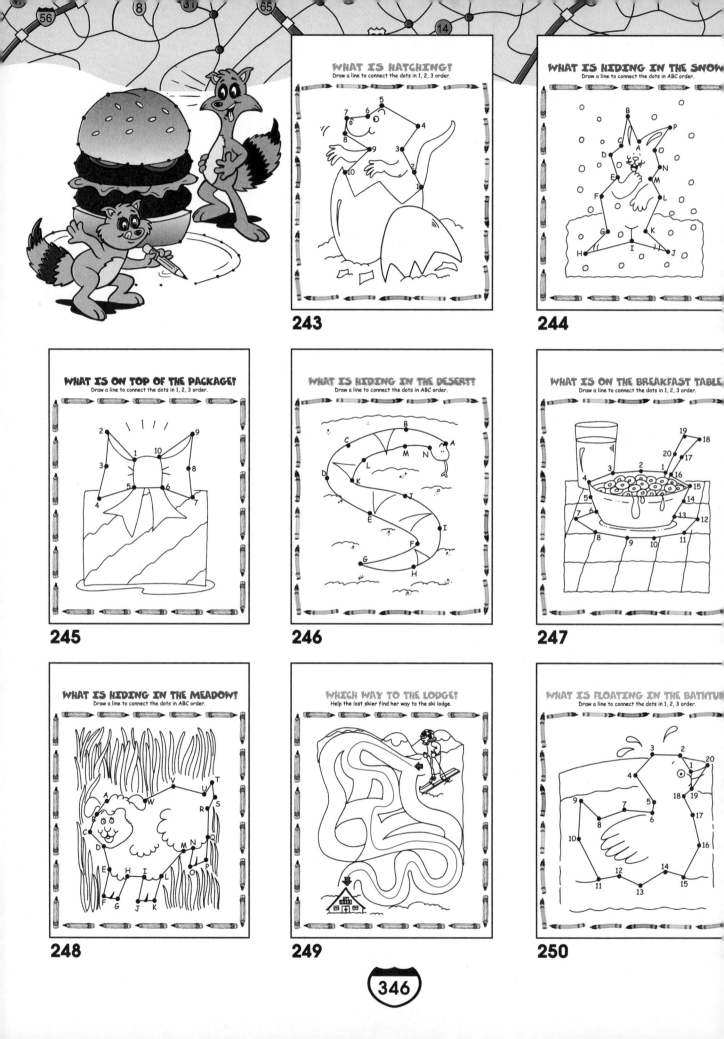

WHAT IS HATCHING?
Draw a line to connect the dots in 1, 2, 3 order.

243

WHAT IS HIDING IN THE SNOW?
Draw a line to connect the dots in ABC order.

244

WHAT IS ON TOP OF THE PACKAGE?
Draw a line to connect the dots in 1, 2, 3 order.

245

WHAT IS HIDING IN THE DESERT?
Draw a line to connect the dots in ABC order.

246

WHAT IS ON THE BREAKFAST TABLE?
Draw a line to connect the dots in 1, 2, 3 order.

247

WHAT IS HIDING IN THE MEADOW?
Draw a line to connect the dots in ABC order.

248

WHICH WAY TO THE LODGE?
Help the lost skier find her way to the ski lodge.

249

WHAT IS FLOATING IN THE BATHTUB?
Draw a line to connect the dots in 1, 2, 3 order.

250

WHAT IS HIDING IN THE RAIN?
Draw a line to connect the dots in ABC order.

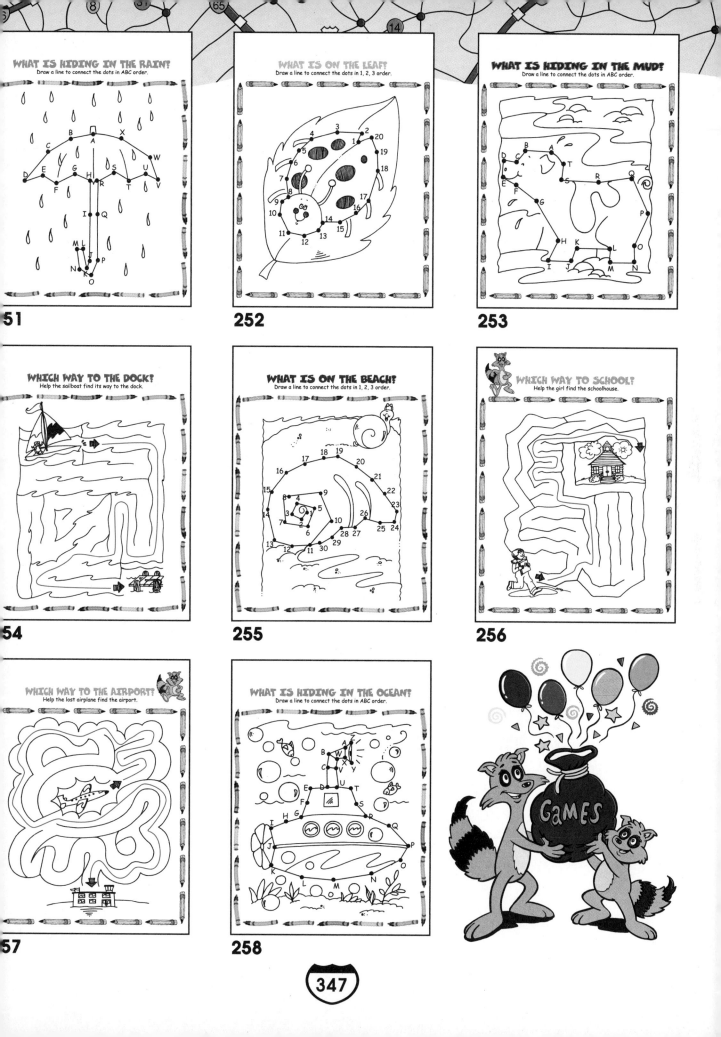

51

WHAT IS ON THE LEAF?
Draw a line to connect the dots in 1, 2, 3 order.

252

WHAT IS HIDING IN THE MUD?
Draw a line to connect the dots in ABC order.

253

WHICH WAY TO THE DOCK?
Help the sailboat find its way to the dock.

54

WHAT IS ON THE BEACH?
Draw a line to connect the dots in 1, 2, 3 order.

255

WHICH WAY TO SCHOOL?
Help the girl find the schoolhouse.

256

WHICH WAY TO THE AIRPORT?
Help the lost airplane find the airport.

57

WHAT IS HIDING IN THE OCEAN?
Draw a line to connect the dots in ABC order.

258

GAMES

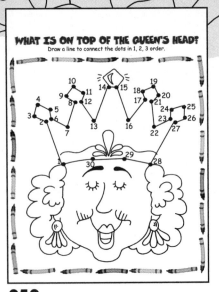

WHAT IS ON TOP OF THE QUEEN'S HEAD?
Draw a line to connect the dots in 1, 2, 3 order.

259

WHAT IS HIDING IN THE WOODS?
Draw a line to connect the dots in ABC order.

260

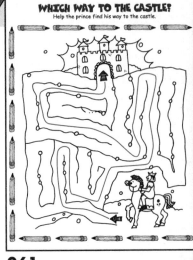

WHICH WAY TO THE CASTLE?
Help the prince find his way to the castle.

261

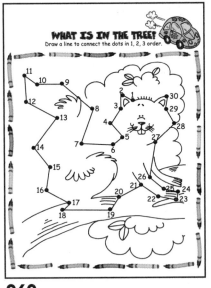

WHAT IS IN THE TREE?
Draw a line to connect the dots in 1, 2, 3 order.

262

WHICH WAY TO THE TOY?
Help the baby find her pull toy.

263

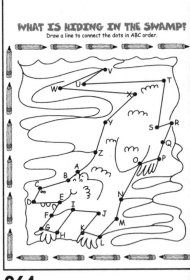

WHAT IS HIDING IN THE SWAMP?
Draw a line to connect the dots in ABC order.

264

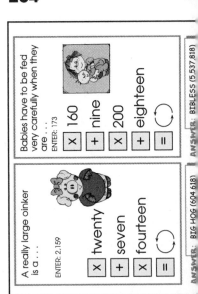

A really large oinker is a . . . .

ENTER: 2,159

×	twenty
+	seven
×	fourteen
=	⟳

Babies have to be fed very carefully when they are . . . .

ENTER: 173

×	160
+	nine
×	200
+	eighteen
=	⟳

293

4

building model planes are two great . . .
ENTER: 443
× thirty
+ seven
× 400
+ four
=
ANSWER: HOBBIES (5,318,804)

southern girl is . . . .
ENTER: 377
× 100
+ thirty
add (4 + 4)
=
ANSWER: BELLE (37,738)

295

Having a best friend is true . . .
ENTER: 788
× 35
+ nine
× two
=
ANSWER: BLISS (55,178)

This girl's name starts and ends with "e."
ENTER: 650
× 54
+ seven
× ten
+ three
=
ANSWER: ELOISE (351,073)

296

A watermelon as large as a bath-tub is a real . . .
ENTER: 1,583
× 100
+ nine
× two
=
ANSWER: BIGGIE (316,618)

Telephone poles are made from . . . .
ENTER: 934
× five
+ three
× four
+ fifty
× three
+ six
=
ANSWER: BIG LOGS (5,607,618)

97

looks almost like a shoe.
ENTER: 3,859
× twenty
+ three
× 1,000
+ forty-five
=
ANSWER: SHOEBILL (77,183,045)

ENTER: 8,000
÷ two
+ ninety-three
× 200
add (9 + 9)
=
ANSWER: BIG BIB (818,618)

298

What you get when you fall down.
ENTER: 1,000,000
× five
+ 8,000
add (2 × 4)
=
ANSWER: BOO BOOS (5,008,008)

The polished table had a . . .
ENTER: 56.2
× twenty
× seven
× seven
=
ANSWER: GLOSS (55,076)

299

Something kids like to do.
ENTER: 10 less than 100
× 523
+ seven
× eight
=
ANSWER: GIGGLE (376,616)

Some rides at a fair can make you . . . .
ENTER: 1 x 1
+ ten
× seventy
+ one
=
ANSWER: ILL (771)

00

on a window is the . . . .
ENTER: the missing number:
43, ____, 45
× five
× seven
+ three
× five
=
ANSWER: STILL (7,715)

lots, you have . . . .
ENTER: 10 – 5
× 580
+ three
× two
=
ANSWER: GOBS (5,806)

301

When you can't stop laughing, you have a bad case of the . . .
ENTER: 50 + 50
× 531
+ seventy-seven
× 100
+ fifteen
=
ANSWER: SILLIES (5,317,715)

The story of David and Goliath is in the . . .
ENTER: 2 less than 10
× 500
× ten
– 2,182
=
ANSWER: BIBLE (37,818)

302

A girl's name with two l's and two e's.
ENTER: half of 1,000
× 640
– 63
– 2,400
=
ANSWER: LESLIE (317,537)

Let's go "dashing through the snow in a one horse open . . ."
ENTER: 5 less than 50
× eighty-two
+ the number of people it takes to ride a unicycle
× 125
=
ANSWER: SLEIGH (461,375)

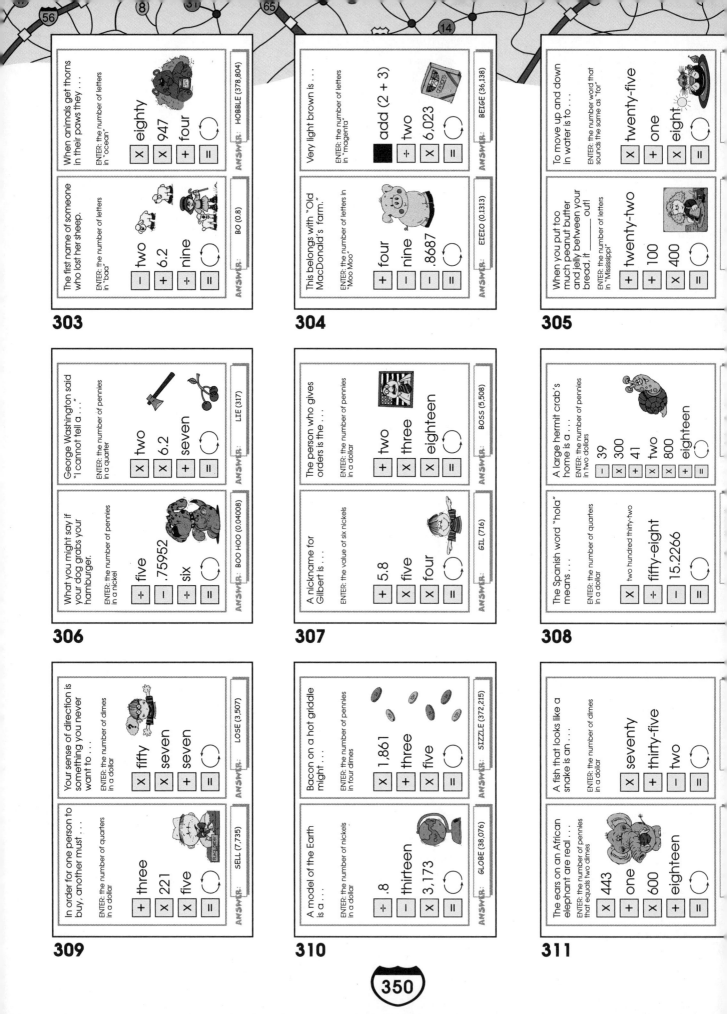

303

When animals get thorns in their paws they . . .
ENTER: the number of letters in "ocean"
× eighty
× 947
+ four
=
ANSWER: HOBBLE (378,804)

The first name of someone who lost her sheep.
ENTER: the number of letters in "baa"
- two
+ 6.2
÷ nine
=
ANSWER: BO (0.8)

304

Very light brown is . . .
ENTER: the number of letters in "magenta"
■ add (2 + 3)
÷ two
× 6,023
=
ANSWER: BEIGE (36,138)

This belongs with "Old MacDonald's farm."
ENTER: the number of letters in "Moo Moo"
+ four
- nine
- .8687
=
ANSWER: EIEIO (0.1313)

305

To move up and down in water is to . . .
ENTER: the number word that sounds the same as "for"
× twenty-five
+ one
× eight
=
ANSWER:

When you put too much peanut butter and jelly between your bread, it _____ out!
ENTER: the number of letters in "Mississippi"
+ twenty-two
+ 100
× 400
=
ANSWER:

306

George Washington said "I cannot tell a . . ."
ENTER: the number of pennies in a quarter
× two
× 6.2
+ seven
=
ANSWER: LIE (317)

What you might say if your dog grabs your hamburger.
ENTER: the number of pennies in a nickel
+ five
- .75952
÷ six
=
ANSWER: BOO HOO (0.04008)

307

The person who gives orders is the . . .
ENTER: the number of pennies in a dollar
+ two
× three
× eighteen
=
ANSWER: BOSS (5,508)

A nickname for Gilbert is . . .
ENTER: the value of six nickels
+ 5.8
× five
× four
=
ANSWER: GIL (716)

308

A large hermit crab's home is a . . .
ENTER: the number of pennies in two dollars
- 39
× 300
+ 41
× two
× 800
+ eighteen
=
ANSWER:

The Spanish word "hola" means . . .
ENTER: the number of quarters in a dollar
× two hundred thirty-two
÷ fifty-eight
- 15.2266
=
ANSWER:

309

Your sense of direction is something you never want to . . .
ENTER: the number of dimes in a dollar
× fifty
× seven
+ seven
=
ANSWER: LOSE (3,507)

In order for one person to buy, another must . . .
ENTER: the number of quarters in a dollar
+ three
× 221
× five
=
ANSWER: SELL (7,735)

310

Bacon on a hot griddle might . . .
ENTER: the number of pennies in four dimes
× 1,861
+ three
× five
=
ANSWER: SIZZLE (372,215)

A model of the Earth is a . . .
ENTER: the number of nickels in a dollar
÷ .8
- thirteen
× 3,173
=
ANSWER: GLOBE (38,076)

311

A fish that looks like a snake is an . . .
ENTER: the number of dimes in a dollar
× seventy
+ thirty-five
- two
=
ANSWER:

The ears on an African elephant are real . . .
ENTER: the number of pennies that equals two dimes
× 443
+ one
× 600
+ eighteen
=
ANSWER:

...these, they would go broke!

ENTER: the number of seconds in one minute

÷ fifteen
+ one
× 10,609
= ◯

ANSWER: SHOES (53,045)

"I will" is ...

ENTER: the number of numerals on a clock face / the number of months in 2 years

+ twelve
÷ three
+ three
× 12.85
= ◯

ANSWER: ILL (77.1)

A boy's name that rhymes with "rely."

ENTER: the number on a clock face that stands for twenty minutes after the hour

× two
− three
× 34.6
= ◯

ANSWER: ELF (173)

When our ice-cream cone falls on the ground, we ...

ENTER: the number of hours between noon and 4 P.M.

× (25 + 25)
− thirty-nine
× five
= ◯

ANSWER: SOB (805)

The opposite of "she."

ENTER: the number of days in a week

+ eight
× two
add (2 + 2)
= ◯

ANSWER: HE (34)

When you hear this ring, school is over.

ENTER: the number on the clock that represents 5 minutes before the hour

+ nineteen
× 258
− two
= ◯

ANSWER: BELL (7,738)

...A baby might say ...

ENTER: the number of people it takes to play on a seesaw

add (3 + 3)
÷ two
− three
− .93994
= ◯

ANSWER: GOO GOO (0.06006)

What Santa's helpers love to say before "Merry Christmas."

ENTER: the number of reindeer named Rudolph pulling Santa's sleigh

− .79798
÷ two
× four
= ◯

ANSWER: HO-HO-HO (0.40404)

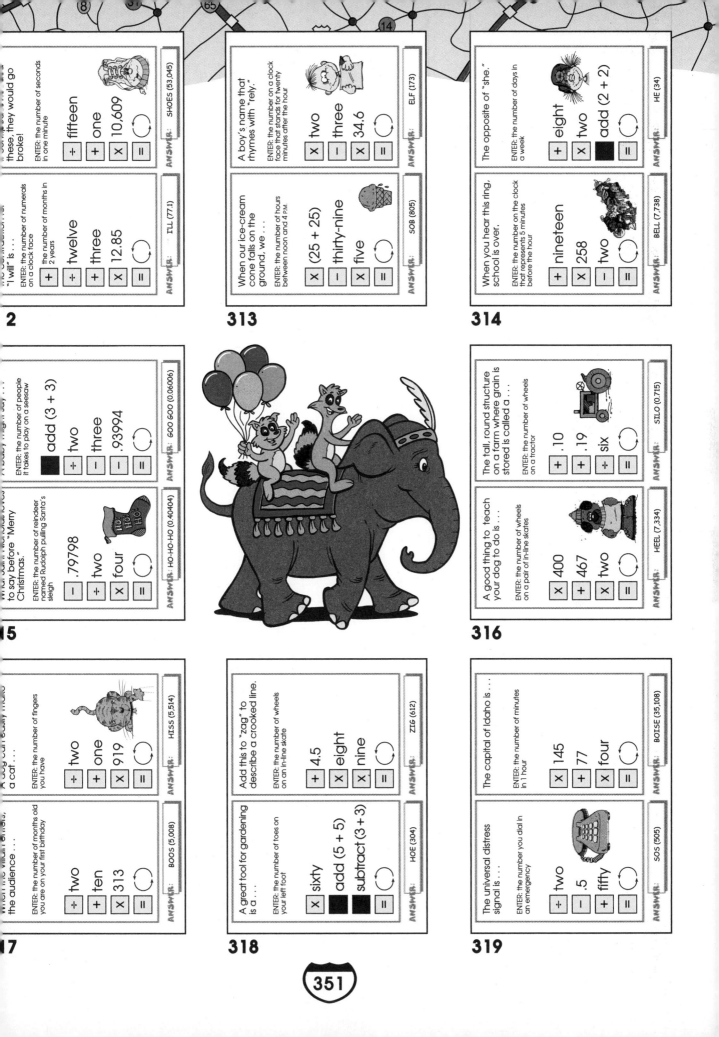

The tall, round structure on a farm where grain is stored is called a ...

ENTER: the number of wheels on a tractor

+ .10
+ .19
÷ six
= ◯

ANSWER: SILO (0.715)

A good thing to teach your dog to do is ...

ENTER: the number of wheels on a pair of in-line skates

× 400
÷ 467
× two
= ◯

ANSWER: HEEL (7,334)

...a cat ...

ENTER: the number of fingers you have

÷ two
+ one
× 919
= ◯

ANSWER: HISS (5,514)

What the villain returns... the audience ...

ENTER: the number of months old you are on your first birthday

÷ two
+ ten
× 313
= ◯

ANSWER: BOOS (5,008)

Add this to "zag" to describe a crooked line.

ENTER: the number of wheels on an in-line skate

+ 4.5
× eight
× nine
= ◯

ANSWER: ZIG (612)

A great tool for gardening is a ...

ENTER: the number of toes on your left foot

× sixty
add (5 + 5)
subtract (3 + 3)
= ◯

ANSWER: HOE (304)

The capital of Idaho is ...

ENTER: the number of minutes in 1 hour

× 145
+ 77
× four
= ◯

ANSWER: BOISE (35,108)

The universal distress signal is ...

ENTER: the number you dial in an emergency

÷ two
− .5
+ fifty
= ◯

ANSWER: SOS (505)

320

A June bug is often mistaken for a . . . .

ENTER: the number of days in a school week

x 80.6
x sixty
+ seven
x fourteen
= ↺

ANSWER: BIG BEE (338,618)

Where can you find elephants and penguins?

ENTER: the number of legs on a horse ÷ 3

+ ninety-three
÷ five
■ divide by 1,000
= ↺

ANSWER: ZOO (0.02)

321

The year both Alaska and Hawaii became part of the United States.

ENTER: the number of stripes on the American flag

+ twenty-eight
x 160
+ one
= ↺

ANSWER: 1959 (6,561)

A name for a boy or girl that rhymes with see.

ENTER: the number of moons revolving around our planet

+
- twenty-six
x fifty-five
+ seven
= ↺

ANSWER: LEE (337)

322

These help you see in the water.

ENTER: the number of ounces in 1 pound

+ 584
x 8,961
+ six
= ↺

The policeman will _____ the stolen money.

ENTER: the number of legs on an octopus

x 800
+ twenty-seven
x five
= ↺

323

When we think of nursery rhymes, we think of Mother . . . .

ENTER: the number of days in the month of January

- six
x two
x seven hundred
■ add six
= ↺

ANSWER: GOOSE (35,006)

What you tell a fly when you want it to go away.

ENTER: the number of toes on both your feet

+ two
+ five
+ two
- .64
+ eight
= ↺

ANSWER: SHOO (0.045)

324

A famous bear's best friend is named . . . .

ENTER: the number for the Spanish number "dos"

x ten
- twelve
x .101
= ↺

ANSWER: BO BO (0.808)

The contraction for "he is."

ENTER: the number of days in February in a leap year

- five
÷ four
x .89
= ↺

ANSWER: HE'S (5.34)

325

Who sells sea shells by the sea shore?

ENTER YOUR RESPONSE: If kitty was given three pieces of tuna for breakfast and for dinner, how many pieces did she have in all?

÷ two
x one before six
x twenty-three
= ↺

I want a big hug or . . . .

ENTER YOUR RESPONSE: Your pet Mittens had five kittens. How many tiny paws are scrambling over your kitchen floor?

- ten
x four hundred
- 427
= ↺

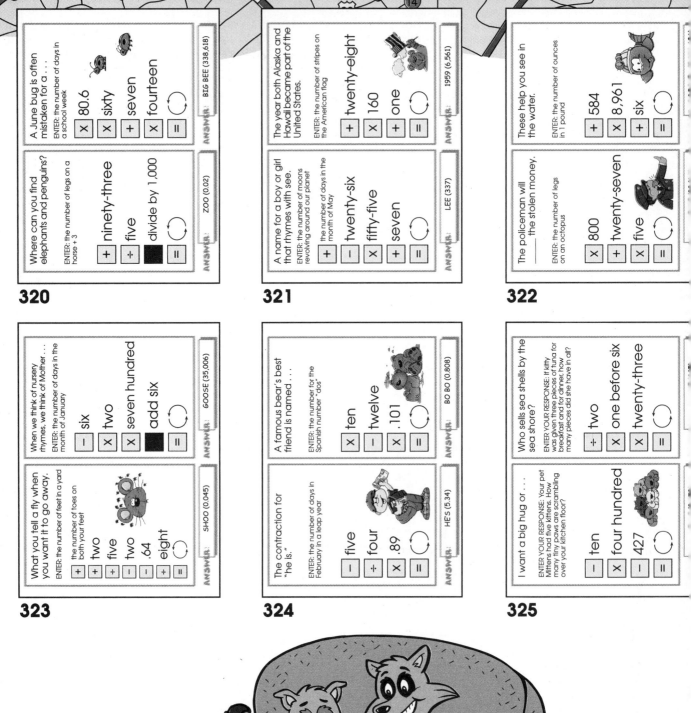